New Religious Movements in the United States and Canada

Recent Titles in
Bibliographies and Indexes in Religious Studies

Theological and Religious Reference Materials: General Resources
and Biblical Studies
G. E. Gorman and Lyn Gorman, with the assistance of Donald N. Matthews

Theological and Religious Reference Materials: Systematic Theology
and Church History
G. E. Gorman and Lyn Gorman, with the assistance of Donald N. Matthews

Healing Faith: An Annotated Bibliography of Christian Self-Help Books
Compiled by Elise Chase

New Religious Movements in the United States and Canada

A Critical Assessment and Annotated Bibliography

Compiled by
DIANE CHOQUETTE

With an Introductory Essay by Robert S. Ellwood, Jr.

G. E. Gorman, Advisory Editor

Bibliographies and Indexes in Religious Studies, Number 5

Greenwood Press
Westport, Connecticut • London, England

Library of Congress Cataloging in Publication Data

Choquette, Diane.
  New religious movements in the United States and
Canada.

  (Bibliographies and indexes in religious studies,
ISSN 0742-6836   ; no. 5)
  Includes indexes.
    1. United States—Religion—Bibliography.
2. Canada—Religion—Bibliography.   3. Cults—United
States—Bibliography.   4. Cults—Canada—Bibliography.
I. Title. II. Series.
Z7834.U6C46 1985 [BL2525]   016.291 '0973   85-9964
ISBN 0-313-23772-7 (lib. bdg. ; alk. paper)

Library of Congress Catalog Card Number 85-9964
ISBN: 0-313-23772-7
ISSN: 0742-6836

First published in 1985

Greenwood Press
A division of Congressional Information Service, Inc.
88 Post Road West, Westport, Connecticut 06881

Printed in the United States of America

10 9 8 7 6 5 4 3 2

Contents

Preface

In 1977, under the direction of Jacob Needleman, visiting scholars and staff members of the newly formed Center for the Study of New Religious Movements in America began to conduct research on religious and human potential movements that had arisen out of the counterculture of the 1960s. Through its association with the Graduate Theological Union in Berkeley, California, the Center also established the New Religious Movements Research Collection in the Graduate Theological Union Library. Since 1977, collecting, organizing, and making accessible primary and secondary materials related to new religious movements has been the aim of the collection's staff. As the librarian for the collection since 1979, I have become increasingly aware of the need for a comprehensive, annotated bibliography useful to both scholars and the general public alike. The present work results from the happy coincidence of an invitation from the Reverend G. E. Gorman to create such a volume as part of a series of bibliographies on topics in religion within Greenwood's Bibliographies and Indexes in Religious Studies program and the availability of fine resources at the libraries of the Graduate Theological Union and the University of California at Berkeley.

Concern evoked by the dramatic growth of high-demand religious groups in recent years in the United States has been felt by several segments of the population. Parents, understandably anxious about their childrens' sudden conversions to unconventional belief systems with their attendant lifestyles, seek advice, assurance, and reliable information. Mainstream church leaders ask for accurate and timely information to serve better the needs of their congregations, especially their young members. Lawyers and mental health professionals have become involved in the "cult phenomenon" also, having particular interests in judicial and psychological ramifications of sudden, intense religious conversions. Scholars in several disciplines, including religion and theology, sociology and anthropology, describe, interpret, and analyze these new religious groups and their social background. Ex-members and members of cults (the term is used here interchangeably with "new religions" and "new religious movements" nonpejoratively in the sense in which Robert Ellwood uses it in his introductory discussion) have written their stories or related them to journalists, who in turn have increased popular awareness of the cult phenomenon.

All of the above groups of people have, in their search for information and understanding, created a substantial, interdisciplinary body of literature. The nature of this body of research, distributed among the specialized literatures of several academic disciplines and the popular press, is such that access to a balanced spectrum of materials on issues and organizations is difficult. Providing such access is a major goal of the present volume.

All of the books, periodicals and periodical articles, dissertations, and unpublished papers described in this bibliography are about new religious and human potential movements. Writings of spiritual teachers and gurus and the doctrinal publications of their organizations are excluded from this volume, but may be sought through information provided in the appendix on selected new religious movement publishers. The terms "cult" and "new religious movement" as used in the annotations generally follow the usage and tone of the authors of the works discussed.

English language items covering cults and related issues in the United States and Canada are the primary focus. Selected writings of some British sociologists, namely Roy Wallis, Eileen Barker, James Beckford, David Martin, and Bryan Wilson, are also found here; their common interests shared with American sociologists of religion add a complementary dimension to the research of those based in the United States and Canada.

The bibliography takes as its historical starting point the counterculture of the 1960s in the United States, although it does include some works giving the historical background of Eastern religions, the occult, and metaphysical religions. As Robert Ellwood notes, the use of the term "new" is certainly relative here: all of the religious beliefs represented in this volume have precedents in American history. Historical studies associate the current crop of cults with the fertile soil that makes their growth possible. Although the literature of new religious movements continues to grow, this volume covers works published through the end of 1983.

The terms "new religious movement" and "cult" have come to denote a wide variety of organizations having some type of religious or spiritual orientation that is unconventional. This bibliography reflects the sense in which those terms have been used by the Center for the Study of New Religious Movements in America, which completed its activities in 1983, and the still thriving New Religious Movements Research Collection at the Graduate Theological Union Library. Emphasis is placed on Hindu, Buddhist, Sikh, Sufi, Neo-Pagan, Witchcraft, Jesus Movement, and Human Potential Movement groups that were founded in the 1960s or experienced renewed growth in the 1960s and 1970s, attracting middle class youth, many of whom had been raised in mainstream churches. New Age communes, UFO groups, Gurdjieff-related groups, and several other types classified by Robert Ellwood are also included. Christian and Jewish groups are generally not represented, the few exceptions being Peoples Temple Christian Church, countercultural Jesus Movement groups, Jews for Jesus, and the Unification Church, which some find to be Christian or Christian-related. Issues that are integral to the cult phenomenon, such as religious liberty, deprogramming, and the brainwashing/conversion debate, are also fully represented. In addition, to demonstrate the effects the new religious consciousness has had on the culture a small, representative selection of items on holistic health, mysticism and physics, and the synthesis of Eastern and Western psychologies is provided. Excluded are the numerous studies related to medical applications of yoga and meditation, which are listed in other bibliographies. Such bibliographies are included here and may be located through the Subject Index.

The bibliography attempts to cover scholarly materials comprehensively, with such research arranged by discipline: historical, sociological and anthropological, psychological and psychiatric, theological and religious, and legal. Collections of essays from more than one academic discipline are brought together in a section on interdisciplinary collected essays, which precedes the sections devoted to specific disciplines.

The opening section on reference works is intended to help the reader find further information. Dictionaries and encyclopedias are excellent sources for definitions of terms used by religious groups and for brief decriptions of cults that have received little or no scholarly or popular attention. The reader will find indexes useful for updating this bibliography and for finding related items of interest. Bibliographies also serve the function of leading one to related readings.

The last three sections of the bibliography, on personal accounts, popular studies, and new religious movements and the spiritualization of knowledge, contain selections from the available literature. Largely stories of ex-members of cults, the personal accounts reveal the anguish and joys of individuals and their families caught in the grip of compelling circumstances; these complement the scholarly research that must stand apart, describing and interpreting those experiences dispassionately. From the tremendous number of articles in newspapers and popular periodicals, a representative selection of the more substantial pieces has been chosen for inclusion. Many more may be found through newspaper and general periodical indexes.

Experience with users of the New Religious Movements Research Collection has shown that they most often inquire after materials on individual cults, issues, or the perspective of a single academic discipline. Therefore, arrangement of the bibliography and its indexes follows these lines of inquiry. The Author/Title Index includes all titles mentioned and all authors, editors, and compilers listed in entries or annotations. The Subject Index contains references to all names of religious and human potential groups, to individuals, and to issues and topics related to the section and subsection headings of the bibliography. I have attempted to be thorough, citing all names and important issues that appear in annotations and titles. For convenience, the citations in the bibliography are numbered consecutively, and these entry numbers are utilized in the indexes and are referred to by Dr. Ellwood in his introductory essay.

Publications of new religious groups now constitute a vast body of literature, deserving of its own bibliography. However, in order to aid the reader in locating some of these publications, an appendix of selected new religious movements publishers is provided. Publishers, for the most part representing well-known groups, have been chosen as a sample of the diversity throughout the United States. Arrangement is by name of the organization with which the publisher is associated. In all cases the publishers produce catalogs that may be requested from the addresses given.

The New Religious Movements Research Collection at the Graduate Theological Union includes books, periodicals, audio materials, and ephemeral publications from many new religious and human potential movements. Particularly in the area of popular literature, which is very selectively represented here, the collection houses many more items than could be listed in this volume. Approximately 90 percent of the items described here are in the collection. The remaining 10 percent were found in the excellent libraries of the University of California, Berkeley. Those individuals interested in using the collection are encouraged to visit the Graduate Theological Union Library during normal business hours when a reference librarian is available to assist users. Others who wish to obtain materials for research should be aware that interlibrary loan services at libraries throughout the country can aid one in finding the nearest location for the books, periodicals, and doctoral dissertations listed here. The Graduate Theological Union Library does not lend materials directly to individuals through the mail. Requests for copies of unpublished papers included in this bibliography may be directed to the New Religious Movements Research Collection. The librarian for the collection welcomes requests for information that cannot be handled in the ways discussed above. Also, additions to the collection are always valued. This bibliography does not claim to be complete, and neither is the collection. Suggestions for items to be included in possible future editions of this bibliography are encouraged.

I would like to thank several people who have been instrumental in the creation of this volume. My deepest appreciation goes to the Reverend G. E. Gorman and to Marilyn Brownstein of Greenwood Press for intelligently and graciously guiding a novice through the intricacies of book preparation. I am grateful to John Baker-Batsel and Claude Welch for granting me a generous amount of time away from my regular duties at the Graduate Theological Union Library so that I could complete this volume in a timely manner. In addition to his fine introductory essay, Robert S. Ellwood Jr. also provided thoughtful suggestions concerning the organization and scope of the bibliography. Thanks are also due to Jacob Needleman for his ideas, particularly during the early stages of planning the volume. Lisa Yount's editorial skills greatly improved my annotations, and her attentive proof-reading relieved me of that onerous task. Although for several reasons we did not produce this volume using a computer, Lisa Thomas cheerfully gave the attempt her all. Thomas Armstrong typed the manuscript with far fewer glitches and more good cheer than any computer can offer. Finally, my gratitude goes to the many friends and colleagues whose constant support, particularly during times of distress in my personal life, made it possible for me to complete this bibliography.

Diane Choquette
Graduate Theological Union Library
Berkeley, California

New Religious Movements
in the United States
and Canada

Introduction
ROBERT S. ELLWOOD, JR.

It is a privilege to introduce this excellent bibliography of contemporary new religious movements in America. With its thoroughness and careful annotation, it answers to a basic need in an area of growing scholarly activity, and it will be much appreciated.

The term "new" is, needless to say, always relative. For the most part, this compilation takes it to refer to groups generated amid the yeasty spiritual ferment of the 1960s. The books and articles in this bibliography are largely about 1960s movements and later groups of a similar sort, and the controversy they have never failed to foment.

This is entirely appropriate, for the sixties were a watershed decade in American life, not least in the area of new religious movements (see 050, 051). To be sure, America has ever been a land of new religious movements, often to an extent that has amazed foreign visitors. Unconventional spirituality on these shores ranges from still-active groups with deep nineteenth-century roots such as Spiritualism, Theosophy, New Thought, and Vedanta to the Beatnik Zen of the 1950s; intellectual influences and even lineages of personal contact can be traced between that lively background and the sixties explosion. Nonetheless, sixties non-normative religion had a special quality created by its association with what was then called the "youth culture" or the "counterculture" (see 057, 060, 061). Its "new religions" received considerably more publicity and engendered markedly more academic interest than the now rather staid descendants of earlier occult and mystical explosions, though a recent trend toward in-depth historical studies in this area can be detected (see 080, 081, 089, 107, 108).

First let us reflect on what is meant by a "new religious movement." Though cumbersome, this term is definitely better than the more popular expressions, "sect" and "cult," because of the heavy stereotyping those words have come to acquire. However, the latter terms do have a traditional descriptive denotation in the sociology of religion, and many writers listed in this bibliography use them in that way. Further, since we are here generally dealing with actual religious groups and not diffuse vogues, groups which are non-normative or unconventional in their setting and often in some tension with it, we are really talking about much the same thing which many sociologists (and others) have labelled as sects and cults (see 200-212).

In the tradition of the sociology of religion descended from Max Weber and Ernst Troeltsch through such authorities as Milton Yinger, sects and cults are religious "withdrawal groups" as opposed to the "church" type of institution. The church represents the normative religion of a society; it basically upholds its operative values, sanctions its social order, and is what most people "are" religiously, if they have not made a deliberate choice to "withdraw" and be something else. The withdrawal group, on the other hand, in effect makes a clear statement that the majority religion is inadequate, corrupt, hopelessly lukewarm, or downright heretical, and that a true believer must "come out from among them" to the extent of making a clean break and aligning with a purer, more open or more faithful assembly. In this tradition, if the withdrawal group attempts a stricter, more intensive following of the majority religion, such as the Amish or Jehovah's Witnesses in a Christian context or certain Hasidic groups in the Jewish tradition, it is called a sect; if, like various Eastern or occult groups, it draws wisdom from "outside" sources and stresses mystical experience, it is a cult.

Many commentators have pointed out that this model, based on the typical European pattern of established church versus more or less permanently marginal alternative groups, does not completely fit the anti-establishmentarian, multidenominational American pattern in which the transit from sect to respectable denomination is a well-traveled road. Nonetheless, as many so-called cultists have found, to their distress, there are "ins" and "outs" in American religious life, with a broad "mainstream" coalition playing the church role. Those perceived as marginal to it labor under some degree of suspicion and also possess certain characteristics which tend to distinguish them from the mainstream groups, quite apart from relative size.

First, because the non-normative group usually means that joiners cut themselves loose from ties of religious identity with family, community, and ethnic group, it must compensate with new experience and new identity tokens that are sufficiently intense to answer for the loss of those "natural" sources of psychological support. It will then emphasize inner experience, a high level of participation, and perhaps a distinctive lifestyle betokened by special dress, diet, and the like. A highly charismatic leader or teacher may replace the authority of family and the clerics of the established church. Talismans of certainty—books, persons, practices of undoubted reliability—reassure the venturer into new spiritual fields. It is typical for such movements to offer a simple, sure teaching and a clear-cut practice, such as chanting or meditation or "charismatic" techniques, which produce immediate experiential and practical results for many.

The emphasis on intensity, participation, and results, however, is likely to make for tension with the environing community, whose church-type religiosity puts religion in a different role. The tension may range from a level little more than indifference to virtual persecution. A moderate degree of tension, which highlights the novel group's distinctiveness and claims without threatening its survival, may actually be to the new religion's benefit.

In connection with the new religious movement's relations to its social environment, we may also note that it may operate in two modes, neither of which is precisely competitive with the mainline churches. New religious movements do not and cannot set up "altar against altar" in every town and neighborhood and are not at their best advantage in competition with the Sunday morning service. Rather, they are likely, on the one hand, to have a center or centers (a school, community, retreat, or meditation hall) which are more intense than what the average parish church offers and, on the other hand, to exercise a diffuse influence, largely among nonmembers, through lectures, books, periodicals, correspondence courses, and even radio and television. That diffuse impact may be much greater than anything comparable within most mainline churches, equalled or excelled only by stellar "electronic church" outlets. Indeed, it is not uncommon for the same person both to have an "official" mainline church connection and to participate at least in the diffuse outreach of a new religious movement, say through doing Transcendental Meditation or taking a yoga class or reading New Thought literature. In order fully to assess the impact of new religious movements, then, we need to take into account both their intensive and diffuse forms of expression.

Many categories can be used to classify religious movements: doctrinal, ritual style, sociological (that is, social class or ethnic group of origin, type of leadership and organizational structure, or nature of individual participation), or geographical. All have value for understanding, and none of them is absolute; however in the context of this volume it seemed that a somewhat open scheme based on family resemblance within each category would be most useful. It will be found that the groups in each of the following nine categories tend strongly to have interlocking histories and overlap in teaching, practices, and sociological style.

Theosophical, Rosicrucian, Gnostic (see 081, 090). These groups have in common a belief in an "ancient wisdom" underlying the religions and philosophies of the world. In the West, it is essentially identical with the Neoplatonist strand which, like an underground river, has watered occult and mystical efflorescences from medieval kabbalism and magic through the Renaissance "Rosicrucian enlightenment," with its Great Chain of Being and macrocosm-microcosm correspondences, down to nineteenth- and twentieth-century occult revivals. Fundamental features are monism, the divine within, the existence and significance of nonordinary levels of reality (e.g., the "astral body" or "etheric double") and of non-ordinary powers such as those usually called psychic or occult, and spiritual growth or initiation through mystical experience. In addition, many in this tradition have affirmed reincarnation and the existence of highly advanced souls, often termed Masters or Adepts, who guide the development of individuals and the planet.

Although this tradition sees itself as having ancient roots, most existing groups are of nineteenth- or twentieth-century origin. The oldest of several American Rosicrucian groups, emphasizing a collection of Western teachings based on Renaissance occultism, is apparently the Fraternitatis Rosae Crucis, founded in 1868; the best known, because of its extensive advertising, is the Ancient and Mystical Order of the Rosae Crucis (AMORC), founded in 1915 by H. Spencer Lewis.

The Theosophical Society was founded in New York in 1875 by the Russian Helena Blavatsky and the American Henry Steel Olcott. It soon became a genuinely international organization which endeavored to correlate the Western occult tradition with cognate Eastern teachings, such as karma and reincarnation. The largest theosophical society is that based in Adyar, Madras, India, but at least two others exist. In addition, theosophy has spawned a number of derivative groups, often based on new revelations from the Masters who have played an important role in the tradition. Among those especially active in the 1960s and after are Anthroposophy, based on the teachings of Rudolf Steiner, a German Theosophist who preferred a more Western and Christian orientation; the Arcane School, established by Alice Bailey; and the colorful "I AM" movement (see 079), conspicuous in the 1930s and returned in a derivative movement, the Church Universal and Triumphant, in the 1960s and 1970s (see 104).

The Ancient Wisdom tradition has long regarded the Gnostic form of early Christianity as among its principal vessels, and its approach has been revived in such groups as the Liberal Catholic Church and the Ecclesia Gnostica, both with Theosophical connections. Gnosticism ancient and modern has emphasized the spiritual nature of human beings, viewing conventional Christian doctrine and festivals as symbolic expressions of intrapsychic processes.

New Thought (see 078, 090). This is a general term for a nineteenth-century movement emphasizing the importance of affirmative thinking. Having roots in Transcendentalism, it taught that, through thinking positive, believing thoughts that affirmed the fundamental goodness and sufficiency of the universe, one could sow the seeds of healing, prosperity, success, and joy. Although New Thought has had a wide influence far outside the relatively small denominations it has engendered, some of them should be mentioned: Unity (1889), Divine Science (1889), Religious Science (1949). Christian Science, although it does not consider itself a part of a larger New Thought movement, clearly emerged from the same milieu. The American New Thought tradition, whether known by that name or some other, has been very much alive in recent decades, both in the teachings of such persons as Norman Vincent Peale and Robert Schuller, and in various "prosperity" and "success" seminars.

Spiritualist/UFO groups. Modern American Spiritualism (see 077, 082, 090) can be traced back to the "tappings" heard by the Fox sisters in upstate New York in 1848 and the enthusiasm they generated. Its roots, however, lie in Swedenborgianism, Mesmerism, and similar phenomena among the Shakers. Although the early Spiritualist vogue died down by the end of the 1850s, it has had modest revivals since, and Spiritualist churches continue to the present. The most important influence of Spiritualism on new religious movements of the 1960s and after, however, has been in its popularization of interest in psychic phenomena and its example of communication of spiritual messages through trance mediumship. Many since then have professed to transmit in this manner deliverances from high spiritual beings on other planes. One thinks of the modern "scriptures" of what has been called "Teaching Spiritualism," such as *Oahspe* (1882) and the *Urantia* book (published 1955).

Another set related to Spiritualism is the plethora of UFO groups (see 138, 264, 696). Soon after the first sightings of "Flying Saucers" or "Unidentified Flying Objects" in 1947, individuals came forward to claim contact with the celestial visitors aboard them. Several of these "contactees" eventually established religious groups, affirming that the "Space Brothers" were so superior to earthlings as to be virtually godlike and that they had important messages for us. Ordinary contact was typically by mediumistic means similar to the Spiritualist, and in fact some major contactees had Spiritualistic backgrounds. Although they played a role in the new religious movements of the 1950s and 1960s, by the 1970s UFO groups were in decline. But a late, bizarre episode was the 1975 mission of two alleged contactees, called Bo and Peep (see 247-249), who led a few hundred people to isolated mountain camps where they were to await UFO visitors.

Occult/Initiatory groups (see 006, 033, 195, 648). This set has rather less historical cohesion than the others and in some cases has been influenced by at least the paradigms of Rosicrucianism, Theosophy, and Spiritualism. However, these groups do stand together as movements which emphasize subjective transformation through systematic training based on secret or occult truths and involving intense personal experiences, usually intentional, which may be called initiatory.

A classic modern example is the groups in the lineage of G. I. Gurdjieff (1872-1949) (see 058, 106). Gurdjieff, who began his public work in Moscow on the eve of the Russian revolution and later resided in France, was a highly charismatic figure who had a powerful impact on his followers. He taught that new states of consciousness can be attained through hard labor, group exercises, and experiences of surprise which unsettle ordinary mental routines. We are asleep, Gurdjieff said, and need the shock of awakening to realize our potential. The Gurdjieff work, as it is called, is perpetuated through several organizations in America and enjoyed some popularity in the late 1960s and the 1970s (see 105, 591).

Other groups of this type represented in the bibliography include Scientology (see 342), the Process Church of the Final Judgment (see 244), Synanon (see 298, 641), and est (Erhard Seminars Training) (see 333, 416, 655). All have in common the intentional induction of intense experience, in these cases usually of a quasi-psychotherapeutic sort brought about by probing questioning, concentration, self-criticism, and even verbal assault. As in classical initiatory rites and the Gurdjieff work, the activity may take place in a sequestered setting and directly or indirectly under the control of an authoritative leader. The underlying teaching typically emphasizes, like Zen, the extent to which our words and concepts and self-images entrap us and the role of "shock therapy" in releasing us from them. The strong tactics of these groups have, needless to say, produced fervent supporters and much controversy. All those named originated around the 1960s or early 1970s.

Quieter and more traditionally occultist groups practicing initiation also exist, such as the Builders of the Adytum, emphasizing Kabbalistic and Tarot lore, and the astrological Church of Light. These groups typically claim that they are modern revivals or surfacings of ancient mystery schools.

Neo-Paganism and its allies (see 037, 294, 610). This is a set which thus far has received insufficient academic study. It is comprised of several diverse strands in America: ethnic, "revivalist" Neo-Paganism, Wicca, ceremonial magic, and Satanism. These have in common a ritualistic, evocational spiritism or polytheism, a "cosmic religion" orientation, and an interlocking sociological network; although these groups and types of groups have significant differences, people in any of them tend to be aware of the others and to sense shared concerns.

The ethnic groups of this type are mostly spiritistic religions of Afro-American background practiced by Latin Americans resident in the United States: Voudon (Haiti), Umbanda (Brazil), Santeria (Cuba). Although little known outside the respective communities, centers of these and similar faiths can be found at various places in this country.

Revivalist Neo-Paganism, largely practised by Americans of European background, consists of groups endeavoring to revive the pre-Christian religions of the Egyptians, Greeks, Celts, or Norsemen, or to construct pagan faiths broadly in their style. Wicca or Witchcraft (see 336, 469, 610) shares with the Neo-Pagans a sense of pre-Christian European spiritual affinity. But although mostly a modern reconstruction in fact, Wicca looks more to traditional folk religion than to the pagan great traditions for its roots. While men and women participate equally in many Wicca groups, the movement is aware of its significance as a custodian of feminine spirituality —indicated by the provocative word "witch"—and have gained an impetus from a recent upsurge of interest among feminists in Wicca and Goddess-worship (see 457).

Ceremonial magic (see 058, 318) on the other hand, stems from a more literary European tradition, that of magical evocation, which, having roots in ancient theurgy, flourished on the fringes of medieval Kabbalism and alchemy. It employs the ritual texts, *grimoires*, and uses such implements as the square altar and the sword and pentacle to evoke gods, demons, and spirits into the magic circle. Most American magical groups, however, are inspired by the 1890s Order of the Golden Dawn in England, and in particular by the Ordo Templi Orientalis (OTO) of the celebrated (and notorious) practitioner of "magick," Aleister Crowley.

Satanism (see 092) is included in this section for convenience, but it should not be confused with Neo-Paganism, Wicca, or magic. It has a quite different relationship to the dominant religious heritage of our culture, the Judeo-Christian, than do these other groups. The former do not see themselves as worshipping Satan, but simply as preferring a different and older pantheon altogether than the Judeo-Christian. However, the Satanist chooses to worship precisely that which that tradition presents as the embodiment of evil, and so is in a peculiar symbiosis with it, whether Satan is regarded as actually evil or simply a much-maligned personification of the life-force and the "natural" impulses. Satanists are of both sorts. While their numbers and importance are far less than the sensational publicity they tend to generate would imply, they represent a segment of the American spiritual spectrum.

As the foregoing indicates, Neo-Pagan and allied groups have a background in Europe, and to a lesser extent in America, going back well before the Second World War; their modern formation is really a product of late romanticism. However, virtually all extant American groups in this category stem from the 1960s generation; they were naturally congenial to the counterculture's interest in ecology, mystical experience, occult symbol systems, and feminism. Theirs has been a movement in considerable flux; most groups in this set have been ephemeral even by new religious movement standards. Nonetheless, as some have disappeared, others have formed: they clearly respond to some deep contemporary need.

Eastern Religions I: From India. Americans have seen India as virtually a second holy land ever since the "Yankee Hindoo" vogue of New England Transcendentalism. However, although Emerson wrote about Indian mysticism and Theosophists incorporated it into their system, the first formal group of Indian religious background was the Vedanta Society (technically, centers of the Ramakrishna Mission) in 1894 (see 087). It has remained perhaps the most intellectually oriented group of this type, attracting such writers as Aldous Huxley and Christopher Isherwood. It was followed in 1920 by the Self-Realization Fellowship, which taught certain yoga techniques.

Since the second World War, and especially in the 1960s, groups of Hindu background have proliferated (see 088, 468). Most have in common a guru or teacher believed to be "God-realized" and to have special spiritual power, a simple but definite form of initiation, intellectual underpinning in some form of Advaita (non-dualist) Vedanta philosophy, and practices based on meditation, yoga, and chanting. Among the best known are the Sivananda Yoga centers (see 299), the Integral Yoga Institute (see 346), the Divine Light Mission (of the "teen-age guru" Maharaj Ji) (see 314), followers of Sathya Sai Baba (see 468) and Sri Aurobindo, Ananda Marga, the Rajneesh movement (see 623) and, largest of all, Transcendental Meditation (see 199). An exception to the usual Indic paradigm is the International Society for Krishna Consciousness, which represents *bhakti* or devotional Hinduism. Strongly rejecting the Advaita Vedanta outlook, it affirms Krishna as a personal god to whom love and service are due (see 285).

Several movements related to the Sikh religion of India can also be found. These include ethnic Sikh groups and the Sikh Dharma of Yogi Bhajan (see 190), who came to America in 1968 and, through several projects, have acquired a significant occidental following, with many converts to Sikhism. Other groups of mostly occidental followers in the West, the Radhasoami Satsang (see 468), Ruhani Satsang, and Eckankar (see 475), have roots in heterodox Sikh movements.

Eastern Religions II: From East Asia. The influx from East Asia arrived a little later than that from India, but it has finally come to have nearly equal importance. Today, this category must be taken to embrace several forms of Buddhism (see 086)—Japanese, Chinese, Korean, Tibetan, and the Theravada Buddhism of southeast Asia—and several of the so-called new religions of Japan (see 083). Like most other "imported" faiths, these have both Asian-American ethnic forms and "export" forms that have appealed to occidental seekers.

The earliest and by far most culturally influential has been Zen Buddhism, which came to America primarily from Japan but which originated in China (see 080). Zen teachers have worked in America since the turn of the twentieth century, aided by the prolific literary output of the Zen writer, D. T. Suzuki; the First Zen Institute of America was founded in New York in 1930. However, the great vogue for Zen did not arise until the 1950s, again abetted by Suzuki and now by other writers ranging from Alan Watts to the "Beat" novelist Jack Kerouac; by the 1960s this enthusiasm had taken the form of a sprinkling of serious Zen centers across the country.

The austerity of Zen, however, did not satisfy all appetites in the psychedelic era. The colorful, Tantric form of Buddhism native to Tibet, carried by refugee lamas and assisted by such popular reading as *The Tibetan Book of the Dead*, was ensconced in several Tibetan religious centers by the end of the decade; the most influential have come to be the Nyingma Institute in Berkeley, California (1969) and the several Kargyupa works of Chogyam Trungpa based in Boulder, Colorado (1970) (see 098, 611).

The Japanese form of Buddhism known as Nichiren, emphasizing a simple form of chanting, burgeoned explosively in its homeland in the post-war era through the aggressive, modernized Soka Gakkai movement. In 1960, Soka Gakkai established headquarters in Santa Monica, California, and quickly formed Nichiren Shoshu of America (later Nichiren Shoshu Academy). The movement spread rapidly among occidental as well as Asian Americans in the 1960s and early 1970s, helped by its "streamlined" form of Buddhism and its atmosphere of happiness and success (see 330).

The Theravada style of Buddhism, less flamboyant and further from areas of American involvement than the Mahayana of Japan or Tibet, attracted the attention of occidental Americans only later. By the 1970s, however, some had discovered the value of its *vipassana* meditation techniques, and several centers were established.

Eastern Religions III: From Islamic Countries. Though often less visible than Hinduism or Buddhism, Islam has been a presence in America even longer, for Muslim traders and immigrants from the Middle East arrived here as far back as colonial times. "Orthodox" Sunni and Shi'a Islam have been primarily ethnic. However, several movements related to Islam or originating in Islamic countries have drawn adherents from other segments of the American population. The most prominent is probably the World Community of Islam in the West (formerly the Nation of Islam), the "Black Muslims." Since the death of its longtime leader, Elijah Muhammad, in 1975, it has played down certain unconventional doctrines and moved toward a more standard interpretation of Islam and greater openness toward the non-black community; it has also experienced division.

Many with little interest in orthodox Islam have been attracted by its mystical wing, known as Sufism, with its rich heritage of poetry, philosophy, and whirling dances. The most influential group has been the Sufi Order, brought to the United States in 1910 by Hazrat Inayat Khan (1881-1927) (see 299). Another is Sufism Reoriented, which emphasizes the teachings of Meher Baba (1894-1969). Baba is regarded as an avatar, or world teacher, by his followers; although he was not formally a Muslim, his doctrine incorporates much of the Sufi outlook (see 614). Largely informal Baba centers are scattered across the country, although the movement is undoubtedly in decline since the master's death and its heyday as a part of the sixties spiritual counterculture (see 310). A Sufi-related group from Indonesia is Subud, which centers on the *latihan*, hours of free, often very active, expression of the divine within; brought to the United States in 1958, it spread rapidly in the sixties and included numerous Gurdjieff followers.

The Baha'i World Faith was inaugurated by the Iranian Baha'u'llah (1817-1892), believed by Baha'is to be the prophet of God for our age, in the succession of Jesus, Muhammad, and others. It emphasizes devotion to God and world unity. Baha'i has spread around the world and has centers in most American cities with a major temple in Wilmette, Illinois. Baha'i was established in the United States as early as 1894. Possessing many adherents, well established in society, and a stable, institutional structure, this faith seems likely to endure.

Christian Movements. New and old Christian movements in America are innumerable. We can here cite only three areas which have particularly received attention from scholars of new religious movements. These are the Unification Church, the Peoples Temple, and the Jesus Movement.

The Holy Spirit Association for the Unification of World Christianity, or Unification Church, founded by the Reverend Sun Myung Moon of Korea, was brought to America in 1959. After a slow start it grew rapidly and drew considerable publicity in the 1970s. Its version of Christianity teaches that Jesus was an unsuccessful messiah and that another, the Lord of the Second Advent, is imminent; many followers identify him with Moon (see 262, 288).

The Peoples Temple Christian Church was founded in 1955 by the Reverend Jim Jones, whose preaching combined personal charisma, miracles, and socialism. By the early 1970s, he had several flourishing congregations, largely black, although Jones himself was white. In 1977 he moved to a settlement in Guyana with approximately one thousand followers. The story of their mass suicide there the following year is well known (see 100, 101).

The Jesus Movement among American young people commenced around 1970 as a sort of backlash against the drug and occult counterculture of the sixties. It started with the conversion of "street people" to evangelical Christianity, usually through certain churches and organizations which found a way to speak to them. While many of these converts simply ended up in evangelical churches or regular youth groups like Intervarsity or Campus Crusade for Christ, a few Jesus Movement groups of the new religious movements type also emerged (see 084, 182, 251). These included the Christian World Liberation Front in Berkeley, California (see 309), which split into two groups in 1975, the Christian Foundation of Tony Alamo and the late Susan Alamo, Calvary Chapel (a pentecostal Assemblies of God church with a large youth ministry in Costa Mesa, California), and the controversial Children of God (see 268, 339), a wandering communal group.

What is the literature about these groups like? A glance at this bibliography will reveal everything from encyclopedic overviews of new religious movements to personal accounts, both positive and negative, of the experiences of individuals within them. One finds studies prepared from the perspective of academic history and sociology as well as from the labors of psychologists and psychiatrists trying to ascertain what makes people join new religious movements and what happens to them when they do. This type of literature leads into the highly controversial area of "brainwashing" and "deprogramming." Other creators of literature approach the field as theologians or experts in religious studies, often either supporting or criticizing one or more new religions from the perspective of another faith. Then there are studies treating the host of legal problems the new religions have created.

Another set of literature involves what might be called the larger context. Many new religions have come from the East; many are based on mystical experience; many have explored "holistic" approaches to health and healing. This is understandable since these are all themes important to the milieu out of which many of them have arisen: a yearning for an alternative culture with fresh attitudes to mind and body is part of what has led people away from conventional religion. Therefore, we have representative titles in this bibliography on science and mysticism focusing on the much-discussed parallels between the vision of reality of the "new physics" and that of the mystics of all ages (see 70, 702); on "holistic health," the approach which emphasizes the importance of a total lifestyle, including nutrition and mental attitude, to health, together with the healing role of spiritual energies (see 710, 712); and on East/West psychology, books and articles that investigate what can be gleaned about human nature by comparing the ways it has been understood in oriental as well as occidental cultures (see 722, 732).

Despite the diversity, however, certain observations may be made about strengths and weaknesses in this body of literature on new religious movements. First, we continue to see the shadow of that tumultuous decade, the 1960s, falling over this collection. We note, to begin with, that only a handful of specific groups out of the hundreds listed in, for example, Gordon Melton's *Encyclopedia of American Religions* (see 004), receives very extensive attention. Those favored by more than one or two monographs or substantial articles are very few. To mention the Hare Krishnas, Scientology, the Unification Church, Synanon, the Peoples Temple, Transcendental Meditation, and Nichiren Shoshu comes close to exhausting the list. It is significant, I think, that these are nearly all of the groups that originated in close association with the celebrated "youth culture" of the sixties.

A second observation is that extensive attention has been given to what happens to one's mind in such religious movements, especially in regard to movements perceived as totalistic: the literature on "brainwashing," "deprogramming," and so forth (see 067, 414, 401).

A corollary observation is that the sixties "youth culture" or "counterculture" was perceived both then and now to be a rebellion of white, middle- and upper-class American young people against "the System" and the values on which they had been raised (see 057, 061). The explosion of attention it received in the media, from Haight-Ashbury "hippies" to bizarre "cultists" and draft resisters, concentrated largely on this aspect of what was happening. (The concurrent civil rights and "Black Power" movements were seen as something quite different.)

So it is that the choice of topics in new religious movements studies consorts well with the impression of the 1960s, that young people raised in the white-picket-fence suburbs of the Eisenhower era were doing strange things: going Eastern, being swept away by totalistic groups that amounted to surrogate families, rejecting science and patriotism to create a chasmic "generation gap." Everything was seen as sharply defined and polarized: the "Establishment" versus the "counterculture"; the old versus the "New Age" values; the inside versus the outside of the "cult." The result was much "anti-cult" literature, together with psychiatric and legal discussion of what was perceived as a youth problem and a cult problem. Other groups, not part of the high-visibility "youth culture," garnered much less attention. Neo-Pagans, members of ethnic Afro-American or Asian-American unconventional religions, members of older unconventional groups from Vedanta to "I AM," tend to be middle-aged. While they may sometimes experience tension within their environment, they do not generate either the glamour or the concerns of "rebellious youth" and "brainwashing cults." Even the eccentrics of older age groups tend to be more open in social style and seen less as affecting the future of society as a whole.

By now, however, we may have reached the penumbra of the sixties' shadow. The bulk of the aforementioned types of literature, essentially prompted by the groups and concerns of that decade, may be behind us. It is becoming increasingly apparent that the sixties' groups are not growing and that their persevering core membership is moving toward middle age. Further, it becomes more and more evident that most joiners leave intensive "cults" on their own within two years (see 227). Although the most fervent of anti-cultists will probably never be appeased, time does its work through developments such as these and the high-decibel debate over brainwashing, deprogramming, and legal tactics vis-à-vis "cults" ought to soften, as those of them which survive quietly become twenty-first century equivalents of Amish and Amanists on the margins of American society.

Scholarly attention should, of course, follow the groups through the coming years. They are passing through stages of growth for which sociological documentation will be quite valuable. They are now tackling the difficult transition from first to second generation of leadership, involving the classic Weberian "routinization of charisma" and socialization of children into the movement, and—as it becomes increasingly clear that the group's eschaton is not just around the corner—endeavors to normalize relations with the surrounding community. All this is transpiring now through efforts to upgrade the professional education of leaders, scholarly activity, public relations, and participation by the groups in community projects.

Out of such longitudinal studies should come insights into what kinds of new religious movements either survive or die, and further which become successful on a large scale and which remain marginal. Rodney Stark (see 172) has done important spadework in listing characteristics of successful new religious movements, ranging from a medium level of tension with the social environment through a normal age and sex range to a high level of achievement in at least one locality. He cites the Mormons as an outstanding example of a successful movement, with their now optimal relationship with society that has engendered both respect and a sense of "difference," their family emphasis which assures a normal age and sex range, and high success in one "home base" locality, Utah. These all imply hypotheses which can be tested through continuing observation of the new movements from the sixties.

For a variety of reasons, however, it does not seem at present that any of the sixties "youth culture" groups has the potential to become that successful, although some may well survive. Scholarly attention should also turn to other important topics in the understanding of new religious movements than the sixties "counterculture" groups and the peculiar set of psychological/legal issues that have clustered around them. This scholarly attention should focus on at least the following areas as worthy of investigation.

1. Other types of new religious movements.

A. Neo-Pagan, Wicca (Witchcraft), and Ritual Magic groups. Although these are often associated with the sixties counterculture, and did have considerable interplay with its "neo-romantic" themes of celebrating nature, exalting fantasy, and questioning the values of a consumer society, the core membership of these groups was and is somewhat older than the "youth culture" of the sixties, often maintaining an outwardly more conventional lifestyle, and has persisted with a different sociology and history. Rather than becoming communal and "totalistic," these groups have kept to the "dense but open" social relations Stark sees as one characteristic of the successful new religious movement. Rather than becoming paternalistic as some of the former groups are accused of being, many groups in this set have enjoyed a considerable influx of interest from the feminist and ecology movements, although others (especially some magicians) are notoriously "right wing." In any case, this set is a significant, though small, social movement which is understudied.

B. Satanism. Although field work in this area is difficult, rumor has it that Satanism is on the rise in the mid-1980s, possibly as a backlash against resurgent fundamentalism, and ought to be investigated.

C. Gnostic and other highly "mystical" Judeo-Christian movements. While explicitly Gnostic churches remain very small, one feels that in the present religious climate there is a potential for growth here. The much larger "New Thought," "success," and "prosperity" movements allegedly based on Christianity have gnostic qualities.

D. New religious movements of ethnic background. As the pluralism of American society becomes more fully acknowledged, milieus which as late as the 1960s might have been viewed as marginal to what was really significant (i.e., a white middle-class "youth culture") are increasingly taken by sensitive observers—not to mention politicians—to be as legitimately American culture as anything else. In the present context, this means that a host of new religious movements and folk religious practices with potential for feeding into new religious movements ought to be taken just as consequentially as the sixties "youth-culture" type. Indeed, all indications are that cultural interaction between ethnic segments of American society will increase and that the future lies here more than in the heritage of the sixties—though its cults of the Native American and the East did much to prepare the way.

What we are talking about here are movements with roots in such communities as the Native American, Afro-American, Asian American, or Jewish—shamanism and the vision quest; Caribbean spiritism and Voudon as they spread into the United States; Korean, Japanese, and southeast Asian "new religions"; Hasidism. These are slowly being enhanced by immigration patterns and slowly drawing interest from outside their original venue. However, many of thse movements have been studied little by scholars.

2. A second category of research and writing that needs to be pursued, and which can be mentioned much more briefly, is biography. While some leaders of new religious movements have "official" in-house biographies, and the present bibliography cites a number of personal accounts, a dearth of

scholarly biographies of their founders and other prominent leaders is apparent. Nevertheless, the personal history and, so far as it can be ascertained, subjectivity of a person capable of creating a new religion is essential to religious understanding.

3. A final area for future research is the comparative study of American and other new religious movements. Considerable work has been done on such movements in Asia, Africa, Latin America, and elsewhere, but apart from superficial allusions, not much has been accomplished to compare them with U.S. movements to see what can be learned about the genesis and destiny of such movements. Admittedly, there are cultural variables one must be aware of, but there may also be a certain chauvinism in assuming that a movement attractive to white American middle-class young people could not have anything in common with a Melanesian cargo cult or Haitian spiritism. In the past, disciplinary lines have tended to cut off the foreign from the domestic, the former being the province of anthropologists and the latter of sociologists. That unfortunate dichotomy is breaking down, and cross-cultural studies in new religious movements need to be an area of scholarly growth.

This bibliography will be a fundamental tool for any future work in this important area of social understanding. Whether particular movements prosper or wither, the methodology and conceptual understandings that inform the excellent scholarly studies represented here and the humanity which underlies the personal statements will illuminate whatever is done from now on. Diane Choquette is to be commended for her careful, informed work of assembling and annotating this collection, and the bibliography itself is recommended to the scholarly world and, it is hoped, to a wide-reading public interested in what is happening in America's spiritual life.

Reference Works

001. Crim, Keith, ed. <u>Abingdon Dictionary of Living
Religions</u>. Nashville: Abingdon Press, 1981.

> Very good source of brief information on beliefs, prac-
> tices and history of world religions. Particularly
> useful for those wishing to understand terms used in
> Eastern religions. The major traditions and some minor
> ones receive lengthy treatment. Many entries include
> a short bibliography. Illustrations.

002. <u>Encyclopedia of Associations</u>. Detroit: Gale Research,
1956- .

> The Religious Organizations section of the first volume
> includes a number of new religious groups, giving the
> address, number of members, publications, and a brief
> description of each organization. This is the only
> published source giving numbers of members, based on
> the organizations' reporting. Updated regularly.

003. Jack, Alex, ed. <u>The New Age Dictionary</u>. Brookline, Mass.:
Kanthaka Press, 1976.

> It is difficult to characterize this dictionary because
> its breadth is as formless as the "New Age" concept is.
> Its definitions are generally brief and popular, with
> little attention to etymology. Does include new
> religious groups, terms used in Eastern religions, and
> spiritual leaders.

004. Melton, J. Gordon. The Encyclopedia of American
Religions. Wilmington, N.C.: McGrath, 1978.

   A two-volume work that offers the most complete listing
   of new religious bodies in the United States. Arranged
   by type, such as "Communal," "Psychic and New Age,"
   and "The Eastern and Middle Eastern Family." Descriptions are generally brief but informative as to doctrine
   and leaders. Melton's Institute for the Study of
   American Religions (Box 1311, Evanston, Ill. 60201) is
   an excellent source for further investigation. Footnotes include citations to a wealth of primary material.
   A second edition is in progress. Index.

005. Riland, George. The New Steinerbooks Dictionary of the
Paranormal. New York: Steinerbooks, 1980.

   Useful for definitions of occult terms and brief biographies of occultists.

006. Shepard, Leslie. Encyclopedia of Occultism and Parapsychology. Detroit: Gale Research, 1978.

   Compiled from Lewis Spence's Encyclopedia of the Occult
   and Nandor Fodor's Encyclopedia of Psychic Science,
   with over 1,000 new entries and updated material added
   by Shepard. Includes terms such as Charismatic Renewal
   and names of contemporary spiritual leaders and organizations. Brief entries. Updated by supplements.

Handbooks, Guides, and Directories

007. The American Buddhist Directory. New York: American
Buddhist Movement, 1982.

   Provides names and addresses of Buddhist organizations
   of all types in the United States and Canada. Tele-
   phone numbers occasionally included. Arranged alphabetically by state with Canada at the end. Plans to
   update every year or two.

008. Baugh, Joanne, ed. Directory for a New World, 1980.
14th ed. Canoga Park, Calif.: Unity-in-Diversity Council,
1980.

   About one hundred organizations, all members of the
   Unity-in-Diversity Council, a New Age organization,
   are described. Entries appear to have been provided by
   the organizations themselves. Includes addresses.
   Although the directory has not been published in a useful form since 1980, this volume is a good supplement
   to The New Consciousness Sourcebook [item 017].

009. Emerging Trends. Princeton, N.J.: Princeton Religion
Research Center, 1979- , v. 1 - .

This monthly publication contains the results of a wide
variety of Gallup International opinion polls concerned
with religion. Occasionally reports on topics such as
attitudes toward cults, interest in yoga and meditation,
and involvement in the Unification Church.

010. Fox, Selena, comp. Circle Guide to Wicca and Pagan
Resources, 1982-1983. 3rd ed. Madison, Wis.: Circle Publications, 1981.

Includes books, periodicals, arts and music, occult
stores and suppliers, and a directory of Wiccan, Pagan,
and Magical groups in the United States and Canada.
The best source for addresses of such groups and the
only comprehensive guide to the Neo-Pagan community.

011. Kirschner Associates. Religious Requirements and
Practices of Certain Selected Groups: A Handbook Supplement
for Chaplains. Washington, D.C.: U.S. Department of Defense,
Department of the Army, Office of the Chief of Chaplains,
1980.

Prepared for Army chaplains, this handbook provides
brief, accurate descriptions of practices and beliefs
of many new religious groups, including Sikh, witchcraft, Islamic, Japanese, Jewish, Hindu, and Christian
related groups. Lists requirements not readily found
elsewhere, such as special holidays, dietary restric-
tions, dress, funeral and burial requirements. Glossary
and index.

012. McDermott, Robert A., ed. Focus on Buddhism: A Guide
to Audio-Visual Resources for Teaching Religion. Chambersburg,
Penn.: Anima Books, 1981.

A heavily annotated listing of films, slides, and
recordings about Buddhism, arranged geographically,
including Buddhism in the West. Only films are listed
for the West. Appendices include sources for additional
information, distributors, and indexes by topic and
title. A very useful guide.

013. McDermott, Robert A., ed. Focus on Hinduism: A Guide
to Audio-Visual Resources for Teaching Religion. 2d. enl. ed.
Chambersburg, Penn.: Anima Books, 1981.

The same type of guide as Focus on Buddhism. Lists
several films, a few recordings, and slide sets pertaining to the United States.

014. Melton, J. Gordon, and Geisendorfer, James V. A
Directory of Religious Bodies in the United States. New
York: Garland Publishing, 1977.

Supplements Melton's Encyclopedia of American Religions
[item 004] by providing addresses. Includes many
new religious groups among the 1,275 bodies listed.
Arranged alphabetically by name and also classified
by type. Not all will agree with Melton's classifica-
tion system, but no one else has made such a good
attempt at classifying alternative religions. Out of
date but still the best resource.

015. Regush, Nicholas, and Regush, June. The New Consciousness Catalogue. New York: G.P. Putnam's Sons, 1979.

A tabloid-size paperback "whole earth catalogue" of the
new consciousness movement. A fairly effective guide
to resources for psychic and spiritual development
through parapsychology, human potential groups, and
spiritual healing. Lists organizations, publications,
and bookstores in a classified arrangement. Lacks an
index but has a detailed table of contents.

016. Ryan, Tim, and Jappinen, Rae. The Whole Again Resource
Guide. Santa Barbara, Calif.: SourceNet, 1982.

Periodicals and a small number of books are classified
by subject matter, such as feminist, nature religions,
New Age, spiritual growth, and yoga. Within each section, periodicals are listed alphabetically; each entry
includes address, price, size, and a brief description
of contents. Geographic, title, and publisher indexes.
The authors intend to publish annually. An excellent
source for many hard-to-locate periodicals published
by small religious groups.

017. Singh, Parmatma. The New Consciousness Sourcebook:
Spiritual Community Guide. Berkeley: Spiritual Community
Publications, 1982.

Includes groups devoted to various New Age activities
such as spiritual growth, holistic health, and ecology,
with special emphasis on peace and nuclear disarmament
work. Groups are listed alphabetically, each with a
brief self-description and address, and geographically
also. Classified listings of publishers, periodicals,
retreats, food and health products, etc. are spotty
in coverage. Not as comprehensive as Melton's Directory
of Religious Bodies [item 014] but more up to date.
Geographical listing is unique and very handy.

Indexes

018. ABC Pol Sci, A Bibliography of Contents: Political
Science and Government. Santa Barbara, Calif.: ABC-Clio,
1969- .

   Published several times a year, this listing of the contents of the latest issues of journals in the fields
   of government, law, and public policy is useful for
   keeping current. Author and subject indexes.

019. Alternative Press Index. Northfield, Minn.: Radical
Research Center, 1970- .

   Useful for its coverage of alternative and radical
   periodicals including titles concerned with feminist
   spirituality, such as Heresies. The early years include
   material on the counterculture and religious communes.
   Published quarterly.

020. Child Development Abstracts and Bibliography.
Lafayette, Ind.: Purdue University, Society for Research in
Child Development, 1927- .

   Repeats material included in Psychological Abstracts,
   but covers pediatrics and physical medicine more ex-
   tensively. Published three times a year. American and
   foreign periodicals are included.   Book notices are
   also included. Arranged by subject with author and
   subject indexes.

021. Index to Legal Periodicals.   New York: Wilson, 1909-   .

   Monthly indexes with annual and three-year cumulations.
   Access by subject and author.   A table of cases and
   book review index also included.

022. Psychological Abstracts. Lancaster, Penn.: American
Psychological Association, 1927- .

   An important bibliography listing new books, journal
   articles, technical reports, and other scientific
   documents. Arrangement is classified.   Data published
   since 1967 is also available for online computer
   searching through the Bibliographic   Retrieval Service
   and DIALOG. Good source for psychological studies of
   new religious movements.

023. Public Affairs Information Service. Bulletin of the
Public Affairs Information Service.   New York: The Service,
1915-.

Very useful subject index for topics related to
legislation and social conditions. Indexes a wide
variety of materials: books, documents, pamphlets,
reports of public and private agencies and periodical
articles. Published weekly with five cumulations
yearly, the last being the annual volume. Can be
searched online through the Bibliographic Retrieval
Service and DIALOG (years since 1976).

024. Reader's Guide to Periodical Literature. New York:
Wilson, 1905-.

Subject and author index for popular periodicals.
Several issues each year with annual cumulations.

025. Religion Index One: Periodicals. Chicago: American
Theological Library Association, 1977-.

Formerly Index to Religious Periodical Literature
(1949-77). Indexes by subject and author about 200
religious and theological periodicals with selected
articles abstracted. Includes a book review index to
scholarly books. Semiannual with cumulations every
two years. Good source for social-scientific studies
of new religious movements. Available through the
Bibliographic Retrieval Service for online searching
as one database with Religion Index Two: Multi-Author
Works [item 026].

026. Religion Index Two: Multi-Author Works, 1976- .
Chicago: American Theological Library Association, 1978- .

Indexes both entire multi-author works and individual
essays within them by subject, authors, and editors.
Entry under editor of each work gives full bibliographic
citation and lists contents. Available through the
Bibliographic Retrieval Service for online searching
as one database with Religion Index One: Periodicals
[item 025]. Published annually.

027. Social Science Citation Index. Philadelphia: Institute
for Science Information, 1973- .

There are three approaches to this excellent index:
1) citation index, arranged alphabetically by cited
author, with references to articles in which a work
is cited; 2) source index, alphabetically arranged by
author, with full bibliographic citations and author's
address if available; and 3) Permuterm subject index,
a system which uses keywords in titles, permutating them
to form all possible pairs of terms. Can be searched online
through the Bibliographic Retrieval Service and DIALOG.

028. Sociological Abstracts. New York: Sociological Abstracts,
1952- .

A classified abstract journal that covers a broad
range of sociological articles in periodicals in various
languages. The last issue of each year is a cumulative
index for the year. A fine source for sociological
studies of new religious movements. Available for online
computer searching through DIALOG and the Bibliographic
Retrieval Service. Frequency varies.

Bibliographies

029. Beckford, James A., and Richardson, James T. "A Bibliography of Social Scientific Studies of New Religious Movements." Social Forces 30(1983): 111-135.

Lists anthropological, psychiatric, psychological, and
sociological publications of the 1960s and 1970s
including North American and Western European books,
journal articles, conference papers, and some theses
and dissertations. Comprehensive, but listed by
author only; no subject access. A revised version is
planned.

030. Cato, Lynn E. UFOs and Related Subjects: An Annotated
Bibliography. Detroit: Gale Research, 1978.

Comprehensive, annotated bibliography arranged by
subject. Includes occult and religious aspects, but
many of these must be found indirectly by searching
through chapters such as "contact claims" and "communication," as there is no subject index. The main
bibliography was published in 1969 by the Library of
Congress. The 1978 edition is supplemented by Kay
Rodgers' select bibliography of 200 items published
between 1969 and 1976. Rodgers' work is not annotated.

031. Clarie, Thomas C. Occult Bibliography: An Annotated
List of Books Published in English, 1971 through 1975. Metuchen, N.J.: Scarecrow Press, 1978.

Clarie offers extensive annotations of most of the
titles he lists. Indexed by author, title, and subject.
Large numbers of titles under astrology, psychical
research, magic, and occult science, reflecting the
interests of many new religious groups.

032. Earhart, H. Byron. The New Religions of Japan: A
Bibliography of Western-Language Materials. 2d ed. Michigan
Papers in Japanese Studies, no. 9. Ann Arbor: Center for
Japanese Studies, University of Michigan, 1983.

Lists over 1,400 primary and secondary writings.
Introductory essay discusses place of new religions
in history of Japan and describes organization of the

bibliography. Annotated section on general works is
followed by unannotated bibliographies for over fifty
religions, some of which have followings in the United
States. Excellent resource by a distinguished scholar.
Name and topic indexes.

033. Galbreath, Robert. "The History of Modern Occultism:
A Bibliographical Survey." Journal of Popular Culture 5
(1971): 726-754.

Bibliographical essay reviews nearly 300 scholarly
and popular items published in the nineteenth and
twentieth centuries. Emphasizes English-language historical studies. Useful guide to background material
concerned with metaphysical occultism.

034. Jarrell, Howard R. International Yoga Bibliography,
1950 to 1980. Metuchen, N.J.: Scarecrow Press, 1981.

Useful listing of books, articles, and periodicals
in Western European languages and theses in English.
No attempt is made to evaluate items. Information
needed for ordering, such as distributors' addresses,
is included. Subject index includes names of Hindu
groups that appear as publishers. Also has author and
title indexes.

035. McDermott, Robert A. "Indian Spirituality in the West:
A Bibliographical Mapping." Philosophy East and West 25
(1975): 213-239.

Bibliographic essay covering Indian spiritual teachings
prominent in the West between 1965 and 1975. Aims at
scholars and interested lay readers. Discusses
works of several Indian teachers and makes some
reference to interpretive studies by Westerners. Best
used to introduce readers to work of Indian gurus.
Includes bibliography of works cited.

036. Medical and Psychological Scientific Research on Yoga
and Meditation. Denmark: Bindu, 1978.

452 scientific reports gleaned from Psychological
Abstracts, Medlars II (a computer data base of medical
literature) and other sources. Most items were published
in the 1970s.   Introductory bibliographic essay is
followed by the bibliography, arranged by author. Many
items have annotations. Includes studies of Transcendental Meditation, Zen meditation, yoga, and other forms
of meditation. Use is hampered by lack of a subject
index.

037. Melton, J. Gordon. Magic, Witchcraft, and Paganism in
America: A Bibliography. Garland Bibliographies on Sects and
Cults, vol. 1. New York: Garland Publishing, 1982.

Classified listing of more than 1,500 items relating to
witches, pagans, and magicians throughout American
history. Particularly useful for materials on contemporary feminist witchcraft and Neo-Paganism. Ninety
percent of the items are at Melton's Institute for the
Study of American Religions. A valuable bibliography
covering neglected areas. First volume in a series
that will cover several new religious groups and prom-
ises to be invaluable. Author index.

038. Popenoe, Chris. Inner Development. Washington, D.C.:
Yes! Inc., 1979. (Dist. by Random House.)

A bookstore catalog with over 600 pages of annotated
titles arranged within subject categories such as
"Contemporary Spiritual Teachers," "Tantra," and "Christianity." An author index is provided along with
publishers' codes and addresses, making this an especially
useful source for tracking down small publishers. Kept
up to date with supplements.

039. Porter, Jack Nusan, comp. Jews and the Cults. Fresh
Meadows, N.Y.: Biblio Press, 1981.

Many books and articles listed here concern Jews and
cults directly, but some items are general scholarly
studies. Most entries are annotated. List of organizations offering help for troubled families and cult
members at the end is now out of date.

040. Rambo, Lewis R. "Current Research on Religious Conversion." Religious Studies Review 8(1982): 146-159.

Most titles listed have been published since 1950.
Scholarly books and journal articles are arranged by
discipline: anthropological, sociological, historical,
psychological, psychoanalytical, and theological. Each
section is introduced by a short overview indicating
important works. Includes many items on new religious
groups; other items may provide fruitful related
reading.

041. Richardson, James T. "New Religious Movements in the
United States: A Review." Social Compass 30(1983): 85-110.

Reviews a selection of scholarly writings published
through 1980. Pays significant attention to quantitative studies, and especially those concerned with type
of people attracted to alternative religions. Bibliography.

042. Robbins, Thomas, comp. Civil Liberties, "Brainwashing"
and "Cults": A Select Annotated Bibliography. Berkeley:
Center for the Study of New Religious Movmeents, Graduate
Theological Union, 1981. Distributed by: New Religious

Movements Research Collection, Graduate Theological Union
Library, Berkeley, California.

   Covers conversion and brainwashing, civil liberties,
   deprogramming, and public policy. Robbins is a sociologist whose strong civil libertarian stance against
   government intervention in cults is reflected in his
   annotations. Author index.

043. Robbins, Thomas. "Sociological Studies of New Religious
Movements: A Selective Review." Religious Studies Review
9(1983): 233-239.

   In this essay Robbins focuses on the contents of
   volumes of collected essays, special issues of journals,
   and monographs. His earlier bibliographic essays are
   better written and include journal articles.

044. Robbins, Thomas; Anthony, Dick; and Richardson, James T.
"Theory and Research on Today's 'New Religions.'" Sociological Analysis 39(1978): 95-122.

   Important bibliographic essay covering sociological
   studies published through 1977. Includes over 200
   titles. Essay is divided into subject areas, including
   "typology," "church-sect theory," and "conversion and
   commitment." Several minor errors occur in bibliographic citations, but generally they do not prevent
   locating the items.

045. Roszak, Betty, comp. A Select Filmography on New
Religious Movements. Berkeley: Program for the Study of New
Religious Movements, Graduate Theological Union, 1979.

   Annotated list of about sixty films, arranged by title.
   Running time, publication date,color of film, subject
   matter, and distributor are included in each annotation.
   Distributors' addresses are given in a separate list.
   Now out of date, but a useful starting point. Still
   available from the Graduate Theological Union Library.

046. Spiritual Counterfeits Project. Bibliography. Berkeley:
Spiritual Counterfeits Project, 1981.

   Selected, annotated bibliography of evangelical Christian
   materials critical of the occult, Transcendental Meditation, Unification Church, and other popular groups.

047. Walsh, Roger N. "Meditation Research: An Introduction
and Review." Journal of Transpersonal Psychology, no. 2
(1979), pp. 161-174.

   A review of the literature is followed by a bibliography
   of nearly eighty scholarly books and journal articles.
   Without trying to be exhaustive, Walsh has chosen works

to demonstrate the evolution and state of the research.
Includes articles reporting research on medical and
clinical psychological uses of Zen and Transcendental
Meditation not listed in this volume.

048. Weiman, Mark. <u>Yoga: A Bibliography</u>. Berkeley: The
Movable Foundation Workshop Press, 1980.

Lists English language books, films, filmstrips, and
recordings. Includes primarily writings of Indians,
some of whom teach in the West. Has glaring omissions;
for example, includes none of Muktananda's work. Also
suffers from lack of indexing.

049. Zimmerman, Marie. <u>Jesus Movement</u>. RIC Supplement, no. 4.
Strasbourg: Cerdic Publications, 1973.

Computer-produced listing of 219 books, journal
articles, and pamphlets in English and Western European
languages published through 1973, arranged by author.

Cultural Background of
New Religious Movements

050. Ahlstrom, Sydney E. "The Traumatic Years: American.
Religion and Culture in the '60s and '70s." Theology Today
36(1980): 504-522.

> Ahlstrom, a noted historian of American.religion,
> discusses what he calls the "revolutionary" changes
> in American culture and religion between 1960 and
> 1975. A good overview, useful for understanding the
> milieu that fostered the growth of nontraditional
> religions. The author also sees the possibility that
> as a whole, new religions may be perpetuating the aims
> of the counterculture--oneness with nature, opposition
> to racism and sexism, and an attempt to humanize the
> social order.

051. Bellah, Robert N. The Broken Covenant. New York: Seabury
Press, 1975.

> This book grew out of a series of lectures, the Weil
> Lectures, which Bellah presented in 1971 at Hebrew
> Union College/Jewish Institute of Religion in Cincinnati.
> The lectures are more about the religious underpinnings
> of American society than about new religious movements.
> Toward the end of the book, Bellah places the growth of
> cults in the context of the cultural crisis of the
> 1960s. He states that the new religious groups strive
> for a median course between humanism and utilitarian
> individualism. Important contribution that has influ-
> enced other sociologists.

052. Bodemann, Y. Michal. "Mystical, Satanic, and Chiliastic
Forces in Countercultural Movements: Changing the World--Or
Reconciling It." Youth and Society 5(1974): 433-447.

> Discusses the counterculture of the 1960s and 1970s.

Claims that mystical, satanic, and millennialistic trends are dangerous because they deny the antagonism between social classes and substitute "small groups of belongingness."

053. Ellwood, Robert S., Jr. "Asian Religions in North America." In New Religious Movements, edited by John Coleman and Gregory Baum, pp. 17-22. Concilium, vol. 161. New York: Seabury Press, 1983.

A brief overview of Hinduism, Buddhism, Sikhism, and Sufism, past and present, among occidental Americans. Notes.

054. Foss, Daniel A., and Larkin, Ralph W. "From 'The Gates of Eden' to 'Day of the Locust': An Analysis of the Dissident Youth Movement of the 1960s and Its Heirs of the 1970s-- the Post-Movement Groups." Theory and Society 3(1976): 45- 64.

A broad overview of the youth movement of the 1960s and early 1970s. The authors see several phases in this movement, giving the unique characteristics of each and describing relationships to earlier and later phases. New spiritual groups are referred to as postmovement groups because they came to prominence after the primary period of social conflict and rein- terpretation of social reality that occurred in the 1960s. Useful, concise descriptions. References.

055. Judah, J. Stillson. "The Attraction of Youth to New Religious Movements: Data from the Hare Krishna Movement, Unification Church, and Jews for Jesus." Paper read at the Pacific School of Religion, Berkeley, California, 22 Jan- uary 1979, photocopied.

A brief overview citing normal adolescent identity confusion, 1960s breakdown of traditional religions, and the rise of the counterculture as significant factors in the growth of new religious groups.

056. King, Winston L. "Eastern Religions: A New Interest and Influence." The Annals of the American Academy of Political and Social Science 387(1970): 66-76.

King considers reasons for the appeal of Eastern religions in the United States: doctrinal flexibility, belief in the interrelatedness of all life, and intuitive orientation. In speculating on the effects of Eastern modes of thinking on Western life, King correctly predicts a meaningful effect on psychotherapy.

057. Musgrove, Frank. Ecstasy and Holiness: Counterculture and the Open Society. Bloomington: Indiana University Press, 1975.

Describes interviews and survey research on counter-culture values. Although Musgrove does not discuss religion as such, his book is useful background reading.

058. Needleman, Jacob. Consciousness and Tradition. New York: Crossroad, 1982.

Series of essays and philosophical discussions on topics related to new religious movements, including magic, Gurdjieff, and the search for the sacred. Includes many references to spiritual disciplines and Needleman's personal search. Index.

059. Needleman, Jacob. The New Religions. New York: E.P. Dutton, 1977.

A readable, descriptive account of the teachings and practices of the Zen Center of San Francisco, Subud, Transcendental Meditation, and other groups. Needleman's main aim, which he accomplishes well, is understanding underlying principles and approaching the spiritual search with thoughtful sympathy. Index and brief list of suggested readings.

060. Passmore, John. "Paradise Now: The Logic of the New Mysticism." Encounter, no. 5(1970), pp. 3-21.

Well-constructed critique of superficial aspects of counterculture values, particularly the search for mystical experiences. Claims that mystical experiences do not necessarily make people better persons, do not promote true community, and are intellectually reactionary. Notes.

061. Roszak, Theodore. The Making of a Counter Culture: Reflections on the Technocratic Society and Its Youthful Opposition. Garden City, N.Y.: Doubleday, 1969.

Roszak joins with the voices expounding the need for religious experience in a materialistic and scientific culture and examines what's going on, who's doing it, and why. Important contribution. Bibliographical notes.

062. Roszak, Theodore. Person/Planet: The Creative Disintegration of Industrial Society. New York: Anchor Press/Doubleday, 1978.

Roszak expands on his earlier study, The Making of a Counter Culture [item 061], and discusses ways in which the yearning for growth and authenticity has spread throughout the culture. He sees great value in this yearning and argues that it can lead to the development of small-scale operations characterized by strong individual participation and allowing for spiritual and personal growth.

063. Roszak, Theodore. Unfinished Animal: The Aquarian
Frontier and the Evolution of Consciousness. New York:
Harper and Row, 1977.

Although Roszak is critical of what he perceives to be
self-indulgent and eclectic occult and mystical groups,
he also finds seeds of a true spiritual awakening in
new religious groups. He surveys and critiques spiritual and quasi-spiritual disciplines with an eye for
the genuine and its importance. A very fine, readable
book. Index of group and personal names.

064. Wills, Gary. "What Religious Revival?" Psychology Today,
no. 11(1978), pp. 74-81.

Wills examines survey data on changing religious
attitudes, cults, and spiritual revival and finds
methodological flaws. He maintains that such problems
in questionnaire design may have led researchers to
think there is a religious revival when in fact no fundamental change has occurred.

065. Wuthnow, Robert. The Consciousness Reformation.
Berkeley: University of California Press, 1976.

Wuthnow uses data obtained by the Berkeley Religious
Consciousness Group, which studied religious, quasi-
religious, and political aspects of the counterculture
in the San Francisco Bay Area (see Glock and Bellah,
eds. The New Religious Consciousness [item 190] for
results) to support his theory that the experimentation
of the counterculture is part of a broad, long-range
cultural shift toward social alternatives. Four meaning
systems are identified, and the impact of each on contemporary social experimentation is assessed. The social
science and mystical meaning systems are considered to
be increasing in influence, while the theistic and
individualistic are declining. A serious, thorough piece
of scholarship. Appendices include statistical tables
and the interview schedule. Index.

066. Yankelovich, Daniel. New Rules: Searching for Self-
Fulfillment in a World Turned Upside Down. New York: Random
House, 1981.

Discussion of survey research data that show a significant change in personal values for many Americans in
the past twenty years. Provides a picture of cultural
flux and shows that the search for self-fulfillment has
ramifications extending beyond new religious movements.

Interdisciplinary
Collected Essays

067. Bromley,David G., and Richardson, James T., eds.
The Brainwashing/Deprogramming Controversy: Sociological,
Psychological, Legal and Historical Perspectives. Studies
in Religion and Society, no. 5. New York: Edwin Mellen
Press, 1983.

Twenty essays grouped by the disciplines mentioned in
the book's subtitle. The authors are scholars who have
studied new religions for several years and as a group
have provided some of the most significant research in
this area. The book strongly rejects a simplistic
mind-control model of conversion in favor of more
complex models that the authors' research supports.
Nothing really new here, many essays are reprints, but
this is an important compilation representing a solid
body of research. It should become a standard in the
field. One good bibliography at the end.

068. Bryant, M. Darrol, and Richardson, Herbert W., eds.
A Time for Consideration: A Scholarly Appraisal of the
Unification Church. New York: Edwin Mellen Press, 1978.

Contributors include Harvey Cox, Herbert Richardson,
Richard de Maria, Warren Lewis, and others. Another
version of Cox's essay appears in Needleman and Baker's
Understanding the New Religions [item 073].Richardson, Bryant,
and Lewis appear here as apologists for the Unification Church. Testa's article is a good critique of
newspaper reportage. De Maria's analysis of conversion
notes the need in our society for vision, which he says
is being met by Unification Church ideology and
community, but he is also critical of the church's
methods and ideology.

069. The Cult Phenomenon: Mental Health, Legal, and Religious Implications. Garden Grove, Calif.: InfoMedix, 1982.

Recordings of talks by Louis J. West, Margaret Singer, Richard Delgado, Barbara Underwood Scharff, Rabbi Robbins, and others, focussing on the destructive aspects of cult life. Sponsored jointly by the Neuropsychiatric Institute of UCLA, the Department of Continuing Education in the Health Sciences of the UCLA Extension, and the Southern California Psychiatric Society.

070. Fichter, Joseph H., ed. Alternatives to American Mainline Churches. Conference Series, no. 14. Barrytown, N.Y.: Unification Theological Seminary, 1983.

Collection of papers presented at a conference sponsored by New Era, an organization connected with the Unification Church. The papers reflect historical and sociological perspectives. The latter approach is found in Rodney Stark and William Bainbridge's conceptual paper, in which they separate religion from its secular imitations and also discuss cult/sect development. David Martin continues in the same vein with his assertion that the search for individual grace or self-mastery is a hallmark of cults. Frank Flinn analyzes Scientology as a fusion of Buddhism and technology. Based on a year of participant-observation study with the Hare Krishnas, Larry Shinn claims that conversion and commitment are more complex than has been recognized and that the religious dimensions of joining that groups have been undervalued. Finally, Joseph Fichter provides a readable description of the "home church" movement of the Unification Church: people who are associated with the UC but are not full-time workers. Overall, a good collection of essays covering some new ground.

071. Horowitz, Irving Louis, ed. Science, Sin, and Scholarship: The Politics of Reverend Moon and the Unification Church. Cambridge, Mass.: Massachusetts Institute of Technology Press, 1978.

A potpourri of contributions, including academic articles, popular magazine pieces, theological studies of Moon's writings, extracts from addresses given by Moon, and statements given to Congressional hearings. Horowitz attempts to put the UC into "the perspective of American social history as well as the international political future." Although there is considerable balance among the essays, the quality is uneven. Still, a useful contribution.

072. Kaslow, Florence, and Sussman, Marvin B., eds. Cults and the Family. New York: Haworth Press, 1982.

This collection of essays was first published as volume 4, numbers 3 and 4 of Marriage and Family Review. Includes psychological and sociological studies and an ex-Unification Church member's account of his

involvement. Edwards's "Moonie brainwashing" account
is typical of such accounts and contributes nothing new.
Kaslow and Schwartz in their introductory essay fail
to differentiate types of cults or to produce a workable
definition of cults. Beckford's research on family
responses to children's involvement in the Unification
Church shows that families differ. Robbins and Anthony
call for more and better longitudinal studies of cults.
A balance of perspectives but uneven quality. Bibliographies.

073. Needleman, Jacob, and Baker, George, eds. Understanding
the New Religions. New York: Seabury Press, 1978.

A variety of essays and reflections on the role of the
new religions in American history, their nature and
significance today, and their phenomenology. The papers
were presented in 1977 at a conference that inaugurated
the Graduate Theological Union's Center for the Study
of New Religious Movements. The twenty-four pieces vary
in quality, with Sydney Ahlstrom's historical essay
being one of the best. Archie Smith takes white scholars
to task for ignoring black religious movements and seeing the new religious movements phenomenon as white and
middle class. Other noted scholars represented here
include Robert Wuthnow, J. Stillson Judah, Robert
Bellah, and Theodore Roszak. On the whole a good contribution, though insecurity regarding methods of study
and the meaning and place of new religions in American
life is evident in some essays. Index.

074. "The New Cults: A Critique." The Humanist, September/
October 1974, pp. 4-33.

Several brief articles displaying different points of
view on the growth of new religions and providing
descriptions of Scientology, ISKCON, witchcraft, and
the occult. Marcello Truzzi's "Nouveau Witches" is a
particularly useful discussion that takes the reader
beyond stereotypes and provides a glimpse into the real
variety of Neo-Pagan groups. A few of the articles
present a "humanist" point of view that is critical of
all beliefs that cannot be scientifically verified.

075. New Religious Movements in America. New York: The
Rockefeller Foundation, 1979.

Abridged version of discussions that took place
during the New Religious Movements Conference held at
the Graduate Theological Union in Berkeley in 1977.
Topics include new religions and mental health, adult
religion, and the development of new religious
organizations. An interesting look at the way scholars
view research on new religious movements and the
problems it presents. See Understanding the New Religions [item 073] for the papers presented at the conference.

076. Shupe, Anson D., Jr. <u>Six Perspectives on New Religions:</u>
<u>A Case Study Approach</u>. New York: Edwin Mellen, 1981.

A survey of approaches to the study of unconventional
religions, including criminological, philosophical,
anthropological, social-psychological, social-structural,
and historical. Shupe has chosen two texts to represent each perspective, which he presents as abstracts
within his discussions. Each case study concludes with
a suggested reading list and questions for discussion,
making this a useful text for the classroom. Shupe
makes clear that no one approach to the study of
fringe religions can present a complete picture.

Historical Studies

077. Atkins, Gaius G. <u>Modern Religious Cults and Movements</u>.
New York: Fleming H. Revell Co., 1923.

> A study of religious movements that started in the
> late nineteenth century and were popular in the 1920s.
> Includes Christian Science, New Thought, Theosophy,
> and Spiritualism. Pays attention to role of changes
> in scientific thinking and the development of
> psychology in creating an atmosphere conducive to
> religious experimentation. Similarities to contemporary
> movements can be seen.

078. Braden, Charles S. <u>Spirits in Rebellion: The Rise and
Development of New Thought</u>. Dallas: Southern Methodist
University Press, 1963.

> Braden's ample history of the metaphysical New Thought
> movement is good background reading for understanding
> a number of related contemporary groups. The emphasis
> on the power of the mind to heal, perhaps with
> different philosophical underpinnings, is strikingly
> similar to the new holistic health movement. Lengthy
> bibliography and index.

079. Braden, Charles S. <u>These Also Believe: A Study of
Modern American Cults and Minority Religious Movements</u>.
New York: Macmillan, 1949.

> Braden includes the I AM Movement (historically
> related to the Church Universal and Triumphant),
> Theosophy, and New Thought among the several religious
> bodies he describes with objectivity. He claims ori-
> ginal studies of Psychiana, Father Divine, and I AM
> and presents substantial chapters on each, including
> analysis of teachings, history, and experiences of mem-
> bers. Annotated bibliography and index.

080. Bridges, Hal. American Mysticism: From William James
to Zen. New York: Harper & Row, 1970. Reprint: Lakemont,
Ga.: CSA Press, 1977.

    A history of mystical experience and thought in the
    United States since 1900. Perhaps of greatest interest
    is the author's discussion of Vedanta, Zen Buddhism,
    and psychedelic drugs. These chapters include many
    references to the literature of their subjects and
    should be useful to readers who wish more in-depth
    treatment than this broad overview supplies. Notes,
    bibliography, and index.

081. Campbell, Bruce F. Ancient Wisdom Revived: A History
of the Theosophical Movement. Berkeley: University of
California Press, 1980.

    Campbell approaches the Theosophical movement with
    appreciation for its contributions and a willingness to
    examine its problems. He also discusses offshoots and
    related movements in enough detail to establish their
    connection to Theosophical ideas. Bibliography and
    index.

082. Ellwood, Robert S., Jr. Alternative Altars: Unconventional and Eastern Spirituality in America. Chicago:
University of Chicago Press, 1979.

    Investigation of alternatives to Judeo-Christian main-
    stream religions and the significance of those religions
    for American spiritual culture. Provides an understand-
    ing of alternative religions throughout American history.
    Focuses on spiritualism, Theosophy, and Zen Buddhism
    as significant examples of religious alternatives.
    Ellwood sees a growth of religion away from other
    social institutions and toward a small-group subjective
    experience. Index.

083. Ellwood, Robert S., Jr. The Eagle and the Rising Sun:
Americans and the New Religions of Japan. Philadelphia:
Westminster Press, 1974.

    Ellwood explores the impact in America of Tenrikyo,
    Nichiren Shoshu, The Church of World Messianity, Seicho-
    no-Ie, and Perfect Liberty. Teachings and history of
    each are described in a readable and sympathetic
    fashion. Addresses for United States offices of the
    religions are provided. A good introduction. Notes
    and index.

084. Ellwood, Robert S., Jr. One Way: The Jesus Movement
and Its Meaning. Englewood Cliffs, N.J.: Prentice-Hall, 1973.

    In this very good, insightful study, Ellwood firmly
    grounds the Jesus Movement in American culture and

religious history. A few specific groups are discussed,
notably the Children of God. Considering the publication date, these descriptions must now be regarded as
historical. As usual, Ellwood's style is imbued with
the personal and is eminently readable. Bibliography
and index.

085. Ellwood, Robert S., Jr. Religious and Spiritual Groups
in Modern America. Englewood Cliffs, N.J.: Prentice-Hall,
1973.

A very fine overview and introduction to both the
current crop of alternative religions and some from
the nineteenth and early twentieth centuries, with
historical links to similar types all the way back to
the Hellenistic period. In the first part of the book
Ellwood gives characteristics of cults and sects and
discusses shamanism. Drawing on important contributors
to the study of religion, he provides a theoretical
framework for the descriptions of a panorama of groups
that occupy the remainder of the volume. Readable
and useful as a college textbook. Bibliography,
addresses of groups discussed, and index.

086. Fields, Rick. How the Swans Came to the Lake: A
Narrative History of Buddhism in America. Boulder, Colo.:
Shambhala, 1981.

Fields, a journalist, has written a thoroughly docu-
mented popular history of Buddhism in America. He
bases his work on interviews, in-depth reading of the
literature, and his own close contact with Buddhists.
Some attention is paid to the origins of Buddhism; then
the author moves quickly to nineteenth-century America.
Fields' book is fascinating for its ample treatment
of lesser known figures but somewhat lacking in full
treatment of Chinese- and Japanese-American Buddhism.
Although this is a long book, the clear style makes
for enjoyable reading. Includes photographs. Sources,
notes, and index of names.

087. French, Harold W. The Swan's Wide Waters: Ramakrishna
and Western Culture. Port Washington, N.Y.: Kennikat Press,
1974.

A history of the Vedanta Society from its inception in
India to its contemporary manifestation in the United
States. French gives an in-depth look at the group's
history prior to 1930 but is brief in his treatment
of Vedanta since then. He maintains that Vedanta has
not grown as much as other religious groups recently
but has shown a new vitality. A useful contribution.
Notes and index.

088. Gelberg, Steven J., ed. Hare Krishna, Hare Krishna:
Five Distinguished Scholars on the Krishna Movement in the
West. New York: Grove Press, 1983.

Gelberg, a member of ISKCON, interviews Harvey Cox,
Larry D. Shinn, Thomas J. Hopkins, A.L. Basham, and
Shrivatsa Goswami. Intended as an introduction to the
movement, this book pays much attention to ISKCON's
historical roots in India. The conversational tone
provides for interesting reading, and a great deal of
information is covered. Includes photographs. Glossary,
bibliography, and index.

089. Jackson, Carl Thomas. The Oriental Religions and American Thought: Nineteenth Century Explorations. Contributions
in American Studies, vol. 55.   Westport, Conn.: Greenwood
Press, 1981.

History of Asian religions in America from the 1700s
to 1900, with emphasis on the 1800s. Claims to be
"the first systematic examination based on wide-ranging
research in the sources." Author plans a sequel to
cover the twentieth century. Islam, Sufism, and Zoro-
astrianism are not included. Focuses on influence of
Hinduism and Buddhism on American writers and religious
leaders rather than on Asians who carried their
religions here. Ends with a chapter on the Parliament
of Religions in 1893. Marginal but interesting. Notes,
bibliography, and index.

090. Judah, J. Stillson. The History and Philosophy of the
Metaphysical Movements in America. Philadelphia: Westminster
Press, 1967.

Spiritualism, Theosophy, Religious Science, Christian
Science, and New Thought are treated as one movement
with diverse expressions. Judah states that all share
a common concern with the practical application of
the "Truth of Being." An emphasis on diet and health
is also found in many of the newer religions, some of
which are metaphysical. Judah describes the teachings,
history, and practices of each group in individual
chapters. An important book. Index.

091. Layman, Emma McCloy. Buddhism in America. Chicago:
Nelson-Hall, 1976.

Includes chapters on each of the major schools of
Buddhism found in the United States. Layman also
discusses what attracts certain Americans to Buddhism
and attempts to identify personality characteristics
of such people as gleaned from visits to many Buddhist
centers. Pays attention to ways in which Buddhism may
offer solutions to social and personal problems.
Glossary, index, and bibliography.

092. Lyons, Arthur. _The Second Coming: Satanism in America_. New York: Dodd, Mead and Co., 1970.

Discusses historical and contemporary forms of Satanism within the context of psychological motivation. The Church of Satan is given special attention as a primary example of an intellectual and benign form of Satanism. Bibliography and index.

093. McLoughlin, William G. _Revivals, Awakenings, and Reform: An Essay on Religion and Social Change in America, 1607-1977_. Chicago: University of Chicago Press, 1978.

Treats recent growth of new religious movements as a "fourth Great Awakening" and relates it historically to earlier revivals. An insightful and thorough account of social factors involved in the contemporary spiritual awakenings.

094. Mathison, Richard R. _Faiths, Cults, and Sects of America: From Atheism to Zen_. Indianapolis: Bobbs-Merrill Co., 1960.

Interesting as a broad survey of many cults and sects, with a sharp eye for charlatans. Written for a general audience, very readable. Index.

095. Melton, J. Gordon. "The Revival of Astrology in the United States: A Perspective on Occult Religion in Modern America." Photocopied. Evanston, Ill.: Institute for the Study of American Religion, 1982.

Melton takes scholars to task for their neglect of the occult background that gives impetus to many new religious movements. He focuses on astrology as having the largest number of participants among occult persuasions.

096. Mickler, Michael L. "A History of the Unification Church in the Bay Area: 1960-74." Master's thesis, Graduate Theological Union, Berkeley, 1980.

Begins with the arrival of UC members from Eugene, Oregon in 1960 and ends with Moon's "Day of Hope" tours in 1974, before the start of the Mose Durst "Oakland Family" era that has been so heavily criticized for its recruitment tactics. Certainly the most detailed history available for that time period. Mickler had access to UC materials no longer publicly available, so his notes and bibliography are invaluable sources.

097. Morita, Yuri. "Daimoku and the Sacred Pipe: The Encounter of Buddhism with the Native American Indians." Master's thesis, Graduate Theological Union, Berkeley, 1981.

A chronicle of a unique collaboration established in
1977 between the Japan Buddhist Sangha, a small Nichiren
Buddhist sect, and the Native American Indian movement
to work nonviolently toward peace. Bibliography.

098. Prebish, Charles. American Buddhism. North Scituate,
Mass.: Duxbury Press, 1979.

Introductory work, important, concise. Describes his-
tory, facilities, personnel, membership rituals,
future plans, and publications of the Buddhist Churches
of America, Nichiren Shoshu of America, San Francisco
Zen Center, Buddhist Vihara Society, Sino-American
Buddhist Association, Nyingma Center, Vajradhatu and
Nalanda Foundation, and Shasta Abbey. Discusses how
Buddhism in this country is developing a distinct
American identity. Bibliography.

099. Raschke, Carl A. The Interruption of Eternity:
Modern Gnosticism and the Origins of the New Religious
Consciousness. Chicago: Nelson-Hall, 1980.

Elegant writing but a questionable use of the term
gnosticism, which Raschke admits he has expanded to
include systems of thought that are critical of
industrialization and advocate seeking salvation
beyond history. Traces gnosticism from the Greco-
Roman period to the present, finding elements in
the Romantics, Gurdjieff, Jung, New Thought, Divine
Light Mission, and ISKCON. Notes and index.

100. Reiterman, Tim, and Jacobs, John. Raven: The Untold
Story of the Reverend Jim Jones and His People. New York:
E.P. Dutton, 1982.

This thoroughly researched, readable book provides
the most complete biography to date of Jim Jones,
showing the existence of troubling personality traits
in him from childhood. Through extensive use of
interviews and documentary materials, Reiterman and
Jacobs also give a comprehensive history of Peoples
Temple. Sources are noted, and there is an index.

101. Reston, James, Jr. Our Father Who Art in Hell.
New York: Quadrangle/New York Times Book Co., 1981.

Reston tells about Jim Jones, the Guyana settlement,
and his own struggle in obtaining information from the
FCC following the Jonestown tragedy. The great value
of this book, which some have called definitive and
others say is flawed by speculation, is the extensive
use of primary material on Jim Jones and Jonestown,
particularly the tapes Jones made of his own talks.
Reston confines his study to the Peoples Temple in
Guyana and diplomatic relationships with that country.
Although Reston describes generally the documents used,
a bibliography would have been a useful addition.

102. Robbins, Thomas, and Anthony, Dick. "Cults, Brainwashing, and Counter-Subversion." Annals of the American Academy of Political and Social Science 446 (1979): 78-90.

   Robbins and Anthony find similarities between today's
   hostility and distrust of authoritarian religious
   groups and the anti-Masonic, anti-Mormon, and anti-
   Catholic agitation of the nineteenth century.

103. Shepherd, William C. "Conversion and Adhesion." In
Religious Change and Continuity, edited by Harry M. Johnson,
pp. 251-263. San Francisco: Jossey-Bass, 1979.

   Shepherd finds similarities in religiosity between
   the Hellenistic world and contemporary America. Serial
   adhesion, in which people move easily from one religious
   commitment to another, and polysymbolism are found in
   both cultures. Author's distinction between adhesion
   and conversion is useful. References.

104. Stupple, David. "The 'I Am' Sect Today: An Unobituary."
Journal of Popular Culture 8(1974): 897-905.

   Discusses the occult I Am movement of the 1930s and
   traces the rituals and beliefs of contemporary groups
   devoted to "Ascended Masters."

105. Veysey, Laurence R. The Communal Experience: Anarchist
and Mystical Communities in Twentieth-Century America.
Chicago: University of Chicago Press, 1978.

   Veysey studies a Vedanta ashram and a Gurdjieff-
   related commune in depth, comparing them to early
   twentieth-century communities in order to see whether
   America is really changing and whether one can trace
   a continuing counterculture in American history. A
   solid, readable piece of scholarship. Notes and index.

106. Webb, James. The Harmonious Circle: The Lives and
Work of G.I. Gurdjieff, P.D. Ouspensky, and Their Followers.
New York: G.P. Putnam's Sons, 1980.

   Webb claims to be the first person to write about
   Gurdjieff and his followers who has not himself been
   involved in their activities. This is a large study
   based primarily on unpublished materials and interviews,
   intertwining biography and history. Gurdjieff's work
   is discussed and sources of ideas are traced. Illustrations. Extensive bibliography and index.

107. Webb, James. The Occult Establishment. La Salle, Ill.:
Open Court, 1976.

   Companion book to his The Occult Underground [item 108]. Discusses aspects of the occult in twentieth-century political
   and social life throughout Western Europe and America,

showing how these ideas, previously underground, have
emerged into the mainstream. Author equates occult
with irrationality. He can be criticized for divorcing
the real intent of occult leaders' writings from the
material he uses for his own thesis. Extensive chapter
notes and index.

108. Webb, James. The Occult Underground. La Salle, Ill.:
Open Court, 1974.

Companion volume to his The Occult Establishment [item 107].
Beginning with the birth of spiritualism in America in
1848, Webb discusses Theosophy, Christian Science,
Gnosticism, secret societies, and related occult groups
and beliefs as they existed in the nineteenth-century
Western world. He interprets these movements as
insecure and fearful reactions to growing rationality
and scientific understanding of the world. Notes and
index.

Sociological and Anthropological Studies

General Works

109. Agehananda Bharati, Swami. The Light at the Center: Context and Pretext of Modern Mysticism. Santa Barbara, Calif: Ross-Erickson, 1976.

> Bharati calls his trenchant critique of mystical move-ments a work of "radical anthropology," the result of "participation" but not participant-observation. A social scientist and a mystic, he discusses what mysticism is and what the mystic does. He is very critical of the spiritual eclecticism he sees in the United States and voices strong opinions about the worth of various Indian gurus. The tone is somewhat arrogant, but many will find this work fascinating reading. Bibliography and index.

110. Anthony, Dick, and Robbins, Thomas. "Spiritual Innova-tion and the Crisis of American Civil Religion." Daedalus, Winter 1982, pp. 215-234.

> The authors see new religions as an effort to create a morality to replace that lost in the breakdown of civil religion, as defined by Robert Bellah. Some groups, such as the Unification Church and Peoples Temple, here designated "civil religion sects," attempt to fill the void with a dualistic conservatism, while at the other extreme, monistic groups such as Meher Baba Lovers avoid authoritarian structures and moral absolutes. Anthony and Robbins have one of the most comprehensive views of new religions and are very aware of the wide variety of these groups.

111. Anthony, Dick, and Robbins, Thomas. "A Typology of Non-Traditional Religious Movements in America." Paper read at the annual meeting of the American Association for the Advancement of Science, n.d. Photocopied.

> The authors organize new religious groups according to meaning systems. Monistic groups such as Eastern religions are subdivided into ascetic and egoistic types. Dualistic groups such as Christian-related ones are divided into traditional and youth-culture types. Implications for group organization, ability to integrate members in society, and types of converts are discussed. A unique typology that organizes the wide variety of groups in a useful way. Bibliography.

112. Anthony, Dick, and Robbins, Thomas. "Youth Culture, Religious Ferment, and the Confusion of Moral Meanings." Paper read at the annual meeting of the Society for the Scientific Study of Religion, 1975, at Milwaukee, Wisconsin. Photocopied.

> The authors argue that the moral absolutism of the Jesus Movement and the moral relativism of Eastern religions offer sharply divergent ways for youth to deal with morality in a pluralistic society. They find that moral relativism suits a pluralistic society better than moral absolutism. References.

113. Anthony, Dick; Robbins, Thomas; and Schwartz, Paul. "Contemporary Religious Movements and the Secularization Hypothesis." In New Religious Movements, edited by John Coleman and Gregory Baum, pp. 1-8. Concilium, vol. 161. New York: Seabury Press, 1983.

> Argues against sociologists who view religion as diminishing in contemporary society, against critics such as Christopher Lasch and Peter Marin who complain of narcissism in new religious groups, and against the "brainwashing" explanation of cults. Concludes that some new religions may offer values and a "trans-rational" mode of thinking to balance scientific rationalism. Notes.

114. Appel, Willa. Cults in America: Programmed for Paradise. New York: Holt, Rinehart and Winston, 1983.

> Appel discusses who joins and leaves cults, what brain-washing is, and what can be done about cults. Her assessment is generally negative, finding cults to be authoritarian groups in which followers are regimented, renounce the world, and believe they are superior to it. Discussion of ex-members is limited to those who have been deprogrammed or have sought psychological counseling. Notes, bibliography, and index.

115. Bainbridge, William Sims, and Stark, Rodney. "Client
and Audience Cults in America." Sociological Analysis
41(1980): 199-214.

> The authors present a geography of cult distribution
> based on data from six directories, Fate magazine,
> Transcendental Meditation initiation records, classi-
> fied telephone directories, and the Gallup Poll.
> Pacific and Mountain states are found to have the highest
> numbers and East, South, and Central states the lowest.
> Geographic distribution found in an earlier study
> (see "Cults in America: A Reconnaissance in Space and
> Time." [item 174]).

116. Bainbridge, William Sims, and Stark, Rodney. "The
'Consciousness Reformation' Reconsidered." Journal for
the Scientific Study of Religion 29(1981): 1-16.

> The authors are critical of Wuthnow's theory of meaning
> systems [see item 065]. Their survey study of 1,439
> respondents and review of Wuthnow's data lead them to
> question Wuthnow's assumption that most people have
> meaning systems. They also find that meaning systems
> based on religious beliefs and promulgated by churches
> and religious movements are the easiest to sustain.

117. Bainbridge, William Sims, and Stark, Rodney. "Friendship, Religion, and the Occult: A Network Study." Review
of Religious Research 22(1981): 313-327.

> The authors report the results of a questionnaire
> administered to 1,439 college students belonging to
> friendship groups. They found that strong interest in
> Yoga, Zen, or Transcendental Meditation was a salient
> factor in friendship, lending support to the idea that
> people join new religious groups because of personal
> relations with members. References.

118. Beckford, James A. "The Articulation of a Classical
Sociological Problematic with a Modern Social Problem:
Religious Movements and Modes of Social Insertion." Paper
read at the annual meeting of the Society for the Scientific
Study of Religion, 22-24 October 1982, at Providence, Rhode
Island.

> Beckford proposes a rich new typology based on the way
> in which members of new religious groups and the groups
> themselves relate to other social groups, processes,
> and institutions. References.

119. Beckford, James A. "Explaining Religious Movements."
International Social Science Journal 29(1977): 235-249.

> Beckford is critical of conventional sociological expla-
> nations for religious movements and suggests further

development of new perspectives such as movement
organization and social networks. A useful contribution. Bibliography.

120. Beckford, James A. "Functionalism and Ethics in Sociology: The Relationship Between 'Ought' and "Function.'"
Annual Review of the Social Sciences of Religion 5(1981):
101-131.

Beckford is critical of evaluations of cults that rely
on the negative or positive contributions they make to
the functioning of individuals, social institutions,
societies and so on. He argues that researchers can
use this approach to make covert value judgements and
asks that value concerns be discussed outright. Complex but well worth reading. References.

121. Beckford, James A. "The State and Control of New
Religious Movements." In Acts of the Seventeenth International
Conference for the Sociology of Religion: Religion and the
Public Domain, pp. 115-130. Paris: Secretariat C.I.S.R., 1983.

Examines ways in which Western countries exert control
over new religious movements. Finds that control is
subtle, bureaucratic, and not significantly different
from control over other comparable organizations.
Points out that although investigations have taken
place they have not appreciably changed public policy.
Concludes that new religious movements have limited
chances of changing the social order because of lack
of widespread support. Notes and references.

122. Beckford, James A. "Talking of Apostasy: Or Telling
Tales and 'Telling' Tales." In Accounting for Action,
edited by M. Mulkay and N. Gilbert. London: Gower Press,
forthcoming.

Discusses theoretical and methodological issues involved
in the approach Beckford has developed for studying the
ways in which people talk about leaving the Unification
Church. Continues to develop ideas put forth in his
"Through the Looking-Glass" (Archives de Sciences
Sociales des Religions, 45 [1978]). Thoughtful,
complex and difficult reading for the non-sociologist.
Bibliography.

123. Bell, Daniel. "The Return of the Sacred? The Argument
on the Future of Religion." British Journal of Sociology
28(1977): 419-449.

Bell argues against sociologists who have predicted
that religion will die out as secularization advances.
As Bell sees it, religion is a human response to the
existential predicaments of culture. However, he
views the cults appearing now as based on magical

thinking, offering instant belief that will not endure.
He believes that new religions rooted in tradition will
arise to give people a sense of continuity. This is
a substantial discussion, including many references to
the writings of poets and scholars of the past two
centuries. Notes.

124. Bird, Frederick. "Charismatic Cults: An Examination
of the Ritual Practices of Various New Religious Groups."
Occasional Publications in Anthropology, Ethnology Series
33(1979): 214-249.

Finds that rituals for meditation, healing, and initiation are prominent in cults. Claims that members of
cults attempt to achieve well-being by practising
rituals authorized by a charismatic leader and felt
to bestow charisma on the practitioners. Notes and
bibliography.

125. Bird, Frederick. "A Comparative Analysis of the Rituals
Used by Some Contemporary 'New' Religious and Para-Religious
Movements." In Religion and Culture in Canada, edited by
Peter Slater, pp. 448-469.

Drawing on his team study of twelve new religious
groups in Montreal, Bird describes and analyzes the
variety of rituals used. Shows that most rituals are
communal and are used for immediate religious experiences. Notes a lack of rites for birth, puberty,
death, and confession in most groups. Includes tables
of the incidence of rituals among the groups and the
extent to which members practice them. Notes.

126. Bird, Frederick. "Initiations and the Pursuit of
Innocence: A Comparative Analysis of Initiation Rites of
New Religious Movements and Their Influence on Feelings
of Moral Accountability." Occasional Publications in Anthropology, Ethnology Series 33(1979): 250-277.

Discusses ways in which initiation rites of new
religious groups tend to lessen moral accountability
and increase feelings of innocence in followers. Claims
that adherents of monastic groups identify with the
leaders' authority and reduce their response to other
authorities in society. In groups where people continue
to work and live in society, adherents reduce moral
accountability by shifting the sense of identity from
the ego to an unchanging, essential self. Notes and
bibliography.

127. Bird, Frederick. "The 'New Religions': Are They
Religious? Are They New?" Paper read at the meeting of
the Canadian Society for the Study of Religion, 28 May 1974,
at Concordia University, Montreal, Canada. Photocopied.

One year into a large, important team research project
studying new religious groups in the Montreal area,
Bird reports on the great diversity in goals, rituals,
and beliefs among the groups. He notes that resem-
blances to traditional religions are strong.

128. Bird, Frederick. "The Pursuit of Innocence: New
Religious Movements and Moral Accountability." Sociological
Analysis 40(1979): 335-346.

Bird contends that new religious groups foster reduced
feelings of moral accountability in adherents by
diminishing accountability to self and others and
supporting moral models that reduce the sense of
difference between actual behavior and moral expectations.
References.

129. Bird, Frederick, and Reimer, William. "New Religious and
Para-Religious Movements in Montreal." In Religion in Canadian
Society, edited by Stewart Crysdale and Les Wheatcroft.
Toronto: Macmillan, 1976.

In this early general report on their team research
project, the authors discuss some of the hard questions:
Are these groups religious even if they don't claim to
be? How new are they? Are they cultic or sectarian?
These questions may be as hard to answer today as they
were in 1976. The authors point to a diversity of
expressions that belies clear distinctions. They maintain that the "newness" of the groups has been exaggerated by both researchers and the media.   Bibliography.

130. Bird, Frederick, and Reimer, William. "Participation
Rates in New Religious and Para-Religious Movements." In
Of Gods and Men, edited by Eileen Barker, pp. 215-238.
Macon, Ga.: Mercer University Press, 1983.

Based on surveys done in Montreal in 1975 and 1980,
this study shows both high participation and high
dropout rates. It is another report from Bird's major
team research project. It supports the "conversion
careers" ideas--that many members of new religious
groups move freely from one group to another.

131. Bird, Frederick, and Westley, Frances. "The Political
Economies of New Religious Movements." Photocopied.
Montreal: Concordia University, 1983.

A useful addition to the study of the ways new religious
groups support themselves. Data from more than a dozen
such groups in the Montreal area show that services
such as classes, retreats, and public lectures are
important means of reaching potential converts but
are rarely more than self-supporting. Scientology and
est courses generate more income, especially when the

instructors donates their time. Sales, donations,
begging, and property rental are also used, but the
latter two are unusual sources of income. Notes.

132. Brent, Peter. "Why the Guru Movement Can't Succeed
Here." Human Nature, February 1979, pp. 31-37.

Brief, clear discussion of the role and function of
the guru in Indian society, including differences
between Eastern and Western world views that Brent
claims will prevent success of the guru institution in
its pure form in the West, although he thinks a
watered-down version may contribute to a more balanced
Western world view.

133. Bromley, David G., and Shupe, Anson D., Jr. "Financing
the New Religions: A Resource Mobilization Approach."
Journal for the Scientific Study of Religion 19(1980): 227-
239.

In one of the few studies of methods of fund-raising
by new religious movements, Bromley and Shupe analyze
methods of public fund-raising used by ISKCON, the
Unification Church, and the Children of God. References.

134. Bromley, David G., and Shupe, Anson D., Jr. "Repression
and the Decline of Social Movements: The Case of the New
Religions." In Social Movements of the Sixties and Seventies,
edited by Jo Freeman, pp. 335-347. New York: Longman, 1983.

Although it is not viewed as the only cause for the
decline of new religious movements in the late 1970s,
social repression is discussed here as a significant
factor. The decline of the Unification Church is used
to demonstrate the power that pro-"status quo" organizations such as the anticult movement have in helping
to maintain social order. References.

135. Campbell, Colin B. "The Cult, the Cultic Milieu and
Secularization." In A Sociological Yearbook of Religion in
Britain: 5, edited by Michael Hill, pp. 119-136. London:
SCM Press, 1972.

Campbell maintains that there is in all societies a
cultural underground comprised of alternative belief
systems. Cult members are continually drawn from this
milieu because they are attracted to alternative
systems. Secularization may encourage the growth of
the "cultic milieu." Notes.

136. Campbell, Colin B. "The Secret Religion of the Educated
Classes." Sociological Analysis 39(1978): 146-156.

Theoretical discussion uses Troeltsch's analysis of
three main types of religion to aid in conceptualizing

the new religious movements. Troeltsch's theory
is described clearly. Campbell believes that the
apparent dilemma of rising secularization along with
increased religiosity can be resolved by Troeltsch's
overarching theory, which sees both as part of the
same trend. Bibliography.

137. Coleman, James. "Social Inventions." Social Forces
49(1970): 163-173.

Coleman contends that people in a complex, impersonal
society are more willing to give up individual freedom
and join communal groups where they can experience
closeness with others and freedom from individual
responsibility. He suggests that such groups may
increase in the future and that the larger society may
allow them greater authority over members, even to the
extent of permitting polygamy or the use of drugs that
are illegal in the larger society. A provocative notion.
References.

138. Evans, Christopher. Cults of Unreason. New York: Farrar,
Strauss and Giroux, 1974.

Evans presents a cross-section of cults, but nearly
half the book is devoted to a critical study of
Scientology. Emphasis on the fantastic elements in
the "science fiction religion," as Evans calls it,
makes for an amusing account. Evans also discusses UFO
cults and a variety of Eastern-related cults that appear
to have been chosen for their eccentric aspects. Index.

139. Foss, Daniel A., and Larkin, Ralph W. "The Roar of the
Lemming: Youth, Postmovement Groups, and the Life Construction Crisis." In Religious Change and Continuity, edited by
Harry M. Johnson, pp. 264-285. San Francisco: Jossey-Bass,
1979.

The authors maintain that the new religious groups that
grew out of the counterculture helped young people find
meaning when faced with a dying counterculture and
what they perceived to be the meaninglessness of
middle-class life. The groups accomplished this by
taking authoritarian stances apart from both construc-
tions of reality and avoiding fear and anguish through
a focus on ultimate concerns. Bibliography.

140. Greeley, Andrew M. "Implications for the Sociology of
Religion of Occult Behavior in the Youth Culture." Youth
and Society 2(1970): 131-140.

Greeley asks sociologists to take seriously the youth
culture's interest in the occult and to study it as a
religious phenomenon.

141. Hall, John R. The Ways Out: Utopian Communal Groups in an Age of Babylon. London: Routledge and Kegan Paul, 1978.

A comparative study of counterculture communal groups, based on field studies made during 1972 and 1973. Of the twenty-seven communes studied, a few are religious: New Vrindaban (ISKCON), The Farm, Krishna Temple in Evanston, Illinois, and the Love Family. Chapters are devoted to time and communal life, social life, work, and satisfaction of wants and needs. Sociological jargon may impede the general reader. Bibliography and index.

142. Hargrove, Barbara. "New Religious Movements and the End of the Age." The Iliff Review, Spring 1982, pp. 41-52.

Traces different forms of apocalypticism found in teachings of new religious groups. Not a major study, but a good beginning one, showing the extent and variety of doctrines about the imminent end of the world.

143. Harper, Charles L. "Religious Cults and the Anti-Cult Movement in the Omaha area." Omaha: Creighton University, 1979. Photocopied.

Harper focuses on the growth of the Unification Church, Church of Scientology, and the Assembly in the Omaha, Nebraska area and their relationships with the local anticult group Love Our Children. It may not be possible to resolve the value conflicts between the two types of groups, but Harper suggests that dialogue may modify the conflict and provide a wider forum for thoughtful appraisal of the fundamental issues involved.

144. Jackson, John A. "Two Contemporary Cults." The Advancement of Science 23(1966): 60-64.

Brief discussion of the function of cults in a changing society, using the Aetherius Society and Scientology as examples. Suggests cult involvement may have therapeutic value by giving alienated individuals a structure for social action. References.

145. Kanter, Rosabeth Moss. Commitment and Community: Communes and Utopias in Sociological Perspective. Cambridge, Mass.: Harvard University Press, 1972.

Synanon is included in this excellent comparative study of the ideas, values, and dilemmas underlying utopian communities and communal life. Historical perspective is provided through discussion of nineteenth-century communes. Sociologists have found Kanter's analytical categories very useful. Bibliography and index.

146. Klapp, Orrin, E. <u>Collective Search for Identity</u>.
New York: Holt, Rinehart and Winston, 1969.

Includes very readable and interesting chapter on cult
movements in which Klapp discusses in a general way
how people find new identities and meaning through
cults. Notes and index.

147. Levine, Edward M. "Religious Cults: Their Implications
for Society and the Democratic Process." <u>Political Psycho-
logy</u>, Fall/Winter 1981-82, pp. 34-49.

Contends that cults such as ISKCON and the Unification
Church are different from cults of earlier times,
because their leaders have organized them to satisfy
their own non-religious interests. Finds cults to be
an ominous sign of the times and attempts to assess
costs to society. Bibliography.

148. Lynch, Frederick R. "Field Research and Future History:
Problems Posed for Ethnographic Sociologists by the 'Doomsday Cult' Making Good." <u>American Sociologist</u>, no. 2(1977),
pp. 80-88.

Discusses ethical and methodological questions raised
by Lofland's study of the Unification Church before it
became a visible, controversial organization. Of
interest to sociologists. References.

149. Martin, David. "The Manifest Destinies of Sects and
Nations." Paper read at the Conference on Conversion,
Coercion, and Commitment, Center for the Study of New
Religious Movements, 11-14 June 1981, at Berkeley, California.
Photocopied.

Commentary on papers of Roland Robertson [item 164]
and William Shepherd [item 564] presented at the
conference. Very fine discussion of tensions between
religious groups and the state in liberal, plurastic
nations. Points out ways in which cults are criticized
for the same things the populace accepts in mainstream
religions.

150. Marx, John H. "The Ideological Construction of Post-
Modern Identity Models in Contemporary Cultural Movements."
In <u>Identity and Authority</u>, edited by Roland Robertson and
Burkart Holzner, pp. 145-189. New York: St. Martin's
Press, 1979.

In this theoretical, abstract essay Marx argues that
since 1960 American society has entered a new phase
in which the basic structures of society are stable
enough to allow for individual experimentation with
new identities and cultural symbols and meanings.
Self-actualization has become important, and individuals

may choose to change identity from time to time.
Although Marx does not talk about religious groups, his
theory may be applied to them. Very scholarly;
challenging for the general reader.

151. Marx, John H., and Ellison, David L. "Sensitivity
Training and Communes: Contemporary Quests for Community."
Pacific Sociological Review 18(1975): 442-462.

Based on a study of the literature, this article
maintains that the existence of encounter groups and
communes points to underlying conflicts in society.
Individuals searching for community are drawn to such
groups because the groups provide collective contexts
for adopting alternative lifestyles and identities.
References.

152. Marx, John H., and Seldin, Joseph E. "Crossroads of
Crisis: I. Therapeutic Sources and Quasi-Therapeutic Func-
tions of Post-Industrial Communes." Journal of Health and
Social Behavior 14(1973): 39-50.

Discusses therapeutic functions of contemporary
communes. Argues that various therapeutic traditions
converged in the 1960s and were appropriate to the
needs of many young Americans. Communes arose as the
most appropriate organizational form for meeting those
needs, in addition to performing other functions.
References.

153. Marx, John H., and Seldin, Joseph E. "Crossroads of
Crisis: II. Organizational and Ideological Models for
Contemporary Quasi-Therapeutic Communes." Journal of Health
and Social Behavior 14(1973): 183-191.

Claims that social organization of contemporary
communes derives from Christian communes of the
nineteenth century and that their ideology derives
from utopian thought of Abraham Maslow and Existen-
tialist-humanistic psychology. General discussion
without reference to individual communes. References.

154. Mosatche, Harriet S. Searching: Practices and Beliefs
of the Religious Cults and Human Potential Groups. New York:
Stravon Educational Press, 1983.

A social-psychological study. Individual chapters are
devoted to descriptions of nine groups, ranging from
the typical (Unification Church and Scientology) to
groups seldom written about (Himalayan International
Institute and Association for Research and Enlightenment). Mosatche gained information through interviews, participant-observation, and extensive reading
in the literature. Her approach is balanced and
objective but fails to reveal anything new. The

concluding chapter, covering issues such as deprogramming and brainwashing, appears intended to soothe
anxious parents of cult members. Bibliography,
glossary, and index.

155. Pope, Harrison. The Road East: America's New Discovery
of Eastern Wisdom. Boston: Beacon Press, 1974.

In this sequel to his Voices from the Drug Culture
Pope sees the rise of interest in Eastern religions
as a consequence of drug use. Pope practiced
Transcendental Meditation and tried different forms
of chanting and yoga. He gleaned other information
from people he met along the way. His book is lively
because so many conversations are reproduced. Pope
admits he is "more opinionated than one normally finds
in rigorous sociology." Bibliography and index.

156. Richardson, James T. "A Data Frame for Commune Research."
Communal Studies Newsletter 4(1977): 1-13.

Richardson presents an outline for organizing information on communes based on a study of the literature
and his own research on Christ Commune. References.

157. Richardson, James T. "Factors in the Success and Failure
of Religious Movements." Paper read at the New Ecumenical
Research Association Conference, 5-9 October 1983, at
Berkeley, California. Photocopied.

Richardson raises more questions than he answers
about what constitutes success and failure in
religious movements. Examples from the Jesus Movement
are used for illustration. Bibliography.

158. Richardson, James T. "Financing the New Religions."
In Of Gods and Men, edited by Eileen Barker, pp. 65-88.
Macon, Ga.: Mercer University Press, 1983.

An examination of fund-raising methods other than
street solicitation. Several different groups are
discussed. Suggests further avenues of research
related to theoretical ideas from studies of
communes. Useful addition to the few scholarly
studies of fund-raising.

159. Robbins, Thomas. "Church, State and Cult." Photocopied.
Berkeley: Center for the Study cf New Religious Movements,
Graduate Theological Union, 1981.

Robbins continues his critique of the medical model
of the cult problem, arguing that authoritarian
religious groups in a pluralistic society present
legal and social problems that must be understood in
the context of changes in the society. Discusses

conflicts that arise as a result of religious movements
meeting needs formerly handled by the family and
churches. Bibliography.

160. Robbins, Thomas, and Anthony, Dick. "New Religious
Movements and the Social System: Integration, Disintegration,
or Transformation?" Annual Review of the Social Sciences of
Religion 2(1978): 1-28.

Robbins and Anthony continue to support their "integrative hypothesis" (the idea that new religious
groups help social dropouts and former drug users either
find more conventional roles in society or redirect
otherwise disruptive energy into nonconventional roles
in communes or monasteries) with findings from research
done since their original statement of the thesis in
"Youth Culture Religious Movements" [item 162].
Bibliography.

161. Robbins, Thomas; Anthony, Dick; and Curtis, Thomas E.
"The Limits of Symbolic Realism: Problems of Empathetic
Field Observation in a Sectarian Context." Journal for the
Scientific Study of Religion 12(1973): 259-271.

Authors discuss problems they encountered while
engaged in participant-observation research with a
Jesus Movement group. In trying to follow Robert
Bellah's model of mixing scientific objectivity with
empathy for the group's beliefs, Anthony discovered
that the Jesus People he was studying could not understand how he could be empathetic without becoming con-
verted. As a result, members repeatedly attempted to
convert him and felt demoralized by their failure.
Bibliography.

162. Robbins, Thomas; Anthony, Dick; and Curtis, Thomas E.
"Youth Culture Religious Movements: Evaluating the Integrative Hypothesis." Sociological Quarterly 16(1975): 48-64.

Authors claim that new religious movements help
alienated people adjust to impersonality of social
institutions by providing a group intermediate between
family and the larger society. They help to integrate
people and manage tensions within the social system.
Monastic orders and tightly knit communes are, however, limited in integrative potential, the authors
believe. They point out that many youth culture religious groups are against drugs and in favor of work
and thus provide converts with some conventional
values. Bibliography.

163. Roberts, Keith Alan. "Religion and the Counter-Culture
Phenomenon: Sociological and Religious Elements in the
Formation of an Intentional Counter-Culture Community."
Ph.D. dissertation, Boston University, 1976.

Roberts focuses on communities that have survived for
at least twenty-five years and those designed for
social reform. He identifies several factors contributing to formation of such groups, including tolerance
by the surrounding community or physical inaccessibility,
social crisis in the dominant culture, inner-worldly
and ascetic religious ethos, and members' belief in
free will. Bibliography.

164. Robertson, Roland. "Exits From and Moves Beyond Society:
Modern Religion and Processes of Globalization." Paper read
at the Conference on Conversion, Coercion, and Commitment
in New Religious Movements, Center for the Study of New
Religious Movements, 11-14 June 1981, Berkeley, California.
Photocopied.

Robertson addresses the issue of what the study of
new religious movements as a field of sociological
inquiry should encompass. He identifies ways in which
societal concerns are becoming increasingly global
and calls for recognition of religious change as an
overall global movement. A provocative article for the
sociologist. References.

165. Robertson, Roland. "Religious Movements and Modern
Societies: Toward a Progressive Problem-Shift." Sociological
Analysis 40(1979): 297-314.

Robertson discusses trends in the history of sociological study cf religious movements. He argues that
the most important aspect of the study of new
religious movements is not why they arise nor whether
they constitute new forms of religiosity but their
general significance with regard to changing conceptions of the relationship between the individual and
society and between groups on the boundaries of
society and the societal mainstream. References.

166. Shepherd, William C. "The New Religions and the
Religion of the Republic." Journal of the American Academy
of Religion Supplement 46(1978): 509-525.

Brief discussion of the history and sociology of
American civil religion, with reference to its
appearance in Norman Mailer's novels. Shepherd
argues that most new religions and self-help groups
are current manifestations of civil religion. Bibliography.

167. Shepherd, William C. "Religion and the Counter Culture--
A New Religiosity." In Religion American Style, edited by
Patrick McNamara, pp. 348-358. New York: Harper and Row,
1974.

Considering production of social solidarity and

creation of a symbolic universe to be the chief functions of religion, Shepherd argues that the counterculture developed a new religious lifestyle based on
drugs and rock music. References.

168. Skonovd, L. Norman. "Apostasy: The Process of Defection from Religious Totalism." Ph.D. dissertation, University of California, Davis, 1981.

Skonovd interviewed seventy people who had left
totalistic cults, fifty-seven of them voluntarily.
From the interviews Skonovd constructs a model of
apostasy that includes several steps. Many quotations
from the interviews provide vivid glimpses of the
complex emotions experienced by leave-takers. Corro-
borates the belief of many researchers that members of
cults are able to think for themselves and do leave
on their own. Bibliography.

169. Skonovd, L. Norman. "Becoming Apostate: A Model of
Religious Defection." Paper read at the annual meeting of
the Pacific Sociological Association, April 1979, Anaheim,
California. Photocopied.

Based on his interviews with thirty ex-members of
new religious groups, Skonovd proposes a model of
defection that relies on cognitive dissonance.
Bibliography.

170. Snow, David A. "The Disengagement Process: A Neglected
Problem in Participant Observation Research." Qualitative
Sociology 3(1980): 100-122.

171. Snow, David A., and Machalek, Richard. "On the Pre-
sumed Fragility of Unconventional Beliefs." Journal for the
Scientific Study of Religion 21(1982): 15-26.

Challenges assumption that unconventional beliefs are
difficult to maintain because they are different and
may be proven false by scientific evidence. Belief
systems such as Scientology are found to have strong
internal logic that insiders can accept. Authors
suggest that social scientists project their own
scientific attitude on others and fail to see that it
is easier to believe than to doubt. References.

172. Stark, Rodney. "How New Religions Succeed: A
Theoretical Model." Paper read at the New Ecumenical Research
Association Conference, 5-9 October 1983, at Berkeley,
California. Photocopied.

Stark's "model of success" comprises seven elements:
cultural continuity, moderate deviancy, effective
mobilization, normal demography, favorable ecology,
lack of secularization, and close internal relations

without resorting to isolation. The presentation is
sketchy, but Stark plans further work on the theory.

173. Stark, Rodney, and Bainbridge, William Sims. "Secularization, Revival, and Cult Formation." Annual Review of the
Social Sciences of Religion 4(1980): 85-119.

    Using statistical studies of numbers and locations
    of cults, the authors argue that secularization
    is the primary cause of renewed religiosity. Because
    Christianity and Judaism arose so long ago and have
    been eroded by the growth of science, they do not suit
    contemporary culture; therefore, the authors say, people
    seek new religious forms.

174. Stark, Rodney; Bainbridge, William Sims; and Doyle,
Daniel P. "Cults in America: A Reconnaissance in Space
and Time." Sociological Analysis 40(1979): 347-359.

    The authors examine geographic distribution of 501
    American cults, manipulating data in several interesting
    ways. Confirming popular opinion, they found that
    the Pacific states have the highest membership relative
    to population. There is considerable variation in
    the types of cults that predominate in different
    regions. A unique study.

175. Stark, Rodney, and Roberts, Lynne. "The Arithmetic of
Social Movements." Sociological Analysis 43(1982): 53-68.

    In this theoretical article the authors play with
    numbers, hypothesizing why it is difficult for cult
    movements to gain large followings in large societies.
    They suggest that in order to survive, new religions
    must appeal to mainstream members of society as well
    as to marginal members. References.

176. Staude, John R. "Alienated Youth and the Cult of the
Occult." In Sociology for the Seventies, edited by Morris
L. Medley and James E. Conyers, pp. 86-95. New York:
John Wiley and Sons, 1972.

    Interprets interest in mysticism and the occult as
    a spiritual renaissance symptomatic of disillusionment
    with science and rationality. Intended for under-
    graduate sociology classes. Discussion questions
    follow the essay.

177. Stone, Donald. "New Religious Consciousness and Personal Religious Experience." Sociological Analysis
39(1978): 123-134.

    Stone's generalizations about characteristics of new
    religious movements are based on data gathered by
    the Berkeley New Religious Consciousness Project. He

suggests that members of religious groups are attracted
by ecstatic religious experiences, developing an
"innerworldly mysticism" compatible with contemporary
secularization. (See also The New Religious Consciousness [item 190]).

178. Thomas, George M. "A Comparative Historical Essay on
Religious Movements and Political Economic Change." Paper
read at the annual meeting of the Society for the Scientific
Study of Religion, 1982, at Providence, R.I. Photocopied.

Argues for studying rise of new religious movements
in a historical context that takes into account
changing worldviews connected to political-economic
change. Sees current alternative religions as
diverse attempts to construct a new worldview using
some gnostic conceptions. A dense paper with lots of
sociological jargon, difficult reading for the nonso-
ciologist.

179. Wallis, Roy. "The Elementary Forms of the New Religious
Life." Annual Review of the Social Sciences of Religion
3(1979): 191-211.

To provide a theoretical structure for understanding
new religious movements, Wallis sets up a typology
based on the way such groups orient themselves to the
world--whether they reject, affirm, or accommodate.
Bibliography.

180. Wallis, Roy. "The Rebirth of the Gods? Reflections
on the New Religions in the West." Belfast: Queen's University,
1978.

An inaugural lecture delivered at Queen's University,
this is an overview in which Wallis makes an important
distinction between authoritarian, "world-rejecting"
groups such as the Hare Krishnas and "world-accepting"
groups such as est and Transcendental Meditation, which
offer techniques for increasing achievement and adjustment.

181. Wallis, Roy. "Sex, Violence, and Religion." Update,
no. 4(1983), pp. 3-10.

Wallis describes unconventional sexual and/or violent
activities of the Children of God, Synanon, and
Charles Manson's Family and suggests that the
charismatic leaders of these groups worked to prevent
any institutional structures from evolving because
such structures could have inhibited their unbridled
use of power. He locates the problem in the group
structure rather than in the personality of the leader.
References.

182. Ward, Hiley H. The Far-Out Saints of the Jesus Communes: A Firsthand Report and Interpretation of the Jesus Movement. New York: Association Press, 1972.

A very good, in-depth early study of eight Jesus People communes. Ward employed participant observation, survey and interviewing techniques, and case study methodologies. A clear and concise presentation, more descriptive than theoretical. Discusses doctrines, attitudes toward sex and race, finances, links with the occult, and possibilities of social action. Bibliography and index.

183. Westley, Frances R. The Complex Forms of the Religious Life: A Durkheimian View of New Religious Movements. American Academy of Religion academy series, no. 45. Chico, Calif: Scholars Press, 1983.

Following the general outline of Durkheim's The Elementary Forms of the Religious Life, Westley focuses on the relationship between beliefs and social organizations and on the function of rituals in new religious movements. She examined these groups to test Durkheim's hypothesis that the structure of society will causally shape the structure of its religious beliefs. Westley predicts that complex societies will have more highly differentiated religious forms. The study is based on data gathered by a research team, of which Westley was a three-year member, at Concordia University in Montreal. Bibliography and questionnaire used in gathering data.

184. Westley, Frances R. "The Cult of Man: Durkheim's Predictions and New Religious Movements." Sociological Analysis 39(1978): 135-145.

Westley applies a series of Emile Durkheim's 1898 predictions about the future of religions to Silva Mind Control and Catholic Charismatics and finds they hold true. The predictions include increased individualism and diversification of beliefs, development of private rituals, and idealized humanity. References.

185. Wilson, Bryan. "New Religious Movements: Convergences and Contrasts." In his Religion in Sociological Perspective, pp. 121-147. New York: Oxford University Press, 1982.

Wilson takes a functional approach to the emergence of new religions. He discusses the changes in society that have led people to seek community in revitalized religious forms that answer their needs better than traditional religions do. This is quite a different approach from the one he takes in Contemporary Transformations of Religion [item 198].

186. Wilson, John. "Making Inferences about Religious Movements." Religion 7(1977): 149-166.

    Wilson criticizes sociological studies of new religious
    movements for lack of depth in interpretation and
    recommends a greater emphasis on analysis of symbolism.
    Bibliography.

187. Zicklin, Gilbert. Countercultural Communes: A Sociological Perspective. Contributions in Sociology, no. 44.
Westport, Conn.: Greenwood Press, 1983.

    A minor contribution to knowledge about rural spiritual
    communes of the late 1960s and early 1970s. Only five
    of the twenty communes studied were spiritual, but
    Zicklin notes that of the twenty, the only communes
    surviving today are two of the spiritual ones. Reaffirms
    the early connections among Eastern religions, drugs,
    and countercultural values. Bibliography and index.

Collected Essays

188. Barker, Eileen, ed. New Religious Movements: A Perspective for Understanding Society. Studies in Religion and
Society, vol. 3. New York: Edwin Mellen Press, 1982.

    Contributors to this collection of nineteen essays
    include Ninian Smart, Bryan Wilson, Eileen Barker,
    Roy Wallis, Anson Shupe, and other important figures
    in the sociology of new religious movements. The essays
    are intended to shed light on our knowledge of ourselves
    as social beings and the societies we inhabit. These
    wide-ranging essays do not confine themselves to
    current religious groups but also add a historical
    dimension. Smart examines some movements in India.
    Christine King discusses Mormons in Nazi Germany.
    Thomas Oden compares ideas of modern encounter groups
    with eighteenth- and nineteenth-century pietistic
    writings. Barker provides a good essay concerning
    research methodology. Glossary of new religious groups
    mentioned in the text. Bibliography.

189. Barker, Eileen, ed. Of Gods and Men: New Religious
Movements in the West. Macon, Ga.: Mercer University Press,
1983.

    Proceedings of the 1981 Annual Conference of the
    British Sociological Association, Sociology of Religion
    Study Group. Includes eighteen essays, both theoretical
    and empirical. Some are concerned with alternative
    religious groups in Western Europe. Important
    researchers among the contributors include the editor
    herself, James Richardson, John Lofland, Anson Shupe,

and Frederick Bird, who continue to report on areas
of research they have been involved in for awhile.
Topics covered include   conversion, anticult movements,
fund-raising, esotericism, and individual studies of a
few groups. Bibliographies and index.

190. Glock, Charles Y., and Bellah, Robert N., eds. The
New Religious Consciousness. Berkeley: University of California Press, 1976.

An important collection of theoretical and empirical
essays, some by novice social scientists who joined
the research team led by the editors. The researchers
studied religious and quasi-religious groups that
contributed significantly to the counterculture in the
San Francisco Bay Area. Includes studies of Synanon,
the Church of Satan, 3HO, ISKCON, and Jews for Jesus.
See Hadden's "Review Symposium" [item 191] for a good
set of reviews of this book. Index.

191. Hadden, Jeffrey K., ed. "Review Symposium: The New
Religious Consciousness, edited by Charles Y. Glock and
Robert N. Bellah." Journal for the Scientific Study of
Religion 16(1977): 305-324.

An interesting series of reviews of Glock and Bellah's
The New Religious Consciousness [item 190]. Thomas
Robbins comments on the studies of Eastern religious
imports, James Richardson finds unexplored comparative
possibilities in the chapters on new Christian movements, Wade Clark Roof finds the case studies of
individual groups impressive and suggestive in ways
not adequately transmitted in the theoretical chapters,
and Dick Anthony critiques the theoretical essays that
Glock and Bellah contributed.

192. Levi, Ken, ed. Violence and Religious Commitment:
Implications of Jim Jones' People's Temple Movement.
University Park and London: Pennsylvania State University
Press, 1982.

Eleven essays divided into four parts. In Part One,
three writers give differing perspectives on whether
Jonestown was an isolated event or could easily occur
again. Richardson's essay is the most scholarly,
carefully pointing out distinctions between Peoples
Temple and other cults. In Part Two, three essays
discuss the social background of cults, who joins them,
and why. Part Three covers reactions to Jonestown.
Part Four is a report of a former member of Peoples
Temple. The editor compiles characteristics of
violence-prone cults in an attempt to tie the essays
together and to generalize about cults and violence,
but he names only Synanon and three others. References
and index.

193. Robbins, Thomas, and Anthony, Dick, eds. In Gods We Trust: New Patterns of Religious Pluralism in America. New Brunswick, N.J.: Transaction Books, 1980.

Eighteen contributions by leading analysts discuss religious ferment and cultural transformation, dis- enchantment and renewal in mainline traditions, new religions and the decline in community, oriental mysticism, and therapy groups. Many articles appeared in the May/June 1978 issue of Society magazine in abridged form. Valuable contribution. Bibliography.

194. "Symposium on Scholarship and Sponsorship." Sociological Analysis 44(1983): 177-226.

A lively set of papers concerned generally with the question of religious sponsorship of sociological research and more specifically with the Unification Church. Irving Horowitz presents the challenge, casting doubt on the possibilities for objective research on new religious groups under such conditions. Bryan Wilson, James Beckford, Thomas Robbins, Eileen Barker, and Roy Wallis respond critically. An altogether thoughtful and important set of papers, demonstrating that there are no simple answers. References.

195. Tiryakian, Edward A., ed. On the Margin of the Visible: Sociology, the Esoteric, and the Occult. Contemporary Religious Movements: A Wiley Interscience Series. New York: John Wiley and Sons, 1974.

A series of essays brought together to illustrate the need for and propriety of sociological investiga- tion of the occult and esoteric. Also includes essays on the social significance of this often-neglected area. Excerpts from a wide variety of esoteric and occult doctrines are presented, but they are too brief to be really useful. Good bibliography. Author and subject indexes.

196. Wallis, Roy, ed. Millennialism and Charisma. Belfast: Queen's University, 1982.

Three of the papers in this collection are concerned with the development of charismatic leaders in cults. Robert Balch's fascinating description of how Bo and Peep (also called The Two) came to see themselves as emissaries of God is a good companion piece to his other articles about them [items 247-249]. Wallis explores the implications of charisma in the Children of God, and Donald Stone argues that Werner Erhard's charisma and ability to convince his followers they can participate in his seemingly supernormal powers contribute to the success of est. Chapter notes.

197. Wallis, Roy, ed. Sectarianism: Analyses of Religious and Non-Religious Sects. New York: John Wiley and Sons, 1975.

Wallis uses the term "sect" to refer to groups having a common ideology which the adherents view as offering a unique access to the truth. Sects also cut themselves off from the rest of society. A cult, on the other hand, is described as individualistic and having no source of authority. By Wallis' definition, the Church of Scientology, which he discusses in terms of societal reaction to it, is a sect. Other items of interest among the nine essays are Francine Daner's essay on why people join ISKCON and James Beckford's comparative study of the organizational aspects of the Jehovah's Witnesses and the Unification Church. Good contributions. Notes following each essay.

198. Wilson, Bryan. Contemporary Transformations of Religion. New York: Oxford University Press, 1976.

Three essays that grew out of the Riddell Lectures, which Wilson delivered at the University of Newcastle. Wilson considers the growth of new religious movements to be unlike that of such movements in any earlier time because the speed of transmission among cultures is so great and possibilities for syncretism are therefore much greater. He also maintains that cults have no real consequence for social institutions, contribute nothing to a culture by which one might live, and are like consumer goods in a secularized world. Provocative and important contribution from a major figure in the sociology of religion.

199. Wilson, Bryan, ed. The Social Impact of New Religious Movements. Conference Series, no. 9. Barrytown, N.Y.: The Unification Theological Seminary, 1981.

A collection of papers presented at a conference sponsored by the Unification Church. Names of participants are familiar. Eileen Barker's extensive social profile of those who join the Unification Church in England is an important contribution. Case studies of the Children of God and Transcendental Meditation are presented by Roy Wallis and by William Sims Bainbridge with Daniel H. Jackson, respectively. James Hunter, David Martin, and Joseph Fichter each discuss the social context in which new religions have arisen. Anson D. Shupe, Jr. and David Bromley show how deprogrammed former Unification Church members have helped to suppress the church by telling their stories to the media.

Cult and Sect Theories

200. Bainbridge, William Sims, and Stark, Rodney. "Cult Formation: Three Compatible Models." Sociological Analysis 40(1979): 283-295.

As a first step toward formulating a theory of cult formation, the authors describe three models: psychopathological, entrepreneurial, and subculture-evolutionary. They find all to be compatible; all offer rewards in the form of compensators. Intended as a theoretical anchor for further empirical research. References.

201. Campbell, Colin B., "Clarifying the Cult." British Journal of Sociology 28(1977): 375-388.

Campbell examines elements of various empirically based concepts of cult and finds them unsatisfactory and confusing. He then sets up an ideal type by using Ernst Troeltsch's "mystic collectivity" concept, which refers to people who do not really form a group but hold syncretic mystical beliefs in common. If such individuals do form a group--a cult--it will be fragile and will dissolve back into the mystic collectivity. Notes.

202. Eister, Allan W. "An Outline of a Structural Theory of Cults." Journal for the Scientific Study of Religion 11(1972): 319-334.

Eister maintains that cults arise because of crises in the culture such as breakdown of traditional religions and disruption of norms of excellence in the arts, literature, and other sources of meaning. References.

203. Glock, Charles Y. "On the Origin and Evolution of Religious Groups." In Religion in Sociological Perspective, edited by Charles Y. Glock, pp. 207-220. Belmont, Calif.: Wadsworth Publishing Co., 1973.

Glock gives a brief account of Weber's "sect-church" theory and how it was refined by H. Richard Niebuhr. He points out that it does not account for cults. By expanding the theory's concept of deprivation, he includes cults. Various forms of deprivation are described, and psychic deprivation, combined with other social conditions, is suggested to give rise to cults.

204. Jackson, John A., and Jobling, Ray. "Towards an Analysis of Contemporary Cults." In A Sociological Yearbook of Religion in Britain, edited by David Martin, vol. 1, pp. 94-105. London: SCM Press, 1968.

Useful discussion of conceptualizations of the cult found in the sociology of religion in the 1960s. The authors attempt to draw together several formulations to include groups with a mystical orientation along with those that are world-affirming but use esoteric practices to enhance success. Bibliography.

205. Nelson, Geoffrey K. "The Concept of Cult." The Sociological Review 16(1968): 351-362.

206. Nelson, Geoffrey K. "The Spiritualist Movement and the Need for a Redefinition of Cult." Journal for the Scientific Study of Religion 8(1969): 152-160.

Nelson calls for a definition of cult that emphasizes the fundamental break between such a group and the religious tradition of its culture. Secondarily, he says, cults are composed of individuals seeking mystical or psychic experiences and concerned with individual problems.

207. Richardson, James T. "From Cult to Sect: Creative Eclecticism in New Religious Movements." Pacific Sociological Review 22(1979): 136-166.

Based on his work with a Jesus Movement group, Richardson discusses changes that occur in a cult that indicate it has developed into a sect. He further suggests a general model for cult/sect development. Bibliography.

208. Richardson, James T. "An Oppositional and General Conceptualization of Cult." Annual Review of the Social Sciences of Religion 2(1978): 29-52.

Richardson refers to several other sociological conceptualizations of cult and then uses his long-term study of a Jesus Movement group to formulate a definition stressing the difference between cultic beliefs and practices and those of the dominant culture. Other aspects are also discussed, including individualism and the transitory nature of cults. Bibliography.

209. Stark, Rodney, and Bainbridge, William Sims. "Of Churches, Sects, and Cults: Preliminary Concepts for a Theory of Religious Movements." Journal for the Scientific Study of Religion 18(1979): 117-133.

The authors identify three forms of cults, based on degree of organization. The least organized are

audience cults, in which people consume doctrine
through the media. Client cults, in which those
offering the services are organized but the clients
are not, are an intermediate level. The most organized
cult movements are those that are truly religious.
References.

210. Wallis, Roy. "The Cult and Its Transformation." In
Sectarianism: Analyses of Religious and Non-Religious Sects,
pp. 35-49. New York: John Wiley, 1975.

Wallis criticizes the concept of cult as based on
beliefs differing from the primary religion of the
culture. He does not find this definition sociologi-
cally useful because it is vague and theologically
oriented. Wallis prefers to distinguish cults by
loose organization, individualism, and acceptance of
the validity of other belief systems. Notes and
references.

211. Wallis, Roy. "Ideology, Authority, and the Development
of Cultic Movements." Social Research 41(1974): 299-327.

Although Wallis' later essays on the concept of
cult are very similar to this one, this is still useful
because of the various religious movements he refers to
as examples. Notes.

212. Wallis, Roy. "Scientology: Therapeutic Cult to
Religious Sect." Sociology 9(1975): 89-100.

Wallis uses the development of Dianetics and Scientology
to illustrate his useful concepts of cult and sect.
His theory allows for the development of the loosely
structured cult of Dianetics into a sect, Scientology,
in which social control emerged and Hubbard centralized
doctrine and authority. Very similar to his "The Cult
and Its Transformation" [item 210]. Notes and references.

Conversion, Brainwashing, and Deprogramming

213. Anthony, Dick, and Robbins, Thomas. "Religious Movements
and the 'Brainwashing' Issue." Paper read at the American
Psychological Association Meetings, September 1979, in New
York.

The authors criticize brainwashing and coercive
persuasion approaches and seek to redirect attention
to the context of cultural confusion and normative
breakdown that they contend enhances the appeal of
esoteric and authoritarian religious groups. Bibliography.

214. Austin, Roy. "Empirical Adequacy of Lofland's Conversion Model." Review of Religious Research 18(1977): 282-287.

Austin interviewed nine male members of Crusade House, a Jesus Movement group, and found that extensive interaction with the group and, for some, tensions within their lives were important factors in conversions. The results of the study are used to critique Lofland's conversion model as presented in his Doomsday Cult [item 288]. References.

215. Bromley, David G., and Shupe, Anson D., Jr. "'Just a Few Years Seem Like a Lifetime': A Role Theory Approach to Participation in Religious Movements." In Research in Social Movements, Conflicts and Change, vol. 2, edited by Louis Kriesberg, pp. 159-186. Greenwich, Conn.: JAI Press, 1979.

The authors, who have done significant research on the Unification Church, address the question of conversion. Based on interviews with and participant-observation of forty-two UC members, they argue that the process of conversion initially involves learning how to act like a convert. Inner psychological change comes later. Their approach emphasizes the freedom of individuals to act as they choose. References.

216. Bromley, David G., and Shupe, Anson D., Jr. "The Tnevnoc Cult." Sociological Analysis 40(1979): 361-366.

After describing the recruitment and authoritarian training practices of the nineteenth-century Tnevnoc cult, the authors reveal that in reality it is the Catholic convent, which was maligned then much as today's cults are now. Anticult critics have found the convent or military analogy wanting, however, because they say those groups, unlike the cults, have entrance standards and do not employ deception in recruitment.

217. Downton, James V., Jr. "An Evolutionary Theory of Spiritual Conversion and Commitment: The Case of the Divine Light Mission." Journal for the Scientific Study of Religion 19(1980): 381-396.

Based on his study of Maharaj Ji's followers, Downton discounts the idea that conversion is a radical personality change. His interviews of DLM members lead him to see conversion and commitment as occurring in evolutionary stages.

218. Greil, Arthur L. "Previous Dispositions and Conversion to Perspectives of Social and Religious Movements." Sociological Analysis 38(1977): 115-125.

Greil asserts that people are influenced to convert to
new perspectives when those close to them share
those perspectives. Choice is involved, particularly
choice of whom one associates with. References.

219. Jules-Rosette, Bennetta. "Disavowal and Disengagement:
A New Look at the Conversion Process in Religious Sects."
Paper read at the Conference on Conversion, Coercion, and
Commitment in New Religious Movements, 11-14 June 1981, at
Berkeley, California.

After examination of many individuals' accounts of
joining and leaving new religious groups, the author
concludes that such accounts are complex rationaliza-
tions of personal choice and cultural innovation.
Bibliography.

220. Kim, Byong-Suh. "Religious Deprogramming and Subjective
Reality." Sociological Analysis 40(1979): 197-207.

An empirical study of deprogramming. Kim interviewed
deprogrammers and deprogrammed youths and also carried
out participant observation research during deprogramming
and rehabilitation sessions. He documents that the
content of beliefs is attacked during deprogramming.
He also shows that by utilizing Shein's model of
coercive transformation of ego identity, deprogramming
itself can be analyzed as coercive persuasion.

221. Lofland, John, and Skonovd, L. Norman. "Conversion
Motifs." Journal for the Scientific Study of Religion
20(1981): 373-385.

The authors refer to several different conversion
studies in formulating six types of conversion:
intellectual, mystical, experimental, affectional,
revivalist, and coercive. References.

222. Lofland, John, and Stark, Rodney. "Becoming a World-
Saver." American Sociological Review 30(1965): 862-874.

Presents a general model of conversion based on
Lofland's early study of the Unification Church.
The model has stages and emphasizes the interaction of
predispositional, situational, and social influences.
The model has been influential in the sociology of
religion. For Lofland's critical reassessment of the
model, see his "Becoming a World-Saver Revisited" in
Conversion Careers [item 226].

223. Long, Theodore E., and Hadden, Jeffrey K. "Religious
Conversion and the Concept of Socialization: Integrating
the Brainwashing and Drift Models." Journal for the
Scientific Study of Religion 22(1983): 1-14.

Long and Hadden find merit in both the brainwashing and "social drift" models of conversion. In the latter model, individuals are influenced gradually through social relationships and may just as easily drift away as become more deeply involved. Pointing out biases in the proponents of each model, the authors integrate the two to create a more complex model. A brief, clear history of Unification Church recruiting methods is used to illustrate the new model. Bibliography.

224. Ofshe, Richard. "The Role of Out-of-Awareness Influence in the Creation of Dependence on a Group: An Alternative to Brainwashing Theories." Paper read at the American Psychological Association Meetings, August 1981.

Ofshe contends that new, sophisticated techniques of social-psychological manipulation are used by totalistic groups such as Synanon. Describing some of these techniques, he states that they go beyond those employed in China or Korea in the following ways: recruits are attracted to the beliefs of the group, they are subjected to very personal attack on their identities, and they tend to be at a point of crisis in their lives.

225. Preston, David. "Becoming a Zen Practitioner." Sociological Analysis 42(1981): 47-55.

Based on participant-observation and interviews with Zen practitioners, Preston's discussion differentiates conversion to Zen Buddhism from conversion to other types of new religious groups. He finds it to be a practical and gradual learning process. References.

226. Richardson, James T., ed. Conversion Careers: In and Out of the New Religions. Sage Contemporary Social Science Issues, no. 47. Beverly Hills: Sage, 1978.

A series of papers offering social-psychological approaches to conversion and commitment in groups such as a UFO cult, a Jesus Movement commune, the Unification Church, a Meher Baba group, and the Divine Light Mission. In addition to case studies, there is an article that discusses deprogramming as a new form of exorcism and one on conversion models. A solid contribution to conversion research.   References.

227. Richardson, James T.; van der Lans, Jan; and Derks, Frans. "Exiting, Expulsion, and Extraction: An Analysis of Ways of Leaving." Paper read at the Annual Meeting of the Association for the Sociology of Religion, August 1981, at Toronto, Canada.

A good theoretical discussion on the ways in which
people leave cults. Points out that reports of high
turnover rates are neglected by some researchers.
Calls for more longitudinal studies and studies of
situations in which a group asks a member to leave.
Bibliography.

228. Robbins, Thomas. "De-Mystifying Cultist Mind Control."
Paper read at the Conference on Conversion, Coercion, and
Commitment in New Religious Movements, Center for the Study
of New Religious Movements, 11-14 June 1981, Berkeley,
California.

A well-reasoned examination of the rhetoric and
assumptions involved in the brainwashing model of
conversion. Argues that while abuses do occur, these
have been exaggerated, which obscures the underlying
value conflicts between cults and society. Bibliography.

229. Robbins, Thomas, and Anthony, Dick. "Brainwashing and
the Persecution of 'Cults'." Journal of Religion and Health,
no. 1(1980), pp. 66-69.

A less comprehensive treatment of propositions advanced
by the authors in "New Religions, Families, and 'Brainwashing'" [item 233].

230. Robbins, Thomas, and Anthony, Dick. "Cults, Brainwashing and Counter-Subversion." The Annals of the American
Academy of Political and Social Science 446(1979): 78-90.

Compares the anticult movement to earlier movements
against Mormons and Catholics in America, finding
similar ideas and rhetoric. Suggests that movements
hostile to religious groups redefine "Americanism"
during periods of cultural confusion and moral
ambiguity.

231. Robbins, Thomas, and Anthony, Dick. "Deprogramming,
Brainwashing, and the Medicalization of Deviant Religious
Groups." Social Problems 29(1982): 283-297.

Authors contend that the new religious movements
phenomenon has been improperly conceptualized as a
mental health problem. They further argue that such
medicalization has helped consolidate an anticult
coalition of parents, clergy, and mental health
professionals. Very good bibliography.

232. Robbins, Thomas, and Anthony, Dick. "The Limits of
'Coercive Persuasion' as an Explanation for Conversion to
Authoritarian Sects." Political Psychology, Summer 1980,
pp. 22-37.

Claims that coercive persuasion may be involved in

conversion to authoritarian cults but not all cults.
Criticizes writings of those who do not differentiate
types of new religious movements, rely only on accounts
of brainwashing provided by those who have been deprogrammed, fail to distinguish forms of coercion, and
impute loss of free will to those who have been indoctrinated. References.

233. Robbins, Thomas, and Anthony, Dick. "New Religions,
Families, and 'Brainwashing.'" Society, June 1978, pp. 77-83.

Critique of brainwashing rhetoric and discussion of
underlying value conflicts between cults and society,
which the authors maintain is the real issue. Strong
stance against deprogramming and temporary conservatorships as threats to personal and religious liberties.
Suggested reading list.

234. Robbins, Thomas; Anthony, Dick; and McCarthy, Jim.
"Legitimating Repression." In The Brainwashing/Deprogramming
Controversy: Sociological, Psychological, Legal, and Historical Perspectives. Studies in Religion and Society,
vol. 5. New York: Edwin Mellen Press, 1983.

With their usual civil libertarian approach, the
authors produce a strong critique of the brainwashing
and coercive persuasion models of cult involvement.
They maintain that brainwashing is an inherently
subjective notion that can be used to socially suppress
deviant groups. Bibliography.

235. Shupe, Anson.D., Jr., and Bromley, David G. "A Role
Theory Approach to Entry and Exit in the New Religions."
Paper read at the Conference on Conversion, Coercion, and
Commitment in New Religious Movements, Center for the Study
of New Religious Movements, 11-14 June 1981, at Berkeley,
California.

The authors apply their role theory approach, presented
in "'Just a Few Years Seem Like a Lifetime'" [item 215],
to deprogramming. They give a detailed account of
decisions concerning how to act that someone undergoing
deprogramming might make. Bibliography.

236. Skonovd, L. Norman. "Deprogramming." Photocopied.
Davis, Calif.: University of California, Department of
Sociology, 1979.

After presenting a phenomenological description of the
deprogramming process, Skonovd concludes that it is
essentially a form of self-transformation requiring
active participation on the part of the one deprogrammed.
References.

237. Snow, David A.; Zurcher, Louis A., Jr.; and Ekland-Olson, Sheldon. "Social Networks and Social Movements: A Micro-structural Approach to Differential Recruitment." American Sociological Review 45(1980): 787-801.

> After studying the literature, distributing a questionnaire to 550 students, and using Snow's data on Nichiren Shoshu of America [item 330], the authors conclude that new members of social movements are recruited via networks of friends, acquaintances, and relatives or in the absence of such networks. Leaving aside psychological considerations, this study seems to verify popular conceptions of "friends converting friends" and the susceptibility of lonely people. References.

238. Stark, Rodney, and Bainbridge, William Sims. "Networks of Faith: Interpersonal Bonds and Recruitment to Cults and Sects." American Journal of Sociology 85(1980): 1376-1395.

> Reviews the sociological literature on recruitment and uses available quantitative data to support the thesis that interpersonal ties play an essential role in recruitment in cults, sects, and traditional churches. The authors claim that deprivation and ideological predisposition are contributing factors that may be overridden by friendship. References.

239. Straus, Roger A. "Religious Conversion as a Personal and Collective Accomplishment." Sociological Analysis 40(1979): 158-165.

> Straus maintains that the potential convert takes an active role in the conversion process, often acting the role of the believer before actual acceptance of beliefs takes place. References.

Individual Groups and Movements

240. Adams, Robert L., and Fox, Robert J. "Mainlining Jesus: The New Trip." Society, no. 4(1972), pp. 50-56.

> The article's title reflects the authors' view that Jesus People replaced their drug ecstasy with religious fervor. Although Jesus communes helped them overcome drugs and learn to work with others, identity crises remained unresolved. Based on interviews and question-naires.

241. Akbar, Na'im. "The Restitution of Family as Natural Order." In The Family and the Unification Church, edited by Gene G. James, pp. 87-104. Conference Series, no. 15. Barrytown, N.Y.: Unification Theological Seminary, 1983.

Compares the role of the family in the Unification
Church to that in the American Muslim Mission.

242. Ambrose, Kenneth P. "Function of the Family in the
Process of Commitment Within the Unification Movement."
In The Family and the Unification Church, edited by Gene
G. James, pp. 23-33. Conference Series, no. 15. Barrytown,
N.Y.: Unification Theological Seminary, 1983.

As one might expect, since the family is central to
the Unification movement, Ambrose claims that within
the UC, family life strengthens the commitment of
members. Not a very deep or interesting paper.
References.

243. Anthony, Dick, and Robbins, Thomas. "The Decline of
American Civil Religion and the Development of Authoritarian
Nationalism: A Study of the Unification Church of Rev.
Sun Myung Moon." Paper read at the annual meeting of the
Society for the Scientific Study of Religion, 1975, at
Milwaukee, Wisconsin.

Argues that the decline of civil religion has given
rise to minority sects that uphold civil religion.
The Unification Church is interpreted as a movement
that has reworked civil religion into a form of
authoritarian nationalism. Bibliography.

244. Bainbridge, William Sims. Satan's Power: A Deviant
Psychotherapy Cult. Berkeley: University of California
Press, 1978.

Very good ethnographic and historical study of
"The Power," Bainbridge's pseudonym for The Process
Church of the Final Judgment. Lacking in comparative
analysis, but fascinating reading, not only because
of Bainbridge's careful observation but because of
the strange nature of the group. Bibliography and
index.

245. Bainbridge, William Sims. "Science, Technology, and
Religion: The Case of Scientology." Paper read at the
New Ecumenical Research Institute Conference, 5-9 October
1983, at Berkeley, California.

Discusses points of compatibility between Scientology
and computers, physics, and science fiction, suggesting
that Scientology may gain respectability if it
appropriates new cosmological theories. Bibliography.

246. Bainbridge, William Sims, and Stark, Rodney. "Scientology: To Be Perfectly Clear." Sociological Analysis
41(1980): 128-136.

Members of Scientology hope to attain the level of

"clear," which is difficult to achieve. The organization claimed to have assisted 16,000 members to reach
this level when the authors prepared their paper.
They show how Scientology has changed the definition
of "clear" from a state of being to status in the
hierarchy of the cult. The processes involved in
becoming clear are described as modern magic.

247. Balch, Robert W. "Conversion and Charisma in the Cultic
Milieu: The Origins of a New Religion." Paper read at the
Annual Meeting of the Association for the Sociology of
Religion, October 1982, at Providence, Rhode Island.

Balch presents an interesting portrait of the
metaphysical seeker, a type of person often looked
upon with disdain by the academic community. He
describes the alternative reality of the seeker's
world and how the UFO cult led by Bo and Peep developed
out of this "cultic milieu." Very interesting reading.

248. Balch, Robert W. "Looking Behind the Scenes in a
Religious Cult: Implications for the Study of Conversion."
Sociological Analysis 41(1980): 137-143.

Study of Bo and Peep UFO cult. Bo and Peep have also
been referred to as the Two. Balch's study of how
people come to join concludes that they quickly
learn new roles rather than experiencing change in
personality.

249. Balch, Robert W., and Taylor, David. "Salvation in
a UFO." Psychology Today, October 1976, pp. 58-66.

Balch and Taylor spent several weeks with followers
of Bo and Peep. They report beliefs and why people
joined. They say the group lacked indoctrination
and structure. This, coupled with the seeker
mentality of members (who moved easily from one
spiritual group to another), contributed to high turnover.

250. Balswick, Jack. "The Jesus People Movement: A Generational Interpretation." Journal of Social Issues, no. 3(1974),
pp. 23-42.

Balswick calls his approach a "phenomenological attempt
at generational analysis, relying strongly upon
participant observation." He compares and contrasts
the Jesus Movement with the counterculture, mainstream
churches, and the fundamentalism of older generations.
Interesting to read in conjunction with Richardson's
recent comparative study, "Experiential Fundamentalism"
[item 306]. References.

251. Balswick, Jack. "The Jesus People Movement: A Sociological Analysis." In Religion, American Style, edited by
Patrick McNamara, pp. 359-366. New York: Harper and Row,
1974.

    Discusses the relationship of the Jesus Movement to
    the counterculture.

252. Barker, Eileen. "Doing Love: Tensions in the Ideal
Family." In The Family and the Unification Church, edited
by Gene G. James, pp. 35-52. Conference Series, no. 15.
Barrytown, N.Y.: Unification Theological Seminary, 1983.

    The Ideal Family is central to Unification theology,
    but as Barker insightfully shows by referring to
    Rev. Moon and his family and UC members and their
    family relationships, the pursuit of the ideal
    paradoxically creates family disunity, a problem that
    threatens the success of the movement.

253. Barker, Eileen. "The Ones Who Got Away: People Who
Attend Unification Church Workshops and Do Not Become
Moonies." Paper read at the Conference on Conversion,
Coercion, and Commitment in the New Religious Movements,
11-14 June 1981, at Berkeley, California. Photocopied.

    Based on questionnaires, interviews, and observations
    of Unification Church introductory workshops in Great
    Britain, Barker's paper attempts to assess factors
    that predispose individuals to join or resist joining
    the UC. Although recruitment techniques in Great
    Britain are slightly different from those in the
    United States, Barker's study is important for com-
    parative purposes. She finds that nine out of ten
    individuals attending two-day workshops do not become
    members. Other findings are difficult to generalize
    from, and Barker discusses these at length. She also
    includes a cogent critique of Margaret Singer's use of
    brainwashing as an explanation for conversion.
    Statistical tables and bibliography.

254. Barker, Eileen. "Whose Service Is Perfect Freedom:
The Concept of Spiritual Well-Being in Relation to the
Reverend Moon's Unification Church." In Spiritual Well-
Being, edited by David O. Moberg. Washington: University
Press of America, 1979.

    A questionnaire distributed to over 500 members of
    the UC in Great Britain and the United States indicated
    that members felt greater spiritual well-being since
    joining. Aspects of the life-style such as community,
    charismatic leader, and the challenge of transforming
    the world are suggested as functioning to increase
    spiritual well-being. Barker's research on the UC
    in England is important.

255. Beckford, James A. "Anti-cult Sentiment in Comparative Perspective: Preliminary Observations." Liberte et Conscience 23(1982): 62-68.

Overview of responses to new religious movements in Europe, Japan, and the United States. Patterns of anticult response in each country are shown to be distinctive. In the United States the distinctive feature is concern with psychological and medical aspects of cult membership. Notes.

256. Beckford, James A. "Conversion and Apostasy: Antithesis or Complementarity?" Paper read at the Conference on Conversion, Coercion, and Commitment in New Religious Movements, 11-14 June 1981, at Berkeley, California.

Beckford studied the social processes involved in joining and leaving the Unification Church in Britain. He maintains that an individual's mode of leaving complements his or her mode of joining. Suggests that the high turnover rate in the UC is part of its mode of operation as an organization offering a challenge and requiring an intense commitment. Bibliography.

257. Beckford, James A. "Politics and the Anti-Cult Movement." Annual Review of the Social Sciences of Religion 3(1979): 169-190.

Examines stereotypes and assumptions about cults and the concept of the person from the point of view of the man in the street, the judiciary, and the social scientist and finds parallels among them. Maintains that the existence of cults raises political questions about the assumptions upon which many Western democracies are based and ought to be taken seriously. Bibliography.

258. Beckford, James A. "Through the Looking Glass and Out the Other Side: Withdrawal from Reverend Moon's Unification Church." Archives de Sciences Sociales des Religions 45(1978): 95-116.

Widens scope of inquiry by studying how people who join or leave the UC account for their actions and how close friends and relatives talk about it. Findings indicate that ex-members are unlikely to be reintegrated into mainstream life. Author criticizes Anthony and Robbins's integrative hypothesis. Bibliography.

259. Benassi, Victor A; Singer, Barry; Reynolds, Craig B. "Occult Belief: Seeing Is Believing." Journal for the Scientific Study of Religion 19(1980): 337-349.

Reports on a series of experiments involving a
magician performing "psychic" tricks for groups of
undergraduates. Even when the magician was introduced
as such, over fifty per cent of the students attributed
the feats to psychic ability. Supports the idea that
susceptibility to occult beliefs is strong among
youth. Bibliography.

260. Brandfon, Jane Hurst. "Pioneer Women in the Nichiren
Shoshu Soka Gakkai." Photocopied. Mount Pleasant, Mich.:
Central Michigan University, n.d.

Brandfon found that although there is nothing sexist
in the doctrines of Nichiren Shoshu, in reality men
are often given roles of greater power than women.

261. Bromley, David G., and Shupe, Anson D., Jr.
"The Archetypal Cult: Conflict and the Social Construction
of Deviance." In The Family and the Unification Church,
edited by Gene G. James, pp. 1-22. Conference Series, no.
15. Barrytown, N.Y.: Unification Theological Seminary, 1983.

The authors, authorities on the Unification Church,
show how through its visibility, conflict with major
institutions, and the work of the anticult movement,
it acquired an image as the stereotypical cult, an
image that they claim bears little resemblance to
reality.

262. Bromley, David G., and Shupe, Anson D., Jr. "Moonies"
in America: Cult, Church, and Crusade. Sage Library of
Social Research, vol. 92. Beverly Hills, Calif.: Sage
Publications, 1979.

The most thorough study of the Unification Church in
America. Using the contemporary "resource mobilization" approach, Bromley and Shupe focus on organizational dynamics rather than on why people join.
The book is chronologically arranged, beginning with
a history of the group in Korea. The later chapters
on the growth of the anticult movement as a reaction
to the church are some of the best. Bibliography
and index.

263. Bromley, David G.; Shupe, Anson D., Jr.; and Ventimiglia,
J. C. "Atrocity Tales, the Unification Church, and the Social
Construction of Evil." Journal of Communication, Summer
1979, pp. 42-53.

Discusses tactics used by deprogrammers to discredit
the Unification Church and how the church, in turn,
legitimizes its actions.

264. Buckner, H. Taylor. "The Flying Saucerians: An Open
Door Cult." In Sociology and Everyday Life, edited by
Marcello Truzzi, pp. 223-230. Englewood Cliffs, N.J.:
Prentice-Hall, 1968.

   A very interesting, enjoyable short article. Buckner
   writes of the growth of flying saucer cults in
   general and connections with the occult, particularly
   in one group he observed.

265. Damrell, Joseph. Seeking Spiritual Meaning: The World
of Vedanta. Sociological Observations, no. 2. Beverly
Hills: Sage, 1977.

   An ethnographic study of a Vedanta temple. Describes
   the history, situation, everyday life, and worldview.
   Damrell discusses his sociological theory and
   methodology through an account of his involvement in
   the spiritual life of the temple. Presents a
   synthesis of field research methods aimed toward
   more accurate understanding of the meaning of
   religious experience. Accessible to the general
   reader. Bibliography and glossary of Hindu terms.

266. Daner, Francine J. The American Children of Krsna:
A Study of the Hare Krsna Movement. New York: Holt, Rinehart
and Winston, 1976.

   A case study intended as a text for introductory and
   intermediate courses in the social sciences. Daner's
   anthropological approach considers ISKCON to be a
   revitalization movement, transforming existing
   institutions into more satisfying ones. Useful for
   its early history of the movement and support of
   Judah's assessment of why people join (see his
   Hare Krishna and the Counterculture [item 285]).
   Glossary and references.

267. Daner, Francine J. "Conversion to Krishna Conscious-
ness: The Transformation from Hippie to Religious Ascetic."
In Sectarianism: Analyses of Religious and Non-Religious
Sects, edited by Roy Wallis, pp. 53-69. New York: John
Wiley, 1975.

   A concise report on why people join and everyday life
   in the group, based on research fully discussed in her
   The American Children of Krsna [item 266]. Notes and
   references.

268. Davis, Rex, and Richardson, James T. "The Organization
and Functioning of the Children of God." Sociological
Analysis 37(1976): 321-340.

   A straightforward history and description of the
   organizational structure of the Children of God up
   to 1976. References.

269. Downton, James V., Jr. Sacred Journeys: The Conversion of Young Americans to Divine Light Mission. New York: Columbia University Press, 1979.

   Over a period of four years Downton maintained contact
   with eighteen DLM members. Fifteen stayed with the
   group throughout. In-depth interviews revealed that
   devotees felt less alienated and aimless and more loving
   and confident than they had before joining. Good
   history of the movement and its adaptation to Western
   society. Bibliography and index.

270. Drakeford, John W. Children of Doom. Nashville: Broad-man, 1972.

   An objective, readable description of the beliefs and
   activities of an early Children of God commune.

271. Foss, Daniel A., and Larkin, Ralph W. "Worshipping the Absurd: The Negation of Social Causality Among the Followers of Guru Maharaj Ji." Sociological Analysis 39(1978): 157-164.

   The authors maintain that disenchanted former youth
   movement participants of the 1960s came to perceive
   life as arbitrary and senseless. They deified Guru
   Maharaj Ji as a mirror of the meaningless universe.
   Bibliography.

272. Garriques, S. L. "The Soka Gakkai Enshrining Ceremony: Ritual Change in a Japanese Buddhist Sect in America." Eastern Anthropologist 28(1975): 133-145.

   Emphasizes the history of Soka Gakkai in America, where
   the authors find that an enshrinement ritual done in
   the convert's home is more important than it is in
   Japan. However, the monastic aspect is more important
   in Japan than in America; in America the lay movement
   has received a greater following.

273. Gordon, David. "The Jesus People: An Identity Synthesis Interpretation." Urban Life and Culture 3(1974): 159-178.

   Posits that the Jesus Movement allows its followers to
   unify a moral code in which they were originally
   socialized with elements of the counterculture in
   order to form new identities for themselves. Gordon
   was a participant observer of rallies, revivals, and
   Bible study groups in 1971 and 1972. Notes and
   references.

274. Greeley, Andrew M. "Superstition, Ecstasy, and Tribal Consciousness." Social Research 37(1970): 202-211.

   Maintains that interest of youth in the occult or
   mystical provides meaning, identity, community, and
   contact with the transcendent. Disagrees with

sociologists who have predicted a decline of importance
for religion as societies modernize.

275. Harder, Mary W. "Sex Roles in the Jesus Movement."
Social Compass 21(1974): 345-353.

Harder found that sex roles in Christ Commune (pseudonym) mimicked those in the larger society: men held
leadership roles and women were expected to be sub-
missive. Bibliography.

276. Harder, Mary W.; Richardson, James T.; and Simmonds,
Robert B. "Life Style: Courtship, Marriage, and Family in a
Changing Jesus Movement Organization." International
Review of Modern Sociology 6(1976): 155-172.

Over a four-year period the authors found that the
Christ Organization (pseudonym) changed from a
communal family style to one resembling the traditional
nuclear family. Sex role expectations were traditional,
with subservience expected from women and sexual
expression reserved for marriage. References.

277. Harrigan, John E. "Becoming a Moonie: An Interview
Study of Religious Conversion." Ed.D. dissertation, University of Maine at Orono, 1980.

Author interviewed a random sample of eighteen male
students at the Unification Seminary. All felt lonely
and alienated prior to joining the church but
experienced increased well-being as members, suggesting
that the church filled needs not met by the larger
society. Bibliography.

278. Hartman, Patricia A. "Social Dimensions of Occult
Participation: The Gnostica Study." British Journal of
Sociology 27(1976): 169-183.

Discusses responses to a questionnaire sent to a sample
of 800 people receiving Gnostica, an occult newspaper.
Younger respondents more frequently reported belief in
the influence of occult forces upon one's life than
older ones did, leading Hartman to conclude that this
may indicate a trend among youths. References.

279. Hashimoto, Hideo, and McPherson, William. "Rise and
Decline of Sokagakkai in Japan and the United States."
Review of Religious Research, no. 2(1976), pp. 83-92.

In the 1960s and early 1970s Soka Gakkai attracted
many members in the United States. By the mid-1970s,
however, the author found the growth rate had slowed
and the organization was tending toward conventionality.

280. Haywood, Carol Lois. "Women's Authority in Metaphysical Groups: An Ethnographic Exploration." Ph.D. dissertation, Boston University, 1982.

Examines patterns of public worship associated with women's power and authority in a Unity parish, a Spiritualist group, and a Theosophical lodge. May be useful to others examining women's roles in alternative religions, an area needing further research. Bibliography.

281. Holloman, Regina E. "Ritual Opening and Individual Transformation: Rites of Passage at Esalen." American Anthropologist 76(1974): 265-280.

Holloman interprets an Esalen encounter/Gestalt workshop in the light of Victor Turner's "ritual process" and maintains that participants experience a type of rite of passage with attendant psychic transformation. References.

282. Hurst, Jane Dygert. "The Nichiren Shoshu Sokagakkai in America: The Ethos of a New Religious Movement." Ph.D. dissertation, Temple University, 1980.

In-depth study of a Japanese new religion that has gained thousands of adherents in the United States since 1960. Pays special attention to the implicit and explicit worldviews of the group. Hurst claims people join to give their lives meaning. Bibliography.

283. Johnson, Paul Doyle. "Dilemmas of Charismatic Leadership: The Case of the People's Temple." Sociological Analysis 40(1979): 315-323.

Johnson focuses on the social dynamics of charismatic leadership and applies his theoretical model of leadership strategies ex post facto to the Peoples Temple. A key element in the model is the precariousness of the leader's power. Bibliography.

284. Johnston, Hank. "The Marketed Social Movement: A Case Study of the Rapid Growth of TM." Pacific Sociological Review 23(1980): 333-354.

Describes how the Transcendental Meditation movement reached many people by using sophisticated marketing strategies tailor-made for different groups, for example students and businessmen.

285. Judah, J. Stillson. Hare Krishna and the Counterculture. New York: John Wiley and Sons, 1974.

The most significant study of the International Society for Krishna Consciousness and its American devotees.

Based on a study of the literature of the movement
and the counterculture, questionnaires, extensive
interviews, and personal participation. Traces the
movement philosophically and historically to the
Vaishnava movement in India. Describes ISKCON's teachings and lifestyle with particular attention to the
appeal of Krishna Consciousness to "hippies" of the
1960s, whom Judah claims were able to place some
countercultural values in a more meaningful context
by joining ISKCON. Well researched and sympathetic.
Glossary of names and terms, bibliography and index.

286. La Magdeleine, Donald R. "Jews for Jesus: Organizational Structure and Supporters." Master's thesis, Graduate
Theological Union, Berkeley, California, 1977.

Includes survey research and reports of interviews
with members. Attempts to assess why people join and
the place of Jews for Jesus within Hebrew Christianity.
A useful study of an organization that has received
little scholarly attention. Bibliography.

287. Lauer, Robert H. "Social Movements: An Interactionist
Analysis." The Sociological Quarterly 13(1972): 315-328.

The authors analyze the development of the LSD movement in terms of the way it interacted with the larger
society. Particularly interesting reading in light
of the movement's turn toward Eastern mysticism, seen
by many as a precursor to the growth of new religious
movements. References.

288. Lofland, John. Doomsday Cult: A Study of Conversion,
Proselytization, and Maintenance of Faith. Enl. ed.
New York: Irvington Publishers, 1977.

Lofland's 1966 study of the Unification Church is updated with a sixty-five page epilogue. Although
considered a classic analysis of the social processes
of the early years of a deviant organization, Lofland's
work has been criticized for neglect of the religious
nature of the group. The epilogue is a minor addition.
Readers looking for a full treatment of the UC in the
1970s should see Bromley and Shupe's "Moonies" in
America [item 262]. References and index.

289. Lofland, John. "White-Hot Mobilization: Strategies
of a Millennarian Movement." In The Dynamics of Social Movements, edited by M. Zald and J. D. McCarthy, pp. 157-166.
Cambridge, Mass.: Winthrop, 1979.

290. Lopez, Alan R. "Reality Construction and Transformation
in an Eastern Mystical Cult: A Sociological Study." Ph.D.
dissertation, University of Connecticut, 1980.

History and description of social processes involved
in the construction of reality in the Yoga Association
of Self-Analysis. Bibliography.

291. Lynch, Frederick R. "'Occult Establishment' or 'Deviant
Religion'? The Rise and Fall of a Modern Church of Magic."
Journal for the Scientific Study of Religion 18(1979): 281-
298.

Lynch finds that the Church of the Sun more closely
resembles a white, middle-class occult establishment
than it does a deviant group.

292. Martin, Ilse. "Inequality, Chastity, and Sign Endogamy
in the New Age Brotherhood." In Sex Roles in Contemporary
American Communes, edited by Jon Wagner, pp. 82-110.
Bloomington: Indiana University Press, 1982.

Martin's participant observation study of the pseudo-
nymous California commune, the New Age Brotherhood,
reveals traditional sexual roles with subordination of
women and a strong emphasis on chastity, which Martin
says contributed to the solidarity of the commune by
diverting energy to the larger group. References.

293. Marty, Martin. "The Occult Establishment." Social
Research 37(1970): 212-230.

Pointing to the absence of research on the growth of
the occult in the 1960s, Marty reports on his analysis
of the content of forty occult periodicals. Their
content was aimed at conventional concerns of middle-
class people. Marty calls this audience the "Occult
Establishment" to distinguish it from the "Occult
Underground" comprised of unconventional youth. A
useful and readable study.

294. Melton, J. Gordon. "The Origins of Contemporary Neo-
Paganism: A Report of Research in Progress." Paper read
to the Popular Culture Association, 17 April 1980, in Detroit,
Michigan. Photocopied.

Although Melton's discussion of the development of
Neo-Paganism and his presentation of survey data are
too brief, his research is a good beginning in a very
neglected area.

295. Nordquist, Ted A. Ananda Cooperative Village: A Study
in the Beliefs, Values, and Attitudes of a New Age Religious
Community. Uppsala, Sweden: Borgstroms Tryckeri, 1978.

In-depth study of a Hindu-related community. Presents
history, beliefs, values, and how members came to be
committed. Information was obtained through interviews, questionnaires, and participant-observation.

Useful addition to quantitative research and the only
such study of Ananda. Questionnaire and other data-
gathering instruments included. Bibliography.

296. Ofshe, Richard. "The Social Development of the Synanon
Cult: The Managerial Strategy of Organizational Transformation." Sociological Analysis 41(1980): 109-127.

Reviews Synanon's development from its inception
through its change to a religious group. Advances
a theory of its transformations based on deliberate
efforts of its managers to gain greater control.
Ofshe's major research on Synanon garnered him a share
in the Pulitzer Prize in 1978. See The Light on
Synanon [item 673] for that story.

297. Ofshe, Richard. "Synanon: The Failure that Founded a
Tradition." In The Self-Help Revolution, edited by A.
Gartner and F. Riessman. New York: Human Sciences Press,
in press.

298. Ofshe, Richard; Berg, Nancy; Coughlin, Richard; Dolina-
jec, Gregory; Gerson, Kathleen; and Johnson, Avery. "Social
Structure and Social Control in Synanon." Journal of Volun-
tary Action Research 3(1974): 67-76.

Discussion of the Synanon "game," a form of encounter
group, and its function in shaping members' actions
and obtaining commitment to the larger group. References.

299. Palmer, Susan. "Performance Practices in Meditation
Rituals among the New Religions." Studies in Religion/
Sciences Religieuses 9(1980): 403-413.

Palmer participated in meditation rituals offered
by Sivananda Yoga Society, Dharmadhatu, the American
Sufi Order, and a Tai Chi Chuan class in Montreal.
Even though the form of the ritual may be a dance,
such as the Sufi dance, these groups define their
rituals as inner-directed meditations. Palmer
discovered elements of social communication and
believes that study of such rituals can provide
insight not only into group social structure but
also into psychological reasons for participating.

300. Pfaffenberger, Bryan. "A World of Husbands and Mothers:
Sex Roles and Their Ideological Context in the Formation of
the Farm." In Sex Roles in Contemporary American Communes,
edited by Jon Wagner, pp. 172-210. Bloomington: Indiana
University Press, 1982.

The author argues that Stephen Gaskin's religious
leadership of The Farm provides values that hold the
commune together, while its conventional sexual roles

tend to work against solidarity. References.

301. Pilarzyk, Thomas. "The Origin, Development, and Decline of a Youth Culture Religion: An Application of Sectarianization Theory." Review of Religious Research 20(1978): 23-43.

    Applies Wallis's sectarianism theory to data on the Divine Light Mission and concludes that internal factors contributed to the group's decline. References.

302. Pilarzyk, Thomas, and Bharadwaj, Lakshmi. "What Is Real? The Failure of the Phenomenological Approach in a Field Study of the Divine Light Mission." Humanity and Society 3(1979): 16-34.

    While attempting to use a phenomenological approach to study a mystical group, Pilarzyk discovered that the two worldviews conflicted, preventing objective research. References.

303. Quarantelli, E.L., and Wenger, Dennis. "A Voice from the Thirteenth Century: The Characteristics and Conditions tor the Emergence of a Ouija Board Cult." Urban Life and Culture 1(1973): 379-400.

    Describes and analyzes a ouija board cult of eight college women. Connects the development of the cult to a wider social interest in the occult, suggesting that it is a micro example of a macro phenomenon. References.

304. Richardson, James T. "Causes and Consequences of the Jesus Movement in the United States." In Acts of the Twelfth International Conference on Sociology of Religion, pp. 393-406. Lille, France: Edition du Secretariat CISR, 1973.

    Maintains that social acceptance of Christian fundamentalism and student frustration with political structures have contributed to the growth of the Jesus Movement. Notes that the movement helps to maintain the status quo. Bibliography.

305. Richardson, James T. "The Jesus Movement: An Assessment." Listening: Journal of Religion and Culture, no. 3 (1974), pp. 20-42.

    Good, brief history and description of the Jesus Movement and its impact on society from its inception to just beyond its initial burst of enthusiasm. References.

306. Richardson, James T., and Davis, Rex. "Experiential Fundamentalism: Revisions of Orthodoxy in the Jesus Movement." Journal of the American Academy of Religion 51(1983): 397-425.

Discussion of differences in beliefs and practices
between fundamentalism and the Jesus Movement. A
major portion of the paper is devoted to how the
Children of God justify using sex as a recruitment
tactic. Bibliography.

307. Richardson, James T., and Reidy, M.V.T. "Form and
Fluidity in Two Contemporary Glossolalic Movements."
Annual Review of the Social Sciences of Religion 4(1980): 183-
220.

Compares and contrasts the Neo-Pentecostal and Jesus
Movements. They were very different initially,
the authors find, but by 1980 they had become so
similar that the authors now consider the Jesus
Movement to be a manifestation of the Neo-Pentecostal
Movement. References.

308. Richardson, James T.; Stewart, Mary; and Simmonds,
Robert B. Organized Miracles: A Study of a Contemporary
Youth, Communal, Fundamentalist Organization. New Bruns-
wick, N.J.: Transaction Books, 1979.

Extensive longitudinal study of the Christ Communal
Organization, pseudonym for a Jesus Movement group
the authors began studying in 1970. Information was
gathered through field and survey research,
personality assessment, and panel research. An important contribution to descriptive analysis. The tone
is very scholarly, sometimes failing to communicate
the flavor of real life in the group. Bibliography
and index.

309. Robbins, Thomas. "Contemporary 'Post-Drug' Cults:
A Comparison of Two Movements." Ph.D. dissertation, University of North Carolina, 1973.

A study of why the Meher Baba cult and the Christian
World Liberation Front, a Jesus Movement group,
appealed to drug users in the late 1960s and how
the two groups differed in reintegrating their
followers into conventional society. Robbins gained
his information via participant-observation and interviews. Bibliography.

310. Robbins, Thomas, and Anthony, Dick. "Getting Straight
with Meher Baba: A Study of Mysticism, Drug Rehabilitation,
and Postadolescent Role Conflict." Journal for the Scientific
Study of Religion 11(1972): 122-140.

Robbins and Anthony used the participant-observation
approach to study followers of Meher Baba and
discovered that the group met followers' needs for
community and reassimilated former dropouts and
drug-users into conventional working roles. Not easy

reading for those unfamiliar with sociological termino-
logy. Bibliography.

311. Robbins, Thomas; Anthony, Dick; Curtis, Thomas E.; and
Doucas, Madeline. "The Last Civil Religion: The Unification Church of Reverend Sun Myung Moon." Sociological Analysis 37(1976): 111-125.

The authors interpret the Unification Church as an
attempt at a totalitarian response to the cultural
fragmentation of mass society. They discuss UC teachings and point out elements of American civil religion
in them. A good analysis. References.

312. Rochford, Edmund Burke, Jr. "Recruitment Strategies,
Ideology, and Organization in the Hare Krishna Movement."
Social Problems 29(1982): 399-410.

In his survey of 200 Hare Krishna devotees, Rochford
discovered recruitment strategy depended a great deal
on local opportunities rather than on ideology or the
organization's structure. In fact, structure and
ideology have been shaped by opportunities such as
the hippie gathering of the late 1960s in San Francisco,
which brought potential converts literally to the group's
doorstep. Bibliography.

313. Rochford, Edmund Burke, Jr. "A Study of Recruitment
and Transformation Processes in the Hare Krishna Movement."
Ph.D. dissertation, University of California, 1982.

From 1975 through 1981, a crucial period for ISKCON
in part because of Prabhupada's death in 1977,
Rochford conducted participant-observation studies,
interviews, and a survey. Avoiding theories of
recruitment that rely solely on psychological pre-
dispositions, he stresses potential converts' opportunities for contact with devotees and how motives
develop during the conversion process. Valuable,
useful history of the movement since the leader's
death. Bibliography.

314. Saliba, John A.,"The Guru: Perceptions of American Devotees of the Divine Light Mission." Horizons 7(1980): 69-81.

Discussion of how Guru Maharaj Ji's followers worship
him and perceive him and his mission. Saliba raises
the question of the DLM's future in light of outside
criticism of the guru and future possible problems of
succession.

315. "Scholars Respond to Jonestown Queries." New Religious
Movements Newsletter, December 1979, p. 1.

Brief report of a survey undertaken by Barbara Hargrove

to determine how and to what extent scholars responded
to media attempts to obtain information and evaluations
of the Jonestown tragedy. She concludes that academic
research and information-gathering centers are needed
so that adequate responses may be given to the public.

316. Schur, Edwin. The Awareness Trap: Self-absorption In-
stead of Social Change. New York: Quadrangle/New York Times
Book Co., 1976.

The human potential movement is taken to task for amor-
phous and simplistic themes. Author examines underlying
assumptions and ideas involved in various self-awareness
therapies. He thinks individual change can go only so
far; changes in public policy are needed to bring about
real social change. Readable. Notes and index.

317. Scott, Gini Graham. Cult and Countercult: A Study of
a Spiritual Growth Group and a Witchcraft Order. Contributions in Sociology, no. 38. Westport, Conn.: Greenwood
Press, 1980.

Scott found through participant-observation of the
Aquarian Age Order and the Inner Peace Movement
(both pseudonyms) that although the two groups maintain similar metaphysical beliefs, they are very
different in all other ways. A useful ethnographic
study that advances understanding of the social psychology of such groups. Bibliography and index.

318. Scott, Gini Graham. The Magicians: A Study of the Use
of Power in a Black Magic Group. New York: Irvington
Publishers, 1983.

Scott studied a magical-religious group she calls
the Church of Hu and reports on the members' beliefs,
rituals, group organization, and social backgrounds.
In the final chapters she discusses the psychological
aspects of the search for power observed in members.
Written to appeal to a general audience. This is one
of the few studies of a magical group. Bibliography.

319. Shinn, Larry D. "The Future of an Old Man's Vision:
ISKCON in the Twenty-First Century." Paper read at the
New Ecumenical Research Association Conference, 5-9 October
1983, at Berkeley, California. Photocopied.

Clear description of the Hare Krishna movement's
economic, recruitment, and organizational status since
the death of Prabhupada. Points out the strength
found in the diverse character and missions of the
American temples and the weaknesses in their economic
and recruitment structures.

320. Shupe, Anson D., Jr. "'Disembodied Access' and Technological Constraints on Organizational Development: A Study
of Mail-Order Religions." Journal for the Scientific Study
of Religion 15(1976): 177-185.

> Shupe's study indicates that occult groups that depend
> on magazine advertising to proselytize and the postal
> service for communication have limited growth oppor-
> tunities. References.

321. Shupe, Anson D., Jr. "Toward a Structural Perspective
of Modern Religious Movements." Sociological Focus, Summer
1973, pp. 83-99.

> Critical of sociological approaches that focus on
> the content of religious movements; suggests that
> researchers pay more attention to the organization of
> group members and the relationship of the group to
> the larger society. Bibliography.

322. Shupe, Anson D., Jr., and Bromley, David G. "Dynamics
of Ideology and Social Organization in Social Movements:
The Case of the Unificationist Movement." Paper read at the
annual meeting of the Southwestern Scciological Association,
March 1981, at Dallas, Texas.

> The authors use the case of the Unification Church
> to demonstrate their thesis that it is normal for
> social movements to change their ideologies as their
> organizations change. Bibliography.

323. Shupe, Anson D.,Jr.,and Bromley, David G. "The Moonies,
and the Anti-Cultists: Movement and Counter Movement in
Conflict." Sociological Analysis 40(1979): 325-334.

> Examines the potential of the Unification Church to
> generate societal conflict. The authors, whc have
> written a major study of the anticult movement (see
> The New Vigilantes [item 324]), consider its origins
> and tactics in relation to the UC. Bibliography.

324. Shupe, Anson D., Jr., and Bromley, David G. The New
Vigilantes: Deprogrammers, Anti-Cultists, and the New
Religions. Sage Library of Social Research, vol. 113.
Beverly Hills, Calif.: Sage, 1980.

> The only in-depth study of the anticult movement;
> companion volume to the authors' "Moonies" in America
> [item 262]. Thoroughly documented, the study employs
> a "resource mobilization" approach to demonstrate how
> family associations, fundamentalist Christians, and
> deprogrammers developed their unique roles and
> strategies. An important, readable descriptive study.
> Bibliography and index.

325. Shupe, Anson D., Jr., and Bromley, David G. "Reverse Missionizing: Sun Myung Moon's Unificationist Movement in the United States." Free Inquiry 8(1980): 197-203.

Brief discussion of several ways in which the Unification Church came into conflict with American society and values. References.

326. Shupe, Anson D., Jr., and Bromley, David G. "Some Problems in Transplanting Oriental Christianity to the U.S.: The Case of Sun Myung Moon." Paper read at the Southwest Conference on Asian Studies, 1980, at Arlington, Texas. Photocopied.

Discusses three areas of conflict between the Unification Church and institutions in American society: the challenge to religious pluralism, the UC's organizational style, and Moon's apparent insensitivity to cultural problems of introducing his movement in the United States.

327. Shupe, Anson D., Jr., and Bromley, David G. "Walking a Tightrope: Dilemmas of Participant Observation of Groups in Conflict." Qualitative Sociology, no. 3(1980), pp. 3-21.

The authors have done major research on two antagonistic groups, the Unification Church and the anticult movement. They discuss several problems that arose, such as pressure from each group to accept its ideology, negotiating over how confidential information would be used, and pressures to take a public stand. Aimed at the sociologist who may find himself/herself in the same type of situation. References.

328. Simmonds, Robert B.; Richardson, James T.; and Harder, Mary W. "Organizational Aspects of a Jesus Movement Community." Social Compass 21(1974): 269-281.

Examines authority structure of Christ Commune, pseudonym for a Jesus Movement group, and its transformations over several years. Authors note that the group they are studying is not the Children of God. Well-written descriptive article. Bibliography.

329. Snelling, Clarence H., and Whitley, Oliver R. "Problem-Solving Behavior in Religious and Para-Religious Groups: An Initial Report." In Changing Perspectives in the Scientific Study of Religion, edited by Allan W. Eister, pp. 315-334. New York: John Wiley and Sons, 1974.

A report of initial participant observation work with four groups, including an ISKCON temple. The authors note that life in the Hare Krishna group was reduced to overcoming sensuality and that aspects of the Protestant ethic were apparent. References.

330. Snow, David Alan. "The Nichiren Shoshu Buddhist Movement in America: A Sociological Examination of Its Value Orientation, Recruitment Efforts, and Spread." Ph.D. dissertation, University of California at Los Angeles, 1976.

Snow found that Nichiren Shoshu recruited thousands of middle and lower middle income Americans between 1960 and 1970. Most were under thirty years of age and were recruited by family or friends. Bibliography.

331. Taylor, David. "The Social Organization of Recruitment in the Unification Church." Master's thesis, University of Montana, 1978.

Based on participant-observation studies, Taylor's thesis provides a very detailed account of recruitment and training sessions held by the UC at its Ideal City Ranch in 1975. Reconstructed conversations capture the intensity of the sessions. Very fine work. Bibliography.

332. Tipton, Steven M. Getting Saved from the Sixties. Berkeley: University of California Press, 1982.

Based on case studies of the Living Word Fellowship, Pacific Zen Center, and est, Tipton's book maintains that joining these groups aided 1960s youths in grappling with ethical and religious questions to find new moral meaning. A thoughtful and important study. Notes, bibliography, and index.

333. Tipton, Steven M. "The Moral Logic of Alternative Religions." Daedalus, Winter 1982, pp. 185-213.

Argues that youth of the 1960s joined alternative religions "to make moral sense of their lives." Reviews biblical, utilitarian, and countercultural moralities. Author uses his research on est to show how its members were aided in mediating the conflict between conventional and countercultural meaning. For a full report of Tipton's valuable research, see his Getting Saved from the Sixties [item 332].

334. Tipton, Steven M. "New Religious Movements and the Problem of a Modern Ethic." In Religious Change and Continuity, edited by Harry M. Johnson, pp. 286-312. San Francisco: Jossey-Bass, 1979.

Discussion of how 1960s youths were able to realize counterculture ideals through the monastic structure of Zen Buddhism. Tipton provides a good look at the way an Eastern ethical system can be synthesized with traditional American forms to help people make moral sense of their lives. Notes and references.

335. Tipton, Steven M. "Zen Master and Student: Moral
Authority in a Ritual Context." Paper read at the Conference
on Conversion, Coercion, and Commitment in New Religious
Movements, 11-14 June 1981, Berkeley, California.

    Tipton describes zazen and the Zen student's inter-
    action with the teacher, claiming that both encourage
    intuitive moral virtue. Description is based on the
    reports of Zen meditators.

336. Truzzi, Marcello. "The Occult Revival as Popular
Culture: Some Random Observations on the Old and Nouveau
Witch." Sociological Quarterly 13(1970): 16-36.

    An early study of contemporary occultism. Much infor-
    mation on urban witchcraft. Sees modern witchcraft
    as being secularized, a "pop religion" reflecting a
    lack of seriousness about the supernatural.

337. Wagner, Melinda Bollar. Metaphysics in Midwestern
America. Columbus: Ohio State University Press, 1983.

    Ethnographic study of Spiritual Frontiers Fellowship,
    an occult group that attracts middle-class, middle-
    aged people. Wagner perceives the organization to be
    an "occult establishment" group and shows how it
    answers the need for meaning in its members' lives.
    Bibliography and index.

338. Wallis, Roy. "A Comparative Analysis of Problems and
Processes of Change in Two Manipulationist Movements:
Christian Science and Scientology." In Acts of the Twelfth
International Conference on Sociology of Religion, pp. 407-
422. The Hague: CISR, 1973.

    Comparative analysis of the problems encountered by
    Christian Science and Scientology in their transitions
    from loosely organized cults to cohesive, authoritarian
    sects. Both solidified by developing transcendental
    ideologies to legitimatize authoritarian control,
    standardization, commitment to the leader, and
    conflict with society. For a very fine and comprehen-
    sive treatment of the development of Scientology,
    see Wallis' The Road to Total Freedom [item 342].

339. Wallis, Roy. "Millenialism and Community: Observations
on the Children of God." In his Salvation and Protest:
Studies of Social and Religious Movements, pp. 51-73. New
York: St. Martin's Press, 1979.

    In this very good analysis of the development of
    the Children of God through 1974, Wallis shows how
    the movement changed in response to new strategies
    the leader believed were revealed to him. Based on
    interviews, participant-observation, and documentary
    materials.

340. Wallis, Roy. "The Moral Career of a Research Project."
In his Salvation and Protest: Studies of Social and Religious
Movements, pp. 193-216. New York: St. Martin's Press, 1979.

Wallis has produced the most significant sociological
studies of Dianetics and Scientology. Here he talks
frankly about the practical and moral problems he
encountered while engaged in the research that resulted
in his book, The Road to Total Freedom [item 342].
Enlightening for the person unfamiliar with participant
observation research in controversial movements.

341. Wallis, Roy. "Recruiting Christian Manpower." Society,
May/June 1978, vol. 15, no. 4, pp. 72-74.

Wallis shows how Moses Berg and his Children of God
coherently justified their use of sexuality in
proselytizing.

342. Wallis, Roy. The Road to Total Freedom: A Sociological
Analysis of Scientology. New York: Columbia University
Press, 1977.

Descriptive and theoretical study of Dianetics and its
development into Scientology, couched in Wallis'
sectarianization theory. Part One is an exposition of
the theory. Part Two discusses the "cult phase," the
loosely structured and individualistic Dianetics.
Part Three covers Hubbard's development of Scientology,
in which he centralized doctrine and authority. In
Wallis's analysis, the group became a sect. Covers
Scientology's conflicts with English and Australian
authorities. Definitive study, very scholarly, yet
interesting reading. Bibliography and index.

343. Wallis, Roy. "Sex, Marriage, and the Children of God."
In his Salvation and Protest: Studies of Social and Religious
Movements, pp. 74-90. New York: St. Martin's Press, 1979.

The marital and sexual arrangements of the Children of
God have been morally condemned by many. Wallis
dispassionately shows how these practices are understandable in the context of the beliefs and social
structure of the group.

344. Wallis, Roy. "The Social Construction of Charisma."
Social Compass 29(1982): 25-39.

Using the Children of God as a case study, Wallis
seeks to demonstrate how "the social nature of the
emergence, recognition, and maintenance of a
charismatic identity" occurs only because of interaction
of a leader with his followers in which both parties
pursue advantages. Puts forth a situational, sociological explanation, which he sees as more relevant to

understanding the development and maintenance of
charismatic relationships than a psychological explanation.

345. Westley, Frances R. "Interpersonal Contamination:
Pollution Fears in the Human Potential Movement." Studies
in Religion/Sciences Religieuses 11(1982): 149-162.

Using an anthropological approach, Westley claims that
members of groups such as est and Arica seek community
but are also afraid of being destroyed by it. She
identifies the fear as identity confusion, "pollution
fear" engendered by a general breakdown of society.

346. Westley, Frances R. "Purification and Healing Rituals
in New Religious Groups." Occasional Publications in
Anthropology, Ethnology Series 33(1979): 195-213.

Discusses body purification rituals of the Integral
Yoga Institute and healing rituals of Catholic
Charismatics. Suggests that such rituals may be
a symbolic response to notions of environmental
disease and moral confusion in American society.
Bibliography.

347. Wise, David. "Dharma West: A Social-Psychological
Inquiry into Zen in San Francisco." Ph.D. dissertation,
University of California at Berkeley, 1971.

In 1970, when Wise studied it, the San Francisco
Zen Center was the largest Zen organization in the
United States. Wise's dissertation begins with a
brief history of Zen in America and goes on to
describe the development of the San Francisco Zen
Center. He examines psychosocial aspects of life in
the Center and includes lengthy quotations from
interviews with members. He describes the Center
as a subculture of disaffected, white, middle-class
young people who find meaning in Zen practice.
Notes and appendix containing the Center's articles
of incorporation.

Psychological and Psychiatric Studies

General Works

348. Anderson, Susan, and Zimbardo, Philip. "On Resisting Social Influence." Photocopied. Stanford: Stanford University, Department of Psychology, 1979.

The authors' thesis is that mind control exists in everyday life whenever information is distorted or withheld systematically. Suggests ways of resisting unwanted influence based on relevant research, interviews with con men, members of cults, and salesmen. References.

349. Appelbaum, Stephen A. Out in Inner Space: A Psychoanalyst Explores the New Therapies. New York: Doubleday, 1979.

A psychiatrist who has sampled the major human potential experiences--est, rolfing, biofeedback, gestalt encounter, and so on-- assesses their meaning for his profession and society. Appelbaum's open and thoughtful approach, combined with a readable style, makes this a useful commentary on the pros and cons of several different systems. References and index.

350. Back, Kurt W., and Bourque, Linda Brookover. "Can Feelings Be Enumerated?" Behavioral Science 15(1970): 487-496.

The authors maintain that properly prepared and administered surveys can elicit useful information concerning the incidence of transcendental or mystical experiences among individuals. In critiquing such surveys they show how three Gallup opinion polls

from the 1960s that apparently indicate a rise in
the incidence of such experiences could be interpreted
differently. References.

351. Chorover, Stephen L. "Organizational Recruitment in
'Open' and 'Closed' Social Systems: A Neuropsychological
Perspective." Paper read at the Conference on Conversion,
Coercion, and Commitment in New Religious Movements,
11-14 June 1981, at Berkeley, California. Photocopied.

Chorover maintains that the brainwashing/conversion
controversy is really about the propriety of closed
and hierarchically structured social relationships;
he says concerns should focus on meaning and power in
these groups, not merely on supposed disease or disorder in the minds of cult members.

352. Clark, John G., Jr. "Cults." Journal of the American
Medical Association 242(1979): 279-281.

Clark makes sweeping, unsupported generalizations
about cults, for example claiming that there are more
than 3,000 that are "absolutist and intolerant."
He claims to have studied sixty "chronically disturbed
and unhappy" people who have been involved in cults.
Intended to inform physicians, the article is
primarily an account of the physical and psychological
disturbance that Clark claims cults cause in their
members. References.

353. Clark, John G., Jr. "Investigating the Effects of
Some Religious Cults on the Health and Welfare of Their
Converts." Paper submitted to the Special Investigating
Committee of the Vermont Senate, 1977.

States that health hazards to cult members are
extreme; suggests that irreversible, catastrophic
personality changes would occur after four years of
cult involvement. Sweeping, unsupported statements
about "all cults" mar Clark's testimony.

354. Conway, Flo, and Siegelman, Jim. "Information Disease:
Have Cults Created a New Mental Illness?" Science Digest,
January 1982, p. 86.

Claims that cults have created a new mental illness
by controlling information received by members.
Based on a survey of over 400 former cult members.
(See Kilbourne [item 369] for a critique of Conway
and Siegelman's statistics.)

355. Cox, Harvey. "Eastern Cults and Western Culture:
Why Young Americans Are Buying Oriental Religions."
Psychology Today, no. 2(1977), p. 36.

Cox discovered that young people who joined Eastern
religious cults in the Cambridge, Massachusetts area
were looking for friendship, authority, and a way to
experience life directly. Cox concludes that the trend
to Eastern religions is a symptom of cultural malaise.
See his Turning East [item 459] for a full treatment
of his ideas.

356. Deikman, Arthur J. "The Evaluation of Spiritual and
Utopian Groups." Journal of Humanistic Psychology, no. 3
(1983), pp. 8-18.

Deikman recognizes the need for discrimination between
the spurious and the genuine among spiritual groups
and suggests paying close attention to how well the
group lives up to its stated aims and to criteria
from traditional spiritual literature.

357. Fauteux, Kevin. "Good/Bad Splitting in the Religious
Experience." American Journal of Psychoanalysis 41(1981):
261-267.

Fauteux argues that the euphoric look and incessant
smiles he has observed on some cult members indicate
infantile pleasure seeking and unhealthy avoidance of
aggression. References.

358. Galanter, Marc. "Charismatic Religious Sects and
Psychiatry: An Overview." American Journal of Psychiatry
139(1982): 1539-1548.

Galanter opens up new areas for psychological inquiry
by switching focus from the individual to the group.
He points out that psychiatric nomenclature was
developed as a typology for mental illness, not social
adaptation. A good article, not only suggesting new
avenues of research but also providing an overview
that demonstrates the author's familiarity with a
wide range of new religious movements literature.

359. Gitelson, Idy B., and Reed, Edward J. "Identity Status
of Jewish Youth Pre- and Post-Cult Involvement." Journal
of Jewish Communal Service 57(1981): 312-320.

Reports on the early stage of a study of vulnerability
to cult recruitment. Seven Jewish ex-cult members
were interviewed and found to have had diffuse
identities before joining cults.

360. Group for the Advancement of Psychiatry. Committee
on Psychiatry and Religion. Mysticism: Spiritual Quest or
Psychic Disorder? GAP Publication, no. 97. New York:
Group for the Advancement of Psychiatry, 1976.

Discusses mystical movements in world religions and

contemporary society. Examines mystical experiences
for psychopathological and healthy elements. Reaches
no certain conclusion about the worth of such
experiences.

361. Halperin, David A., ed. Psychodynamic Perspectives on
Religion, Sect, and Cult. Boston: John Wright, 1983.

Collection of essays concerned primarily with the
psychology of and therapy with those disturbed by
involvement in authoritarian, totalistic new religious
groups. Section One covers historical parallels,
such as Gnosticism, the Albigensian Cathari, and
the Mormons. Second section contains studies on the
nature of cult affiliation and two articles concerned
with Jewish identity. Therapeutic approaches such as
psychoanalytic, family therapy, and self-help make
up the third section. A useful collection. References
and index.

362. Hargrove, Barbara. "Mental Health and the New Religions."
Iliff Review 40(1983): 25-36.

Suggests caution when attributing mental illness to
cult affiliates ; calls for more thoughtful approaches
to distinguishing healthy from unhealthy involvement
and asks regular social institutions to respond more
positively to the idealism of youth.

363. Hastings, Arthur. "A Transpersonal Viewpoint on New
Religious Movements." Paper read at the Conference on Conversion, Coercion, and Commitment in New Religious Movements, 11-14 June 1981, at Berkeley, California. Photocopied.

Briefly describes transpersonal psychology, in particular its emphasis on spiritual growth. Criticizes
new religious groups in general for exclusivity,
leadership pathology, and failure to promote spiritual
growth. References.

364. Hauser, James. "Adolescents and Religion." Adolescence
16(1981): 309-320.

In this overview of research on adolescent religiosity
Hauser pays particular attention to needs fulfilled
by and possible benefits of joining new religions.
References.

365. Horton, Paul C. "The Mystical Experience as a Suicide
Preventive." American Journal of Psychiatry 130(1973):
294-296.

Discusses cases of three suicidal adolescents who
found relief from their distress in mystical

experiences. Suggests that therapists regard mystical
experiences as therapeutic allies, not simply as
delusions. References.

366. Jones, Connie A. "Women and Authoritarianism in New
Religious Movements." Paper read at the annual meeting of
the Society for the Scientific Study of Religion, 21-24
October 1982, at Providence, Rhode Island. Photocopied.

> Reports on a study of authoritarianism in members of
> eleven San Francisco Bay Area religious groups. For
> comparative purposes, mainline Christian churches
> were included along with new religious groups.
> Women were found to be no more or less prone to authori-
> tarian attitudes than men, but authoritarianism did
> vary significantly among the groups. Statistical
> tables, test instrument, and bibliography. For a full
> report of the study see McBride and Schwartz [item
> 376].

367. Kaslow, Florence, and Schwartz, Lita Linzer. "Vulner-
ability and Invulnerability to the Cults: An Assessment of
Family Dynamics, Functioning, and Values." In Marital and
Family Therapy: New Perspectives in Theory, Research and
Practice, edited by Dennis A. Bagarozzi, Anthony P. Jurich,
and Robert W. Jackson, pp. 165-190. New York: Human
Sciences Press, 1983.

> This study of the family backgrounds of ex-cult members
> is a tentative first step toward identifying family
> characteristics of such people. The sample of nine
> ex-cult members was too small for the finding of
> unhealthy family background to be very significant.
> References.

368. Kemp, Katherine V. "The Fate of Aggression in Organized
Cults." Paper read at the Conference of the American
Psychological Association, May 1978, at Atlanta, Georgia.
Photocopied.

> Using anecdotal material, Kemp argues that cult
> members exhibit an apparent lack of aggression but
> actually direct a great deal of hostility outside the
> groups.

369. Kilbourne, Brock K. "The Conway and Siegelman Claims
Against Religious Cults: An Assessment of Their Data."
Journal for the Scientific Study of Religion 22(1983): 380-
385.

> By applying a standard correlation analysis to the
> Conway and Siegelman "information disease" data
> [item 354], Kilbourne finds that the statistics do
> not support the authors' conclusion. Indeed, they
> support the conclusion that positive and even therapeutic
> effects can be associated with cult membership. Referen-
> ces.

370. Levine, Edward M. "Religious Cults: Havens for the Emotionally Distressed, Idealists, and Intellectuals, and Strongholds of Authoritarian Personalities." Paper read at the Conference on Conversion, Coercion, and Commitment in New Religious Movements, 11-14 June 1981, at Berkeley, California. Photocopied.

> Examines incentives new religious groups provide to those who join, as well as motives of converts and cult leaders. Joiners and leaders are found to have a variety of psychological weaknesses. Levine's narrow concept of religion and spirituality leads him to make sweeping judgments about the lack of such qualities in these groups. References.

371. Levine, Edward M. "Rural Communes and Religious Cults: Refuges for Middle-Class Youth." In Adolescent Psychiatry, vol. 8, edited by Sherman C. Feinstein, Peter L. Giovacchini, John G. Looney, Allan Z. Schwartzberg, and Arthur D. Sorosky, pp. 138-153. Chicago: University of Chicago Press, 1980.

> Compares psychosocial aspects of communes and authoritarian religious cults. Argues that cults appeal to some middle-class young people because the nuclear family and society in general do not instill strong values based on tradition. Anxiety over an uncertain future causes some to seek direction in authoritarian cults, where, it is implied, they are taken advantage of. References.

372. Levine, Saul V. "Cults and Mental Health: Clinical Conclusions." Canadian Journal of Psychiatry 26(1981): 534-539.

> Good, balanced overview of clinical findings related to the mental health of cult members and ex-members. Levine's own experience involved work with or interviews of over 400 cult members and clinical work with eighty-three ex-cult members. His conclusions note both positive and negative effects and recommend further well-controlled research.

373. Levine, Saul V. "Youth and Religious Cults: A Societal and Clinical Dilemma." In Adolescent Psychiatry, vol. 6, edited by Sherman C. Feinstein and Peter L. Giovacchini, pp. 75-89. Chicago: University of Chicago Press, 1978.

> Based on extensive interviews with 106 members of several popular new religious groups, Levine's article maintains that cult membership gave new meaning to their lives. He warns against the dangers of fanaticism for some people with borderline personality disorders but claims that most people will be involved temporarily and will not be harmed. References.

374. Levine, Saul V., and Salter, Nancy E. "Youth and
Contemporary Religious Movements: Psychosocial Findings."
Canadian Psychiatric Association Journal 21(1976); 411-420.

> Reports on interviews with 106 cult members. Members
> reported personal dissatisfaction as a primary reason
> for joining a group. Many claimed to benefit from
> involvement, leading the authors to conclude that
> most people who join cults are not harmed and some
> are helped. References.

375. Lifton, Robert Jay. Thought Reform and the Psychology
of Totalism: A Study of "Brainwashing" in China. New
York: W.W. Norton, 1961.

> Classic, important study of thought reform. Chapter
> 22, which describes eight criteria for identifying
> thought reform, is often referred to by those who
> claim that cults use mind control. "Milieu control,"
> the total control of human communication, is a key
> criterion for Lifton. Critics have argued, however,
> that milieu control is found in only a small percentage
> of cults. Notes and index.

376. McBride, James, and Schwartz, Paul. "Reflections on
Authority and Authoritarianism in the New Religious Move-
ments." Paper read at the Conference on Conversion,
Coercion, and Commitment in New Religious Movements, 11-14
June 1981, Berkeley, California. Photocopied.

> Reports on a comparative study of ethnocentric and
> fascistic tendencies among members of new religious
> groups and mainstream Christian churches. Employed
> versions of the E and F scales, updated by Nevitt
> Sanford, co-author of the classic study The Authori-
> tarian Personality, (1950). A Hare Krishna group
> showed the strongest tendencies of this kind, while a
> Meher Baba group showed the least such tendencies, even
> less than the Lutheran group. Useful study. Biblio-
> graphy.

377. Miller, Edward V.B. "Authoritarianism: The American
Cults and Their Intellectual Antecedents." Ph.D. dissertation, University of Hawaii, 1979.

> In this long dissertation, Miller explores authoritari-
> anism in est and the Collegiate Association for the
> Research of Principles, an organization of the Unifica-
> tion Church. He relates that authoritarianism to
> the political climate of Nazi Germany and concludes
> that cults are symptoms of a society ready to accept
> another Hitler. He says they represent a decline of
> the superego and a growth of infantilism. Biblio-
> graphy.

378. Naranjo, Claudio. "Charisma, Pseudo-Certainty, and Grace." Paper read at the Conference on Conversion, Coercion, and Commitment in New Religious Movements, 11-14 June, at Berkeley, California. Photocopied.

> Naranjo finds the "spiritual supermarket" to be both the expression of a need and an exploitation of that need. He discusses aspects of narcissism in spiritual leaders and followers, treating it as part of spiritual growth, and warns that discerning true spiritual teachers requires a refined ability to assess the motives of others. References.

379. Newman, Ruth G. "Thoughts on Superstars of Charisma: Pipers in Our Midst." American Journal of Orthopsychiatry 53(1983): 201-208.

> Discusses the interdependent relationship between a charismatic leader and his/her followers and the psychological implications for society. References.

380. Pavlos, Andrew J. The Cult Experience. Contributions to the Study of Religion, no. 6. Westport, Conn.: Greenwood Press, 1982.

> Pavlos's intention--to present an accurate, readable book on cults, explaining cult conversion and cult-related behavior in psychological terms--is good. Unfortunately, he has merely produced stereotypical generalizations about why people join cults. Bibliography and index.

381. Richardson, Herbert W., ed. New Religions and Mental Health: Understanding the Issues. New York: Edwin Mellen Press, 1980.

> This collection of fifteen essays presents a range of issues related to legislative proposals such as temporary conservatorship that attempt to regulate the activities of new religions. The point of view is clearly against any such state interference. Conversion is approached from a theological perspective, and several writers (for example, Richardson, Anthony, Robbins, and Chorover) argue well against deprogramming and brainwashing explanations. The essays convey the power of mental health professionals to label deviant behavior as unhealthy and to control individuals.

382. Richardson, James T. "Psychological and Psychiatric Studies of New Religions." In New Directions in the Psychology of Religion, edited by Lawrence Brown. New York: Pergamon Press, forthcoming.

> Summarizes and evaluates several studies published

through 1981. Critical of studies by Margaret Singer
and John Clark. Bibliography.

383. Sargant, William. Battle for the Mind: A Physiology
of Conversion and Brain-Washing. Garden City, N.Y.:
Doubleday, 1957.

This book is frequently referred to by those
advancing brainwashing arguments to explain conversion
to cults. Sargant notes parallels between brainwashing of prisoners of war and religious conversion
in evangelical contexts. Bibliography and index.

384. Scheflin, Alan, and Opton, Edward. The Mind Manipula-
tors. New York: Paddington Press, 1978.

Authors discuss mind control, behavior modification,
and psychosurgery. In the section on "Religious
Brainwashing," the authors discuss brainwashing and
deprogramming and conclude that while there may
be some substance to the brainwashing charges, it is
difficult to assess how much. "Substitute family
function" is mentioned as the key attraction of cults.
Extensive notes and index.

385. Schein, Edgar H.; Schneier, Inge; and Barker, Curtis
H. Coercive Persuasion: A Sociopsychological Analysis of
the "Brainwashing" of American Civilian Prisoners by the
Chinese Communists. New York: W.W. Norton, 1961.

Schein sees coercive persuasion as a progression of
phases: unfreezing, changing, and refreezing.
Chapter 11, in which he discusses parallels between
religious orders, prisons, and similar settings, is
sometimes referred to in connection with new religious
groups. Schein maintains that social pressures in
such settings can be as coercive as physical constraints. Bibliography and index.

386. Schwartz, Lita Linzer, and Isser, Natalie. "Psycho-
historical Perceptions of Involuntary Conversion." Adolescence 14(1979): 351-360.

Discusses aspects of conversion to authoritarian
religious groups in terms of criteria for thought
reform described by Lifton [item 375], Sargant
[item 383], and others. References.

387. Schwartz, Lita Linzer, and Zemel, Jacqueline L.
"Religious Cults: Family Concerns and the Law." Journal
of Marital and Family Therapy 6(1980): 301-308.

Discusses psychological problems encountered by some
in totalitarian groups and suggests that misrepresentation and fraud in recruiting may be a basis for
legal redress. References.

388. Shapiro, Eli. "Destructive Cultism." American Family Physician, no. 2(1977), pp. 80-83.

According to Shapiro, young adults in totalistic religious cults are susceptible to a sociopathic illness he calls "destructive cultism," which is characterized primarily by extreme personality change.

389. Ungerleider, J. Thomas, and Wellisch, David K. "Coercive Persuasion (Brainwashing), Religious Cults, and Deprogramming." American Journal of Psychiatry 136(1979): 279-282.

Reports on psychosocial characteristics of fifty cult members and former members. Each was interviewed and given several standard psychological and psychiatric tests. No data emerged to indicate that individuals could not make sound judgments, though they were found to have a strong ideologic hunger, suggesting that the cults served to nourish that hunger. References.

390. Ungerleider, J. Thomas, and Wellisch, David K. "Cultism, Thought Control, and Deprogramming: Observations on a Phenomenon." Psychiatric Opinion, January 1979, pp. 10-15.

Psychological testing of two people who had resisted forcible deprogramming and then returned to their religious group revealed an absence of psychosis, including major affective disorders. Authors suggest that other needs revealed by the testing may have been met by group membership. They question the involvement of mental health professionals and the legal system in deprogramming. References.

391. Vaughan, Frances. "A Question of Balance: Health and Pathology in New Religious Movements." Journal of Humanistic Psychology, no. 3(1983), pp. 20-41.

From the perspective of transpersonal psychology, Vaughan suggests that the authenticity of a spiritual group can be judged by the extent to which the group fosters transcendence of the ego as opposed to unhealthy regression to pre-egoic dependence. Bibliography.

392. Verdier, Paul A. Brainwashing and the Cults. North Hollywood: Wilshire Book Co., 1977.

Verdier's approach is sensationalistic, and the power he attributes to hypnosis and thought reform is extraordinary. The underlying assumption is that human beings do not have free will and that malevolent conditioning therefore must be counteracted with

constructive behavior control. Provides a test,
based largely on Lifton's [item 375] thought reform criteria,
for determining whether a person has been brainwashed.
References.

393. Welwood, John. "On Spiritual Authority: Genuine and
Counterfeit." Journal of Humanistic Psychology, no. 3(1983),
pp. 42-60.

Suggests criteria for recognizing a true spiritual
leader, but claims that because spiritual groups are
filled with human frailties, the would-be member needs
some prior training in an awareness discipline such as
meditation.

394. West, Louis J., and Singer, Margaret T. "Cults, Quacks,
and Nonprofessional Psychotherapies." In Comprehensive
Textbook of Psychiatry, III, edited by Harold I. Kaplan;
Alfred M. Freedman; and Benjamin J. Sadock. 3d. ed. Baltimore:
Williams and Wilkins, 1980.

A general article in which cults, human potential
groups, and various forms of nonprofessional psychotherapies are described in uniformly negative terms.
References.

395. Wilber, Ken. "Legitimacy, Authenticity, and Authority
in the New Religions." Paper read at the Conference on
Conversion, Coercion, and Commitment in New Religious Movements, 11-14 June 1981, at Berkeley, California. Photocopied.

Wilber, using a transpersonal psychology approach,
makes a good attempt at the difficult and rarely
performed task of establishing criteria for
distinguishing beneficial new religious groups from
detrimental ones. While many have attempted to define
"destructive cultism," few have considered the complex
questions of authenticity and legitimacy. References.

396. Wright, Fred, and Wright, Phyllis. "The Charismatic
Leader and the Violent Surrogate Family." Annals of the
New York Academy of Sciences 347(1980): 266-276.

Reviews literature relevant to psychology of cult members, leaders, and cults themselves. Attempts to understand sources of extreme violence exhibited by a few
cults, but cites only "overcontrolled hostility" as
shown in some clinical studies of cult members. Authors
fail to explain why violence occurs in some cults and
not others. References.

397. Zerin, Marjory Fisher. "The Pied Piper Phenomenon and
the Processing of Victims: The Transactional Analysis
Perspective Re-examined." Transactional Analysis Journal
13(1983): 172-177.

Zerin claims that the individual responsibility model
put forth by Transactional Analysis does not apply to
cult members because they are brainwashed. Conclusions
are based largely on quotations from a publication
by Margaret Singer which is not listed in the meager
references. Brief and shallow.

398. Zerin, Marjory Fisher. "The Pied Piper Phenomenon:
Family Systems and Vulnerability to Cults." Ph.D. dissertation, The Fielding Institute, Santa Barbara, California,
1982.

An attempt to identify family system factors in
adolescent vulnerability to cult recruitment. Twelve
families were studied, using psychological tests.
Results supported the hypothesis that vulnerable
youth lack inner direction and have weak relationships
with their fathers. Psychological tests used are
printed in the appendix. Bibliography.

Therapy with Ex-Cult Members

399. Ash, Stephen Mark. "Cult-Induced Psychopathology:
A Critical Review of Presuppositions, Conversion, Clinical
Picture, and Treatment." Ph.D. dissertation, Rosemead
School of Psychology, La Mirada, California, 1983.

Ash addresses the lack of professional knowledge
about cult-induced psychopathology and its therapeutic
treatment. His definition of a cult as a totalitarian
closed system run by a leader having absolute control
and requiring absolute submission from his followers
makes obvious his contention that cults are inherently
unhealthy. Ash's survey and critique of the psychological literature is comprehensive but biased against
any literature that presents cults in a positive
light. Bibliography.

400. Clark, John G., Jr. "Problems in Referral of Cult Members." Journal of the National Association of Private
Psychiatric Hospitals, no. 4(1978), pp. 27-29.

Clark expresses frustration and anger with hospital
psychiatrists who fail to take as seriously as he does
the mental illness of cult followers.

401. Clark, John G., Jr.; Langone, Michael D.; Schecter,
Robert E.; and Daly, Roger C.B. Destructive Cult Conversion:
Theory, Research, and Treatment. Weston, Mass.: American
Family Foundation, 1981.

Provides guidelines for treatment of troubled persons,
reviews the mental health literature on cults, and
offers a tentative theory of conversion. The authors

are concerned with cults that "regularly effect drastic
and destructive personality changes in many converts"
such as ISKCON, the Unification Church, and the Church
of Scientology. Clark has been criticized for generaliz-
ing from the clinical cases he has seen to all cults
and for reducing spiritual needs to psychological ones.
He is one of the severest critics of cults.

402. Feinstein, Sherman C. "The Cult Phenomenon: Transition,
Repression, and Regression." In Adolescent Psychiatry,
vol. 8, edited by Sherman C. Feinstein, Peter L. Giovacchini,
John G. Looney, Allan Z. Schwartzberg, and Arthur D. Sorosky,
pp. 113-122. Chicago: University of Chicago Press, 1980.

Reviews psychological studies of cult members published
through 1979. Concludes that most people attracted to
cults are not fundamentally ill psychologically but
are in a vulnerable state of development. Suggests
that psychiatrists offer counseling so that ex-cult
members may view cult involvement as a growth
experience. References.

403. Galper, Marvin F. "Adolescent Identity Diffusion and
the Extremist Religious Cult." Paper read at the Annual
Meeting of the Western Psychological Association, 22 April
1977, at Seattle, Washington. Photocopied.

Brief discussion of recent cultural changes that have
alienated youth from mainstream society. Based on
his counseling of thirty former members of totalistic
cults, Galper's conclusion is that such groups inhibit
psychological growth and produce a pseudo-resolution of
identity crises. References.

404. Goldberg, Lorna, and Goldberg, William. "Group Work
with Former Cultists." Social Work 27(1982): 165-170.

Claims that cult members suffer from mind control
and "post mind control" syndrome when they leave cults.
Describes stages of "post mind control" syndrome and
how the authors deal with it in therapy groups.
References.

405. Gordon, James S. "The Cult Phenomenon and the Psychotherapeutic Response." Paper read at the Conference on
Conversion, Coercion, and Commitment in New Religious
Movements, 11-14 June 1981, at Berkeley, California. Photocopied.

In a clear, readable manner Gordon suggests issues for
mental health professionals to consider when counseling
those who have left new religious groups. Stresses
understanding positive and negative aspects of
individuals' involvement, distinguishing among
various groups, and respect for the spiritual quest.
References.

406. Grof, Christina, and Grof, Stanislav. "Spiritual Emergency: Understanding and Treatment of Transpersonal Crises." Paper read at the Seventh International Transpersonal Conference, 1982, at Bombay, India.

Approaching the subject from the standpoint of transpersonal psychology, the authors discuss altered states of consciousness resulting from meditation and other spiritual practices. They criticize psychiatry for labeling such experiences psychotic. Paper suggests ways of distinguishing transformative experiences, valued by transpersonal psychologists, from psychosis.

407. Langone, Michael D., "Treatment of Individuals and Families Troubled by Cult Involvement." Update, no. 1(1983), pp. 27-39.

Langone's treatment guidelines for other clinicians are based on his clinical experience with approximately seventy-five families and ex-cult members as well as his association with psychiatrist John G. Clark, Jr., who has counseled over 500 people disturbed by cult involvement. The guidelines consider the ethical issues, especially in situations where families cannot accept a child's informed cult involvement, and suggest family counseling in those cases.

408. Levine, Edward M. "Deprogramming Without Tears." Society, no. 3(1980), pp. 34-38.

Levine fails to make distinctions among different types of new religious groups, charging all cults with deceit, manipulation, intolerance, and authoritarianism. He claims that deprogramming is necessary, even if it causes unhappiness to those who have found security and relief from distress in cults, because individuals must be made to think freely and the groups they join are not truly religious anyway. A thoroughly cynical approach.

409. Levine, Saul. "The Role of Psychiatry in the Phenomenon of Cults." In Adolescent Psychiatry, vol. 8, edited by Sherman C. Feinstein, Peter L. Giovacchini, John G. Looney, Allan Z. Schwartzberg, and Arthur D. Sorosky, pp. 123-137. Chicago: University of Chicago Press, 1980.

Based on interviews with over 200 cult members and psychotherapy with about fifty members, Levine offers suggestions to help psychiatrists deal effectively with troubled members of authoritarian cults and their parents. Balanced approach. References.

410. Levinson, Peritz. "Religious Delusions in Counter-
Culture Patients." American Journal of Psychiatry 130(1973):
1265-1269.

An abrupt increase in the incidence of messianic delusions was noted among patients admitted to a psychiatry
service in a large city. Levinson discusses clinical
features of delusions, influence of counterculture
values, and treatment of patients. References.

411. Lockwood, George. "Rational-Emotive Therapy and
Extremist Religious Cults." Rational Living 16(1981): 13-17.

Lockwood advocates using logic and empirical proofs
in confronting beliefs of those involved in totalistic
cults. He prefers that people avoid any religious
beliefs based on faith. References.

412. Maleson, Franklin G. "Dilemmas in the Evaluation and
Management of Religious Cultists." American Journal of
Psychiatry 138(1981): 925-929.

Maleson speaks frankly about problems he encountered
in attempting to counsel two cult members, including
parents' insistence on a brainwashing explanation and
the cult members' desire to stay with the group.
These attitudes frustrated Maleson's desire to treat
underlying mental problems that had been present
before conversion. References.

413. Schwartz, Lita Linzer, and Kaslow, Florence W. "Religious Cults, the Individual, and the Family." Journal of
Marital and Family Therapy 5(1979): 15-26.

Identifies a weak father-child relationship as a
critical factor in vulnerability to religious cults.
Suggests concurrent or conjoint family therapy when
members and former members seek counseling. References.

414. Singer, Margaret T. "Coming Out of the Cults."
Psychology Today, January 1979, pp. 79-82.

Singer describes problems of adjustment she has
observed among those who have left new religious
groups. It is worth noting that seventy-five per
cent of her study sample had been deprogrammed.

415. Singer, Margaret T. "Therapy with Ex-Cult Members."
Journal of the National Association of Private Psychiatric
Hospitals 9(1978): 14-18.

Singer advocates deprogramming or reentry counseling
followed by group therapy for all who have been
indoctrinated by cults, here described as extremely
authoritarian social groups.

Individual Groups and Movements

416. Babbie, Earl, and Stone, Donald. "An Evaluation of the est Experience by a National Sample of Graduates." Biosciences Communication 3(1977): 123-140.

Analyzes data on the subjective experience of est obtained through questionnaires sent to a representative sample of participants. Self-reports indicate improvements in mental health, sexual relationships, and relationships with family and friends. The authors did not design or carry out the study and are careful to point out methodological problems such as lack of control groups, no measurement of change other than subjective, and the need for longitudinal study. References.

417. Baer, Donald M., and Stolz, Stephenie B. "A Description of the Erhard Seminars Training (est) in the Terms of Behavior Analysis." Behaviorism 6(1978): 45-70.

Authors are impressed by est's array of self-control techniques. Their description of est training in behavior analysis terms is, however, wordy and dull. References.

418. Berger, Alan L. "Hasidism and Moonism: Charisma in the Counterculture." Sociological Analysis 41(1981): 375-390.

Compares the authority of the zaddik, Hasidic communal leader and holy man, with that of Sun Myung Moon. The zaddik is found to gain authority by adhering to tradition based on a transcendent source, while Moon's authority is self-established idolatry. References.

419. Bird, Frederick; Pandya, Rooshikumar; and Westley, Frances R. "The Pursuit of the Therapeutic." Paper read at the annual meeting of the Pacific Sociological Association, 7 April 1983, at San Jose, California. Photocopied.

The authors administered a questionnaire to members of a Creative Awareness group and a Rajneesh Sannyasin group in Montreal to determine psychotherapeutic effects of membership. Members reported enhanced well-being, better social relations, and a greater feeling of personal integration. The authors discuss how the practices of the groups produce such changes.

420. Boadella, David. "Violence in Therapy." Energy and Character 11(1980): 1-20.

Examines dangers of violence in therapy groups, including Eva Renzi's description of an assault in a Rajneesh center therapy session. References.

421. Buckley, Peter, and Galanter, Marc. "Mystical Experience, Spiritual Knowledge, and a Contemporary Ecstatic Religion." British Journal of Medical Psychology 52(1979): 281-289.

Based on interviews with five members of the Divine Light Mission and a questionnaire administered to 119 members, this article claims that desire for mystical experience and the presence of a charismatic leader help to explain the appeal of the group. References.

422. Dean, Roger A. "Moonies: A Psychological Analysis of the Unification Church." Ph.D. dissertation, The University of Michigan, 1981.

Dean interviewed and had many informal conversations with thirty-eight members, former members, and parents of members and former members of the Unification Church. The results challenge stereotypes of Moonies as unthinking zombies. Dean identifies certain types commonly found among church members such as the authority seeker, the ideals seeker, and the social nonconformist. Bibliography.

423. Dean, Roger A. "Youth: Moonies' Target Population." Adolescence 17(1982): 567-574.

Discusses the identity crisis that young people in our society experience and how the idealistic lifestyle of the Unification Church offers meaning. References.

424. Deutsch, Alexander. "Tenacity of Attachment to a Cult Leader: A Psychiatric Assessment." American Journal of Psychiatry 137(1980): 1569-1573.

Deutsch discusses a small communal religious group, which he does not identify, and attempts to discover why a few members stayed loyal to the leader after he had become cruel and irrational. They denied his irrationality or interpreted it as a teaching tool or "divine madness," and they stayed with him although they were not isolated, coerced, or threatened. Deutsch suggests that they became dependent on the leader and allowed themselves to regress under his authority. References.

425. Deutsch, Alexander, and Miller, Michael J. "A Clinical Study of Four Unification Church Members." American Journal of Psychiatry 140(1983): 767-770.

Interviews with and psychological testing of four women UC members revealed predisposing characteristics

such as idealism, sexual conflict, and naivete.
Although the sample was small, the findings provide
some support for Galanter's "relief effect" [item 430].
References.

426. Deutsch, Alexander, and Miller, Michael J. "Conflict,
Character, and Conversion: Study of a 'New Religion' Member."
In Adolescent Psychiatry, vol. 7, edited by Sherman C. Fein-
stein and Peter L. Giovacchini, pp. 257-268. Chicago:
University of Chicago Press, 1979.

In an attempt to assess psychological vulnerability
to cults, the authors present a case study of a female
member of the Unification Church. Psychological tests
and interviews revealed lifelong religiosity and
conflicts over sexual and aggressive impulses. The
authors claim that the woman exhibited long-term
ability to transform her aggression into helpfulness,
an adaptation that found expression in the UC.
References.

427. Finkelstein, Peter; Wenegrat, Brant; and Yalom, Irvin.
"Large Group Awareness Training." Annual Review of Psychology
33(1982): 515-539.

A good review of literature on est, which the authors
suggest warrants more objective research. References.

428. Galanter, Marc. "Psychological Induction into the
Large-Group: Findings from a Modern Religious Sect."
American Journal of Psychiatry 137(1980): 1574-1579.

Galanter studied 104 persons who attended a sequence
of Unification Church introductory workshops. He found
that after the first two-day workshop, seventy-one
percent elected to drop out, and after the full twenty-
one day sequence, nine percent joined the UC. Such
figures counter brainwashing arguments. Psychological
tests revealed that the joiners had relatively weak ties
to family and friends. References.

429. Galanter, Marc. "The 'Relief Effect': A Sociological
Model for Neurotic Distress and Large-Group Therapy."
American Journal of Psychiatry 135(1978): 588-591.

Random sample of 119 "premies" (Divine Light Mission
members) at a national festival answered a questionnaire.
They reported that membership had improved their
psychological health, leading Galanter to posit that life
in the group had relieved neurotic distress.

430. Galanter, Marc. "Unification Church ('Moonie') Dropouts:
Psychological Readjustment after Leaving a Charismatic
Religious Group." American Journal of Psychiatry 140(1983):
984-989.

Of sixty-six former UC members studied, thirty-six percent reported serious emotional problems after leaving but had readjusted and were stable nearly four years later. Those who were deprogrammed were more negative toward the UC and had coerced others to leave. Continuing his exploration of the "relief effect," Galanter suggests that stress from loss of the group caused the ex-members to experience temporary difficulties. References.

431. Galanter, Marc, and Buckley, Peter. "Evangelical Religion and Meditation: Psychotherapeutic Effects." Journal of Nervous and Mental Disease 166(1978): 685-691.

Claims that ritual meditation of Divine Light Mission devotees is associated with a decline in neurotic distress. The authors found the DLM to be an impressive therapy setting.

432. Galanter, Marc, and Diamond, Luiza Cohn. "Relief of Psychiatric Symptoms in Evangelical Religious Sects." British Journal of Hospital Medicine 26(1981): 495-497.

Report of the authors' study of representative members of the Divine Light Mission and the Unification Church. Major finding is a decline in drug use and neurotic symptoms after conversion. References.

433. Galanter, Marc; Rabkin, Richard; Rabkin, Judith; and Deutsch, Alexander. "The Moonies: A Psychological Study of Conversion and Membership in a Contemporary Religious Sect." American Journal of Psychiatry 136(1979): 165-170.

As a result of their study of Unification Church workshops and 237 members of the UC, the authors reject brainwashing as an explanation for conversion because subjects were there voluntarily and did not report abuse or coercion. Psychological studies of the 237 members indicated that thirty percent had sought professional care for drug use prior to joining the UC. Data indicated some reduction of distress as a result of membership.

434. Galper, Marvin F. "Indoctrination Methods of the Unification Church." Paper read at the annual meeting of the California State Psychological Association, 13 March 1977, at Los Angeles. Photocopied.

Galper interviewed thirty ex-members of the UC whom he had treated as patients. He concludes that UC indoctrination produces a psychologically damaging trance state. References.

435. Glass, Leonard; Kirsch, Michael A.; and Parris, Frederick
N. "Psychiatric Disturbances Associated with Erhard Seminars
Training: I. A Report of Cases." American Journal of Psychia-
try 134(1977): 245-247.

   Five people who had psychiatric disturbances requiring
   emergency care following est training are discussed in
   this first such case report in psychiatric literature.

436. Haaken, Janice, and Adams, Richard. "Pathology as
Personal Growth--A Participant-Observation Study of Lifespring Training." Psychiatry 46(1983): 270-280.

   Well-written overview of a Lifespring Basic Training
   workshop from a psychoanalytic perspective. Argues
   that the training undermines the ego and promotes
   regression to the extent that reality testing is
   impaired. The study was restricted to the training
   period, hence does not imply long-term disturbances
   in participants.

437. Hosford, Ray E.; Moss, C. Scott; Cavior, Helen; and
Kerish, Burton. "Research on Erhard Seminar Training in a
Correctional Institution." Catalog of Selected Documents in
Psychology, no. 1(1982), pp. 8-9.

438. Jones, Connie A. "Exemplary Dualism and Authoritarianism
at Jonestown." Paper read at the Conference on Conversion,
Coercion, and Commitment in New Religious Movements,
Center for the Study of New Religious Movements, 11-14 June
1981, at Berkeley, California. Photocopied.

   A discussion of the social and psychological dynamics
   within the Peoples Temple that led to the development
   of illegitimate authoritarian practices that resulted in
   tragedy. Jones creates a fairly plausible argument
   against the brainwashing theory by finding authoritarian
   personality traits in both Jim Jones and his followers.
   Bibliography.

439. Judah, J. Stillson. "Attitudinal Changes among Members
of the Unification Church." Paper read at the Conference
of the American Association for the Advancement of Science
and the Society for the Scientific Study of Religion,
February 1977, at Denver, Colorado. Photocopied.

   Reports results of his nationwide survey of several
   hundred UC members. Findings indicate they became
   more conservative politically, less materialistic, and
   felt their lives were more meaningful after joining
   the church.

440. Kachel, Arthur Theodore."An American Religious Community
Using Hallucinogens in 1970." Ph.D. dissertation, Columbia
University, 1975.

Case study of the relationship between drug use and
religious experience among Stephen Gaskin's Monday
Night Class (before they moved to Tennessee and
became The Farm). Kachel found that although the group
created its religious life out of hallucinogenic
experience, the use of drugs declined as religious
development occurred. Bibliography.

441. Kilbourne, Brock K., and Richardson, James T. "The
Communalization of Religious Experience in Contemporary
Religious Groups." Unpublished paper. Reno: University of
Nevada, 1983.

The first empirical study comparing Unification Church
members with Catholics and Protestants. A much larger
percentage of UC members indicated prior religious
searching and a preference for communal religious
experiences, which the authors claim indicates that
they chose the Unification Church for the particular
communal religious experience it offers. Bibliography.

442. Kriegman, Daniel H. "A Psycho-Social Study of Religious
Cults from the Perspective of Self Psychology." Ph.D.
dissertation, Boston University, 1980.

Clinical study of members of the Divine Light Mission,
whom Kriegman refers to as "fanatics." He found
narcissistic personality disorder in twelve. Difficult
for those unfamiliar with psychological language to
understand. Bibliography.

443. Persinger, Michael A.; Carrey, Normand J.; and Suess,
Lynn A. TM and Cult Mania. North Quincy, Mass.: The Christopher Publishing House, 1980.

The authors' viewpoint is essentially cynical, finding
"commercial ploys" and "psychological manipulations"
in any "cult-like behavior." Transcendental Meditation
as a technique and movement is relentlessly criticized.
Many scientific studies of TM are examined for flaws,
but citations for the studies are not provided. The
selected bibliography is very small, reflecting little
of what is discussed. Index.

444. Richardson, James T.: Harder, Mary W.; and Simmonds,
Robert B. "Thought Reform and the Jesus Movement." Youth
and Society 4(1972): 185-202.

Authors note similarities between conversion processes
in a Jesus Movement commune (presumably "Christ
Commune," a group they have studied for several years)
and Lifton's [item 375] model of thought reform,
though they say the cult processes are not as
extreme as Chinese thought reform.

445. Ross, Michael W. "Clinical Profiles of Hare Krishna Devotees." American Journal of Psychiatry 140(1983): 416-420.

Psychological tests administered to forty-two members of a Hare Krishna temple revealed no psychopathology. The longer they had been in the group, the less anxious, alienated, and outgoing they were. Only two of the forty-two were alienated from their families. An important study supporting the notion that members of ISKCON are not psychologically impaired. References.

446. Russie, Roger Eugene. "The Influence of Transcendental Meditation on Positive Mental Health and Self-Actualization, and the Role of Expectation, Rigidity, and Self-Control in the Achievement of These Benefits." Ph.D. dissertation, California School of Professional Psychology, Los Angeles, California, 1976.

The Personal Orientation Inventory was administered to TM meditators and control groups in order to evaluate TM as a psychotherapeutic agent. TM was found to be effective in enhancing self-esteem, developing relationships, increasing self-acceptance, and increasing ability to express feelings spontaneously. TM was not found effective in improving ability to accept anger and aggression or to apply values to life. References.

447. Simmonds, Robert B. "Level of Discourse and Self-Concept Within a Fundamentalist Christian Milieu: Conversion to the Jesus Movement." Paper read at the annual meeting of the Society for the Scientific Study of Religion, October 1978, at Hartford, Connecticut. Photocopied.

This paper is based on the same data Simmonds used for his dissertation [item 448], but here the data is used to support a theory of conversion based on both negative factors (preconversion disillusionment and negative self-concepts) and positive ones (spiritual ideals offered by Christ Commune, which allowed members to regain hope and to place their negative self-concepts in the positive light of Christian humility). References.

448. Simmonds, Robert B. "The People of the Jesus Movement: A Personality Assessment of Members of a Fundamentalist Religious Community." Ph.D. dissertation, University of Nevada at Reno, 1977.

Reports on the results of psychological testing of ninety-six members of Christ Communal Organization (pseudonym). Scores indicated maladaptive personalities as compared to a normative sample. Many subjects reported heavy drug use and unhappiness prior to conversion but not after joining the group, leading

Simmonds to hypothesize that they had switched depen-
dency from drugs to a rigid religious belief system.
References.

449. Simmonds, Robert B.; Richardson,James T.; and Harder,
Mary W. "A Jesus Movement Group: An Adjective Check List
Assessment." Journal for the Scientific Study of Religion
15(1976): 323-337.

Self-concepts of eighty-three members of the Jesus
Movement commune the authors call Christ Commune were
compared with those of a normative sample of college
students. The commune group scored lower on self-
confidence, self-control, and personal adjustment.
References.

450. Simon, Justin. "Observations on Sixty-seven Patients
Who Took Erhard Seminars Training." American Journal of
Psychiatry 135(1978): 636-691.

Simon recommended est to patients who were in psychotherapy with him and reports that sixty-one percent
of them, particularly those with good ego strength,
had positive experiences that enhanced the effects of
their psychotherapy. References.

451. Westley, Frances R. "Merger and Separation: Autistic
Symbolism in New Religious Movements." Journal of Psychoanalytic Anthropology 5(1982): 137-154.

Westley finds fascinating parallels between the
symbologies of autistic children and of some human
potential groups. Rituals of both autistic children
and human potential groups are shown to be concerned
with merging with the world or separating entirely from
it and with highly rigid conceptions of the inner
world. Westley does not imply that adherents of
human potential groups are autistic; rather, she
intends to shed light on the cultural etiology of
such groups. Bibliography.

Theological and Religious Studies

452. Bak, Felix. "The Church of Satan in the United States."
<u>Antonianum</u> 50(1975): 152-193.

> Bak concentrates on the most sensational elements of
> the Church of Satan, as gleaned from Anton La Vey's
> writings and popular periodical accounts. He discusses
> theology and rituals and compares the Satanic mass
> to the Roman Catholic mass.

453. Biersdorf, John E. <u>Hunger for Experience: Vital
Religious Communities in America</u>. New York: Seabury Press,
1975.

> Report of the Insearch Study of promising religious
> commmunities, as defined by a group of church and
> synagogue executives, scholars, ministers, and
> lay leaders in 1972. With the exception of Tail of
> the Tiger, a Tibetan Buddhist community under the
> direction of Chogyam Trungpa, all communities are
> within the Judeo-Christian heritage.

454. Bergeron, Richard. "Towards a Theological Interpretation of the New Religions." In <u>New Religious Movements</u>,
edited by John Coleman and Gregory Baum, pp. 74-80. Concilium,
vol. 161. New York: Seabury Press, 1983.

> Bergeron finds monism and gnosis to be common
> characteristics of all new religious movements not
> part of the Judeo-Christian heritage. His dynamic
> typology shows clearly the points of contact and
> fundamental divergence between Christianity and
> gnosis. Both are treated as valid religious expres-
> sions.

455. Bryant, M. Darrol, and Hodges, Susan, eds. Exploring Unification Theology. 2d. ed. Conference Series, no. 1. Barrytown, N.Y.: Unification Theological Seminary, 1978.

Collection of papers and conversations that grew out of a series of meetings between Unification Church members and college and university teachers of religious studies. Rodney Sawatsky contributes a historical and sociological analysis of the UC; Elizabeth Clark examines the role of women in Unificationist theology; Henry Van der Goot reflects on the UC theology of creation; and Darrol Bryant critically explores the church's eschatology.

456. Chidester, David. "Being Human: Symbolic Orientation in New Religious Movements." Journal of Dharma 7(1982): 430-451.

Identifies different worldviews and concepts of human identity as the challenge presented by new religious movements. Using a few prominent groups as examples, author describes different religious worldviews and asks for greater tolerance of religious diversity.

457. Christ, Carol. "A Religion for Women: A Response to Rosemary Ruether." Womanspirit, Fall Equinox 1980, pp. 11-14.

Christ argues that feminist goddess worship does have historical roots going back thousands of years, that it helps women to integrate intellect and intuition, and that men play significant roles in some goddess-worshipping groups. Article is response to Ruether's "Goddesses and Witches" [item 486].

458. Cox, Harvey. "Something Versus Nothing--the Real Threat of the Moonies." Christianity and Crisis 37(1977): 258-263.

Although Cox does not find Unification theology promising, he points out that naive, idealistic youth may find it to be so for three reasons: 1) it claims to be Christian yet incorporates appealing aspects of Eastern religions; 2) it attempts to unify religion and science; and 3) it offers a religiously grounded social vision. He adds that the Christian churches are lacking in these areas.

459. Cox, Harvey. Turning East: The Promise and Peril of the New Orientalism. New York: Simon and Schuster, 1977.

Cox studied several Eastern religious groups, participating in Zen and Tibetan Buddhist meditation. He describes his personal experiences and reflects on the relation of Eastern religions to Christianity, American culture, and the needs of followers. Although

he claims meditation meets needs of those who
practice it, he is critical of the way Eastern forms
may be stripped of meaning in a capitalist consumer
culture. A sensitive study. Bibliography and
index.

460. Eck, Diana. "Dialogue and the 'New Religious Movements.'"
Current Dialogue, Summer 1983, pp. 10-21.

Surveys the state of interfaith dialogue among
Christian churches and new religious groups in America.
Useful for descriptions of materials published by
Christian denominations for educating and witnessing.

461. Ellwood, Robert S., Jr. "The Study of New Religious
Movements in America." Council on the Study of Religion Bulletin 10(1979): 69.

Reviews some works and trends in the study of new
religious movements and suggests that this study may
lead to more integrated study of traditional and
nontraditional religions.

462. Fichter, Joseph H. "Hammering the Heretics: Religion
vs. Cults." Witness, January 1983, pp. 4-6.

Fichter notes failure of Christian churches to engage
in ecumenical dialogue with cults. He suggests
recognizing what is true in others' doctrines, without
discrimination or harassment, in accord with the
Vatican decree on ecumenism.

463. Foster, Durwood. "The Challenge of the New Religious
Movements." Pacific School of Religion Bulletin, June 1981,
pp. 3-7.

In this short, thoughtful article, Foster asks the
Christian churches to learn from the positive aspects
of new religious groups, such as rehabilitation of
drug users, use of spiritual techniques, and communal
emphasis, without ignoring the need for responsible
criticism.

464. Gallup, George, Jr., and Poling, David. "The Yearnings
of Youth." In their The Search for America's Faith, pp. 15-
40. Nashville: Abingdon Press, 1980.

Using results of Gallup opinion polls, authors
discuss the strong spiritual desires of young people,
the fact that the mainstream churches are not meeting
these needs, and how new religious groups do meet
these needs.

465. Gilkey, Langdon. "The Khalsa Goes West." Paper read at
the Conference on Conversion, Coercion, and Commitment in
New Religious Movements, 11-14 June 1981, at Berkeley,
California. Photocopied.

> Gilkey's remarks are the result of a week of participa-
> tion in the life of the Sikh Khalsa's summer solstice,
> a general meeting and central religious event.
> It is clear from his description of Yogi Bhagan, the
> group's members, and their beliefs and practices that
> he was immensely impressed by the moral integrity,
> strength, and commitment of the members. As a point
> of criticism he notes that the Sikh Khalsa has yet to
> develop a theology.

466. Hammann, Louis J. The Puzzle of Religion: The Parts
and the Whole. Washington, D.C.: University Press of
America, 1977.

> Analyzes the components of religion and develops a
> model for comparing religions, avoiding making judg-
> ments on the validity of beliefs. Applies the model
> to the Church of Scientology, Tenrikyo, and the Hare
> Krishna movement.

467. Haramgaal, Ya'aqov. "Deprogramming: A Critical View,"
American Zionist, May/June 1977, pp. 16-19.

> Very critical of deprogramming, which Haramgaal
> compares to forced conversions of Jews to Islam and
> Christianity throughout history.

468. Harper, Marvin Henry. Gurus, Swamis, and Avatars:
Spiritual Masters and Their American Disciples. Philadelphia:
Westminster Press, 1972.

> Harper taught church history in India, where he
> became interested in gurus and their disciples.
> Writing for an American audience, he presents the
> history and teachings of several Hindu cults as
> they exist in India. Includes Meher Baba, Radhasoami
> Satsang, Sathya Sai Baba, ISKCON, Vedanta Society,
> and several other gurus and groups. The treatment
> of the groups' existence in America is brief. Harper
> recognizes the appeal Hinduism holds for its followers
> and is sympathetic to the religious needs of those
> who join Hindu cults. Chapter notes and index.

469. Heenan, Edward F., ed. Mystery, Magic, and Miracle:
Religion in a Post-Aquarian Age. Englewood Cliffs, N.J.:
Prentice-Hall, 1973.

> Collection of descriptive and theoretical articles
> on the religious dimensions of witchcraft, the Jesus
> Movement, and drug use. Heenan's introduction calls

the 1970s a "Second Reformation" in which elements of
mystery rejected by the Protestant Reformation were
rediscovered.

470. Jennings, Ray. "Moonies: A Movement in Search of a
Theology." The American Baptist, January 1982, pp. 11-13.

Jennings attended the Unification Church conference
in Tenerife, Canary Islands, in 1981. Though critical
of the UC's theology, he considers it to be a Christian
sect.

471. Judah, J. Stillson. "Programming and Deprogramming."
Paper read at a conference sponsored by the University of
Toronto and Toronto School of Theology, March 1977, at
Toronto, Canada. Photocopied.

Balanced though somewhat dated look at the deprogramming
controversy.

472. Kang, Wi Jo. "The Unification Church: Christian
Church or Political Movement?" Japanese Religions 9(1976):
19-32.

Although Kang believes the UC is a heretical movement,
his major disagreement is with its political involvement. He views as "unChristian" the strong anti-
communist stance of the UC and its belief in the
special importance of the United States.

473. Kelley, Dean M. "De-programming: What's Going on Here?"
Unpublished photocopy, n.d.

Kelley rejects the brainwashing notion in favor of
one involving religious zealotry. Describing new
religious groups as "high-demand" movements having
historical parallels, Kelley speaks strongly against
deprogramming and in favor of the right of the individual to be passionately religious.

474. Kliever, Lonnie D. "Unification Thought and Modern
Theology." Religious Studies Review 8(1982): 214-221.

Study of the theology of the Unification Church. Kliever finds Unificationism to be eclectic, esoteric,
and appropriate to the modern world.

475. Lane, David Christopher. The Making of a Spiritual
Movement: The Untold Story of Paul Twitchell and Eckankar.
Del Mar, Calif.: Del Mar Press, 1983.

Lane's investigative study reveals Twitchell's
connection with the Radhasoami movement in India.
Through textual studies Lane demonstrates how Twitchell
created the religion he claimed was the oldest path

to God, using sources he later denied. A fine bit of
sleuthing.   In an appendix, Lane discusses parallels
between Radhasoami and other new religious movements
such as the Divine Light Mission. Chapter notes.

476. Melton, J. Gordon. "UFO-Contactees--A Report of Work in
Progress." In Proceedings of the First International UFO
Congress, edited by Curtis G. Fuller. New York: Warner
Books, 1980.

Reports on the nature of religious response to UFOs,
based on a survey of thirty-five people who claimed
to have had contact with UFOs.

477. Moellering, Ralph. "Ancient and Modern Gnosticism."
Currents in Theology and Missions 10(1983): 221-232.

Briefly discusses the characteristics of ancient
Gnosticism and notes several new religious groups
that include these characteristics.

478. Moody, Jonathan Frederic. "Ethics and Counter Culture:
An Analysis of the Ethics of Hare Krsna." Ph.D. dissertation,
Claremont College, 1978.

Descriptive analysis of religious ethics of International Society for Krishna Consciousness, based on
literature and discussions with devotees of one
temple. ISKCON is perceived as born out of the context
of the counterculture and as a counterculture in itself.
Author finds dynamic tension between regulation and
spontaneity in lives of members. Bibliography.

479. Needleman, Jacob; Bierman, A.K.; and Gould, James A.,
eds. Religion for a New Generation. New York: Macmillan,
1973.

Anthology intended to stimulate philosophical and
religious inquiry in the classroom. Essays on aspects
of social living, such as war, sexuality, religion,
racial tension, and ecology, promote the close connection between the counterculture and the growth of new
religions. Now appears outdated. Index.

480. Nordstrom, Louis. "The Vajra World of Chogyam Trungpa."
New Religious Movements Newsletter, December 1979, pp. 7-10.

General description of the Tibetan Buddhist teachings
at the Naropa Institute and how Trungpa has adopted
Western psychological language to present his
teachings.

481. Parsons, Arthur. "Yoga in a Western Setting: Youth in
Search of Religious Prophecy." Soundings 57(1974): 222-235.

Good analysis of the practice of a Kundalini Yoga
group in the Boston area. Parsons shows how the
practitioners adopted the practice of the group but
brought Western explanations to the experience.

482. Perry, Whitall N. Gurdjieff in the Light of Tradition.
Pates Manor, Eng.: Perennial Books, 1978.

Highly critical study of the enigmatic teacher's
writings, first published as a series of articles in
Studies in Comparative Religion, 1974 to 1975. Perry
claims that Gurdjieff's writings are not part of a
spiritual tradition but rather are "science fiction."
Index.

483. Rambo, Lewis R. "Charisma and Conversion." Paper read
at the Conference on Conversion, Coercion, and Commitment
in New Religious Movements, Center for the Study of New
Religious Movements, 11-14 June 1981, at Berkeley, California.
Photocopied.

Rambo views conversion as a dynamic process involving
interaction of the religious leader, group, and potential follower, with all parties bearing moral responsibility for their actions. References.

484. Raschke, Carl A. "The Human Potential Movement." Theology
Today 33(1976): 253-262.

Raschke finds neo-Pietistic elements in the human
potential movement--a search for self-perfection through
therapy. Brief yet articulate critique, pointing out
political naivete, narcissistic tendencies, and dangers
of psychological manipulation in the movement.

485. Rose, Steve. Jesus and Jim Jones. New York: Pilgrim
Press, 1979.

Rose explores ethical, religious, and societal
questions related to the Peoples Temple tragedy. He
suggests evaluating religious groups according to underlying values they demonstrate. Almost half of the book
is taken up by several appendices of responses of
religious leaders in the Disciples of Christ, the
denomination to which Peoples Temple belonged.

486. Ruether, Rosemary Radford. "Goddesses and Witches:
Liberation and Countercultural Feminism." Christian Century
97(1980): 842-847.

Ruether tackles problems of historical truth, separatism,
and other dangers she sees in forming a feminist
spirituality. Scholarly, cogent critique of
feminist witchcraft.

487. Smart, Ninian. "The Moonies: Are They Christian?"
Paper read at the Conference on Conversion, Coercion, and
Commitment in New Religious Movements, Center for the Study
of New Religious Movements, 11-14 June 1981, at Berkeley,
California. Photocopied.

Smart was called upon in 1980 by the High Court of
London to give evidence as an expert witness on
whether the Unification Church can be considered
Christian. Descriptively, avoiding normative judgments, he finds that the UC shares enough themes with
Christian traditions (though not with mainstream
churches) to be considered Christian. Smart is careful
to differentiate between normative and descriptive
uses of the term Christian. Scholarly but readable.

488. Smith, Archie, Jr. "An Interpretation of the Peoples
Temple and Jonestown: Implications for the Black Church."
Pacific School of Religion Bulletin, February 1980, pp. 1-4.

Smith believes that the vision of Peoples Temple, a
new social order, addressed the needs of blacks to
unite spirituality, justice, and social change but
lacked a self-critical dimension.

489. Sontag, Frederick. "Marriage and the Family in the
Unification Church Theology." In The Family and the Unification Church, edited by Gene G. James, pp. 217-234. Conference Series, no. 15. Barrytown, N.Y.: Unification Theological
Seminary, 1983.

Description and critique comparing elements of Unification theology relating to marriage and the family to
Marxist thought and traditional Christian theology.

490. Sontag, Frederick. Sun Myung Moon and the Unification
Church. Nashville: Abingdon Press, 1977.

Sontag traveled to many UC centers and interviewed
members and Sun Myung Moon himself in an attempt to
understand the movement. He found a genuine new
religious movement with problematic elements in its
activities. Bibliography includes many popular
articles.

491. Woods, Richard. The Occult Revolution: A Christian
Meditation. New York: Herder and Herder, 1971.

The revival of interest in magic, sorcery, witchcraft,
and the devil is seen as part of the religious response
to the impact of technological change and the failure
of the Christian churches to provide acceptable values
for belief and commitment.

492. Zaehner, Robert Charles. Our Savage God. London: Collins, 1974.

> Provocative appeal for reasoned thinking. Uses Charles Manson as an example of the destructive uses of mysticism. Lots of references to Plato, Aristotle, and Hindu texts. Scholarly and sometimes difficult reading. Bibliography and index.

Christian and Jewish Responses to New Religious Movements

493. Amirthan, Samuel. "The Challenge of New Religions to Christian Theological Thought." International Review of Mission 67(1978): 399-406.

> Argues that Christianity has not been and still is not prepared to meet the challenges of religious pluralism. Calls for a view of Christian truth that is inclusive, accepting other religions.

494. Bach, Marcus. Strangers at the Door. Nashville: Abingdon Press, 1971.

> Bach claims the new religious movements' challenge to the Christian churches is a new one because it involves "foreign faiths," not sectarianism. He thoughtfully discusses the teachings of a few Eastern groups, including a description of his early interest in Vedanta. He invites Christian churches to view other religions as expressions of the "Cosmic Christ." Index.

495. Boa, Kenneth. Cults, World Religions, and You. Wheaton, Ill.: SP Publications, 1977.

> Intended to prepare Christians against cults. Provides brief, fairly objective descriptions of doctrines and rituals of major world religions and several new religious groups. Each entry includes a brief biblical evaluation. Bibliography of similar books.

496. Breese, Dave. Know the Marks of Cults. Wheaton, Ill.: SP Publications, 1979.

> An example of extreme evangelical Christian anti-cultism. Breese finds cults undeserving of study, since outside of Christianity are only "death, hopelessness, darkness, and heresy." He uses biblical citations to counter some superficial general characteristics of cults.

497. Burtner, William Kent. Coping with Cults: How They
Work in America. Kansas City: National Catholic Reporter
Cassettes, 1980.

> Series of talks revolving around the Unification
> Church; includes case studies. Tells parents how to
> help involved children. Explains deprogramming.
> Prepared by a Dominican priest.

498. The Challenge of the Cults: An Examination of the
Cult Phenomenon and Its Implication for the Jewish Community.
2d. ed. Philadelphia: Jewish Community Relations Council
of Greater Philadelphia, 1979.

> Reviews psychological and sociological aspects of
> cults, finding them to be undemocratic and objection-
> able from the standpoint of Jewish ethical teaching.
> Suggests that the Jewish community develop education
> programs, engage in public action, and provide support
> for ex-cult members and their families. Includes a
> bibliography, primarily of popular anticult sources.

499. Coleman, John. "The Religious Significance of New
Religious Movements." In New Religious Movements, edited by
John Coleman and Gregory Baum, pp. 9-16. Concilium, vol. 161.
New York: Seabury Press, 1983.

> Coleman identifies neo-Orientalism as the major new
> religious challenge to Christianity. To meet this
> challenge, Coleman maintains Christianity must develop
> its own authentic esotericism. Scholarly.

500. Duddy, Neil T. The God-Men: An Inquiry into Witness
Lee and the Local Church. 2d. ed. Downers Grove, Ill.:
InterVarsity Press, 1981.

> Duddy, along with other members of the Spiritual
> Counterfeits Project, an evangelical Christian organi-
> zation, critiques teachings and social structure of
> the Local Church on biblical grounds. Glossary and
> notes.

501. Elkins, Chris. What Do You Say to a Moonie? Wheaton,
Ill.: Tyndale House Publishers, 1981.

> A former Moonie turned Baptist (see his Heavenly
> Deception [item 584] for that story) speaks out against
> common myths about members of the UC, describes the
> Unificationist theology, and suggests that Christians
> remain friendly and helpful to Moonies.

502. Enroth, Ronald M. Youth, Brainwashing, and the
Extremist Cults. Grand Rapids, Mich.: Zondervan, 1977.

> An evangelical Christian approach intended for the

general reader. Enroth displays sympathy toward deprogramming. He attempts to distinguish "extreme"
cults from others, noting that the former brainwash
their converts.

503. Enroth, Ronald M.; Ericson, Edward; and Peters, C.B.
The Jesus People. Grand Rapids, Mich.: Eerdmans, 1972.

An accurate, readable description of the Jesus Movement
as it was in 1971. Teachings and activities of a few
groups are presented in a generally favorable light.
However, authors are critical of the exaltation of
feeling, denigration of the intellect, and simplistic
mentality they find among the Jesus groups. Index.

504. Enroth, Ronald M., et al. A Guide to Cults and New
Religions. Downers Grove, Ill.: InterVarsity Press, 1983.

Evangelical Christian responses to Rajneeshism, est,
Eckankar, the Hare Krishna movement, Transcendental
Meditation, and the Unification Church. These groups,
chosen to represent a spectrum of new religious leaders
and teachings, are described in objective tone, followed
by criticism using biblical citations. Reading list
of materials with the same viewpoint.

505. Haddon, David, and Hamilton, Vail. TM Wants You!
A Christian Response to Transcendental Meditation. Grand
Rapids, Mich.: Baker Book House, 1976.

Using a question-and-answer format, Haddon and Hamilton,
the latter a former TM teacher, discuss the practice
of TM and scientific studies of it. They provide a
biblical critique of its theology and claim that TM is
a "typical representative of the spirit of the Anti-
christ."

506. Johnston, William. Christian Zen. 2d rev. ed. San
Francisco: Harper and Row, 1981.

A Jesuit priest provides guidelines for Christians
wishing to deepen their inner lives through Zen
meditation.

507. Larson, Bob. Larson's Book of Cults. Wheaton, Ill.:
Tyndale House Publishers, 1982.

Short descriptions of a wide variety of religious
groups organized by type: "pseudo-Christian cults,"
"personality cults," "occult/mystical cults," and
"minor cults." Evangelical Christian perspective,
sometimes including ridicule of strange beliefs or
rituals. Bibliography and index.

508. Mangalwadi, Vishal. The World of Gurus. New Delhi:
Vikas Publishing, 1977.

> Discusses the historical, social, and intellectual
> background of Indian guruism. Evaluates several gurus,
> using conservative Christian-based criteria for judging
> the truth or falsity of religious claims. Finds
> Jesus Christ to be the only true teacher. Footnotes
> and index.

509. Martin, Walter. The New Cults. Santa Ana, Calif.:
Vision House, 1980.

> Martin's intention is to inform Christians of the
> basic teachings of several of the best-known new
> religious groups and to point out where those teachings
> differ from biblical Christianity. Less strident than
> most evangelical Christian responses, Martin's work is
> generally well researched and readable. Bibliographies
> provided for each group discussed.

510. National Council of the Churches of Christ in the U.S.A.
Commission on Faith and Order. "A Critique of the Theology
of the Unification Church as Set Forth in 'Divine Principle.'"
Occasional Bulletin of Missionary Research, July 1977,
pp. 18-23.

> An official study document that finds many aspects of
> Unification doctrine to be at variance with essential
> dimensions of Christian doctrine and states that the
> UC is not a Christian church. For another point of
> view on this issue, see Smart [item 487].

511. New Religious Movements Up-Date. Aarhus, Denmark:
Dialogue Center, 1977-1981, vol. 1-5.

> This periodical is aimed at educating Christian
> churches about new religious movements. Research
> standards are high; even those uninterested in the
> Christian interpretation will find the articles infor-
> mative. Good source for news items about groups in
> Europe. Published quarterly. Continued as Update
> [item 524].

512. Newport, John P. Christ and the New Consciousness.
Nashville: Broadman Press, 1978.

> One of the best evangelical/conservative Christian
> responses. Descriptions of a wide spectrum of groups
> are free of the sneering judgments found in some other
> works of this genre. Newport discusses doctrinal
> differences between Christianity and "new consciousness"
> groups without resorting to the questionable use of
> biblical passages. Chapter notes include references to
> good scholarly works.

513. Patton, John E. The Case Against TM in the Schools.
Grand Rapids, Mich.: Baker Book House, 1976.

   Written at a time when Transcendental Meditation was
   being taught in some New Jersey schools. Delves into
   the teachings of TM in an attempt to show its religious
   nature. Patton, a lawyer, feels that trying to abolish
   TM in public schools is futile. (See TM in Court [item
   573] for the story of how this did nonetheless come to
   pass.)

514. Quebedeaux, Richard, and Sawatsky, Rodney, eds. Evan-
gelical-Unification Dialogue. Conference Series, no. 3.
Barrytown, N.Y.: Unification Theological Seminary, 1979.

   This transcript of eight days of dialogue between
   evangelical Christians and Unificationists provides a
   detailed differentiation of theologies and another
   approach to understanding theological differences
   besides the typical evangelical critique.

515. Rudin, A. James. Jews and Judaism in Reverend
Moon's Divine Principle: A Report. New York: The American
Jewish Committee, 1976.

   A vehement critique of anti-Jewish elements in the
   central text of the Unification Church.

516. Rudin, Marcia R. "The New Religious Cults and the Jewish
Community." Religious Education 73(1978): 350-360.

   Finds the impact of new religious movements on the
   Jewish community threatening; particularly critical of
   theologies of Hebrew Christians and the Unification
   Church. Asks the Jewish community to offer its youth
   more love, community, and ways to serve humanity.

517. Saliba, John A. "The Christian Church and the New
Religious Movements: Towards Theological Understanding."
Theological Studies 43(1982): 468-485.

   Criticizes Christian denominations for lack of
   interest in new religious movements and evangelicals
   for hostile anticult stances. Calls for compassionate
   interfaith dialogue. Scholarly approach.

518. Saliba, John A. "The Christian Response to the New
Religions: A Critical Look at the Spiritual Counterfeits
Project." Journal of Ecumenical Studies 18(1981): 451-473.

   Useful, scholarly corrective and critique of the
   evangelical Christian anticult response. Saliba
   asks that Christians engage new religions in true
   ecumenical dialogue, avoiding condemnation.

519. Sire, James W. Scripture Twisting: 20 Ways the Cults
Misread the Bible. Downers Grove, Ill.: Intervarsity Press,
1980.

Sire, a conservative Christian, focuses on groups that
diverge significantly from orthodox Christianity,
applying his list of twenty kinds of mistakes to the
ways in which gurus and spiritual teachers use the
Bible. Intended as a guide, the book is arranged by
type of error, such as "inaccurate quotation,"
"overspecification," "selective citing," and "confused
definition." General index and Scripture index.

520. Skousen, Max. Christianity and est. Marina del Rey,
Calif.: DeVorss, 1978.

Skousen argues from an esoteric Christian standpoint
that est and Christianity are complementary; both have
transformation and regeneration as their goals.

521. Spero, Moshe Halevi. "Cults: Some Theoretical and Practical Perspectives." Journal of Jewish Communal Service
53(1977): 330-338.

Claims cults constitute a "critical social crisis"
for the Jewish family. Discusses psychosocial aspects
of cult involvement and offers suggestions for Jewish
social service agencies in helping to meet needs of
Jewish youth.

522. Spiritual Counterfeits Project. Journal. Berkeley,
Calif.: Spiritual Counterfeits Project, v. 1, 1977- .

Biblical critiques and evangelical Christian response
to a wide variety of new religious movements. Quality
of research varies; for instance, the special issue
on Eckankar was very well researched, but many articles
lack depth and scholarship. Published irregularly.

523. Spiritual Counterfeits Project. Newsletter. Berkeley,
Calif.: Spiritual Counterfeits Project, v. 1, 1975- .

Published several times a year. The same viewpoint
and topics as their Journal (1977-) but contains
shorter articles and news about SCP.

524. Update. Aarhus, Denmark: Dialogue Center, 1982- .

This periodical continues New Religious Movements Up-
Date (1977-1981) and has the same Christian viewpoint.
The articles, however, are more scholarly and less
polemical. Good source for brief news items about
new religious groups in Europe. Book reviews. Published
quarterly.

525. Vandana. <u>Gurus, Ashrams, and Christians</u>. London:
Darton, Longman, and Todd, 1978.

An Indian Catholic nun talks from within the Hindu
spiritual traditions about the nature of ashram life
and the guru-disciple relationship. Several gurus
and their Indian ashrams are described critically.
Vandana reflects on aspects of Indian religious life
that may contribute to the deepening of the Christian
spiritual life. Notes and glossary.

Legal Studies

526. "Alternative Religions: Government Control and the First Amendment." New York University Review of Law and Social Change 9(1979-1980): 1-126.

> Proceedings of a colloquium including Richard Delgado, Thomas Robbins, Jeremiah Gutman, Marcia Rudin, Paul Traub, Leo Pfeffer, Dick Anthony, and Paul Chevigny. Delgado's paper, "Religious Totalism as Slavery," calls for prosecuting cults for violation of the Thirteenth Amendment. Rudin, arguing that cults are a danger to society, is offset by Pfeffer, who contends that cults today are not different from those in earlier times and should be protected by the First Amendment. Robbins argues, as he does elsewhere, that the real problem of cults is social control, not mind control. Anthony presents a proposal for a "nonideological" counseling program for those troubled by cult involvement. The papers, followed by panel discussions, are a good representation of diverse viewpoints.

527. American Jewish Congress. Commission on Law, Social Action, and Urban Affairs. The Cults and the Law. Bulletin no. 1. New York: American Jewish Congress, 1978.

> A comprehensive review of legal and legislative developments relating to cults at federal, state, and local levels through 1977. Intended to stimulate the Jewish community to protect itself from cult proselytizing.

528. "The Anti-Religion Movement: An Abstract of Contemporary Terrorism, Kidnapping, and Violation of Religious and Civil Liberties in America." Los Angeles: Alliance for the Preservation of Religious Liberty, n.d.

A compilation of newspaper articles, personal testimony, and statements from the American Civil Liberties Union and the National Council of Churches against deprogramming. The publishing organization (now virtually inactive) has been called a cult "front"; even in its more active days, however, concerned mainstream Christians worked along with members of new religious groups in APRL.

529. Aronin, Douglas. "Cults, Deprogramming, and Guardianship: A Model Legislative Proposal." Columbia Journal of Law and Social Problems 17(1982): 163-286.

Aronin assumes that existing laws are inadequate to deal with cults and proposes a model conservatorship statute similar to the failed New York state Lasher bills. The model hinges on showing that the cult involved normally practices coercive persuasion, that from the circumstances of the individual's involvement one may infer that he or she has been subjected to coercive persuasion, and that his or her psychological state might have resulted from coercive persuasion. The actual legislation appears as an appendix following a lengthy discussion. Notes.

530. Babbitt, Ellen M. "The Deprogramming of Religious Sect Members: A Private Right of Action Under Section 1985 (3)." Northwestern University Law Review 74(1979): 229-254.

Babbitt discusses a section of the law that prohibits any private conspiracy that intends to deprive a citizen of a constitutional right in terms of its potential cause of action for a victim of deprogramming. She finds a reasonable probability of success for a section 1985(3) suit. Notes.

531. Baird, Robert D. "Religious or Non-Religious: TM in American Courts." Journal of Dharma 7(1982): 391-407.

Discussion of the metaphysical system underlying Transcendental Meditation and with what justification the teaching of it in public schools was found to violate separation of church and state.

532. Bates, Frank. "Child Law and Religious Extremists: Some Recent Developments." Ottawa Law Review 10(1978): 299-312.

Discusses case law concerning parents' rights to retrieve children under the age of minority from religious groups. Notes with dismay the unwillingness of courts to make value judgments about religions. Argues that social science studies show that children raised in minority religions have a much greater risk than others of developing psychological problems and

that courts should favor the welfare of children over
religious freedom. Notes.

533. Beebe, Robert L. "Tax Problems Posed by Pseudo-Religious
Movements." Annals of the American Academy of Political and
Social Science, November 1979, pp. 91-105.

Discusses the development of law relating to religion,
in particular new religions, and tax administration.
Beebe points out that new religions present the most
difficulties in this area.

534. California. Senate. Select Committee on Children and
Youth. Hearing on the Impact of Cults on Today's Youth.
Northridge: California State University, August 24, 1974.

Transcript of a fact-finding hearing intended to
determine if teenagers under eighteen are being "kid-
napped" and brainwashed by new religious groups.
Members, former members, and relatives of members of
The Love Family, Alamo Foundation, Children of God, and
Divine Light Mission provide testimony.

535. Coleman, Lee, and Solomon, Trudy. "Parens Patrie Treatment:
Legal Punishment in Disguise." Hastings Constitutional Law
Quarterly 3(1976): 345-362.

Criticizes state intervention to force involuntary
psychiatric treatment of those who are deemed unable
to care for themselves. Argues that the state controls
and punishes deviants in this way. Cults are not
directly discussed, but temporary conservatorships over
cult members have been based on the parens patrie doctrine. Notes.

536. "Cults and the Constitution." The Center Magazine 15
(1982): 8-39.

Report on a conference held at the Hutchins Center.
Includes papers by psychiatrist Louis West, former
Moonie Gary Scharff, sociologist James Richardson,
law professor Richard Delgado, and professor of
religion William Shepherd. The papers vary in quality
and viewpoint. Several other people participated in
a discussion that is also included.

537. Delgado, Richard A. "Ascription of Criminal States of
Mind: Toward a Defense Theory for the Coercively Persuaded
("Brainwashed") Defendant." Minnesota Law Review 63(1978): 1-
34.

Addresses the use of coercive persuasion as a criminal
defense, noting that the defense could be used by
cultists who might be induced by their leaders to
commit criminal acts. Argues that a coercively persuaded
defendant acts with intentions that are those of his/her

"captors" and is, therefore, not culpable. Joshua
Dressler provides a critique of Delgado's argument on
pp. 335-360 of this issue. Notes.

538. Delgado, Richard A. "Limits to Proselytizing." In The
Brainwashing/Deprogramming Controversy, edited by David G.
Bromley and James T. Richardson, pp. 215-233. New York:
Edwin Mellen Press, 1983.

Argues for state intervention in cults, based on his
contention that adherents are damaged by mind control.
Suggests conservatorships, "cooling-off" periods
before commitments are made to groups, and civil suits.
Delgado is the most articulate spokesperson for such
controls.

539. Delgado, Richard A. "Religious Totalism: Gentle and
Ungentle Persuasion under the First Amendment." Southern
California Law Review 51(1977): 1-98.

Lengthy and very important legal brief arguing in favor
of court-ordered deprogramming, mandatory cooling-off
periods for prospective cult members, requests for
rescue, and other remedies for alleged cult mind
control. Delgado feels that cults are sufficiently
harmful to individuals and society to override protection of them under the First Amendment. Extensive
footnotes include many useful references, although they
tend to be negatively critical assessments.

540. Dodge, Joseph. "The Free Exercise of Religion: A Sociological Approach." Michigan Law Review 67(1969): 679-728.

Dodge proposes what he claims to be a value-free
sociological method for determining whether the
state's interest or the religion's interest is stronger
in cases where free exercise of religion is claimed.
Using the theoretical work of Robert Bellah, Dodge ranks
religious interests according to functions of religious
systems rather than beliefs. His complex model appears
to give more weight to world religions such as
Christianity and less to "primitive" religions such as
those of American Indians, because the latter do not
"advance civilization." This model could work against
some cults. Notes.

541. Dressler, Joshua. "Professor Delgado's Brainwashing
Defense: Courting a Determinist Legal System." Minnesota
Law Review 63(1979): 335-360.

Criticizes Richard Delgado's use of coercive persuasion
as a criminal defense, claiming that it is logically
impossible to "frame a coercive persuasion defense that
is both consistent with present criminal law and juris-
prudential doctrines and is also morally acceptable."
An important critique. Delgado's article appears earlier
in the same issue.

542. Emory, Meade, and Zelenak, Lawrence. "The Tax Exempt
Status of Communitarian Religious Organizations: An
Unnecessary Controversy?" Fordham Law Review 50(1982): 1085-
1112.

Discusses cases in which new and unconventional religious
communities have not been granted tax-exempt status.
Although members live communally, sharing all income and
goods as part of their religious beliefs, courts have
ruled that individuals benefit by receiving food,
clothing, and the like and that therefore the community
should be taxed. Points out that these rulings are
inconsistent with the tax-exempt status of traditional
monasteries and convents and argues that the differential treatment violates the First Amendment. Suggests
taxing members for benefits they receive as a way of
preventing abuses; legitimate religious organizations
may not be strongly affected but illegitimate ones may
be. Notes.

543. Greene, Robert H. "People v. Religious Cults: Legal
Guidelines for Criminal Activities, Tort Liability, and
Parental Remedies." Suffolk Law Review 11(1977): 1025-1058.

Review of legal issues surrounding religious cults.
Discusses criminal and civil liability of religious
groups, leaders, and members, as well as deprogramming,
guardianship, and habeas corpus. Cautions courts
against infringing civil and religious liberties of
cult members.

544. Gutman, Jeremiah S. "Government Intrusions into New
Religions." Church and State, December 1979, pp. 10-16.

Gutman contends that governmental interest in new
religious groups constitutes a violation of the First
Amendment. He points out instances in which the
government has interfered with new religious groups but
has left mainstream religions alone on the same issues.
A civil libertarian approach; particularly strong against
deprogramming.

545. Harman, Willis W. Assessment of Future National and
International Problem Areas. Volume II-E Potential Use and
Misuse of Consciousness Technology. Menlo Park, Calif.:
Stanford Research Institute, Center for the Study of
Policy Research and Analysis, and National Science Foundation,
Washington, D.C., 1977.

Results of an assessment of six global problems,
including unemployment, chronic stress on individuals
and society, and management of large, complex systems.
Analyzes potential use and misuse of traditional
techniques of consciousness exploration, biofeedback,
and psychoactive drugs, and discusses possible abuses
of power by religious groups.

546. Heins, Marjorie. "'Other People's Faiths': The Scientology Litigation and the Justiciability of Religious Fraud." Hastings Constitutional Law Quarterly 9(1981): 153-197.

Heins represented several churches of Scientology in lawsuits brought against them by former Scientologists who claimed fraudulent misrepresentation of the benefits to be derived from auditing, Scientology's main practice. Mind control and breach of contract were also claimed. Plaintiffs argued that Scientology is not a religion and therefore its beliefs are not protected by the First Amendment. Heins discusses issues involved and warns courts to be wary of claims of fraud deriving from religious belief. Footnotes.

547. Hill, Daniel G. Study of Mind Development Groups, Sects, and Cults in Ontario: A Report to the Ontario Government. Toronto: Office of the Special Advisor, 1980.

In his capacity as Special Advisor to the Attorney General of Ontario, Hill, with his staff, produced a comprehensive general study of deprogramming, new religious and quasi-religious groups in relation to public concerns, possible legislation, and social policy issues. He heard recommendations from scholars, educators, ex-cult members and current members, concerned citizens, religious leaders, psychiatrists, and others. The report's conclusions call for a heavy burden of proof to fall on those who would seek legislative control of cults, but it also recognizes the importance of public concern. Bibliography.

548. Homer, David R. "Abduction, Religious Sects, and the Free Exercise Guarantee." Syracuse Law Review 25(1974): 623-645.

Discusses kidnapping and deprogramming of members of cults and justifiable state intervention. Argues that substantial proof of great actual or potential harm to society must be offered in order to justify legal intervention. Notes.

549. Johansen, R.B., and Rosen, Sanford J. "State and Local Regulation of Religious Solicitation of Funds: A Constitutional Perspective." The Annals of the American Academy of Political and Social Science 446(1979): 116-135.

Authors discuss the wide variety of state and local solicitation ordinances, pointing out challenges concerning the constitutionality of such ordinances. They suggest that criminal law and regulation of time, place, and manner of solicitation are less problematic methods for dealing with abuses.

550. Korns, William A. "Cults in America and Public Policy." Editorial Research Reports 1(1979): 267-283.

Overview of the new religious movements phenomenon, with special attention to prevailing views on First Amendment issues, tax exemption questions, and political involvement of cult leaders. Selected bibliography.

551. Levine, Mark. "The Free Exercise Clause as a Defense to Involuntary Civil Commitment: Bringing Mental Illness into Religion." Albany Law Review 39(1974): 144-156.

Argues that individuals deemed mentally ill because of their religious beliefs and involuntarily committed to mental institutions are denied free exercise of religion. Levine feels they have a right to refuse commitment unless they are found to be dangerous or to pose a grave and immediate threat to the state. Notes.

552. Massachusetts. General Court. Senate. Committee on Commerce and Labor. Commonwealth of Massachusetts Public Hearing, Senator John G. King, Commerce and Labor, March 21, 1979. Lexington, Mass.: American Family Foundation, 1979.

Transcription of testimony for and against a bill concerning fund-raising methods used by religious groups. Although the bill is not printed in the document, one can infer that it encountered difficulties in passage because it was directed primarily at selected groups, notably the Unification Church.

553. Moore, Joey P. "Piercing the Religious Veil of the So-Called Cults." Pepperdine Law Review 7(1980): 655-710.

Overview of federal and state studies of recruitment, indoctrination, deprogramming, fund-raising, and tax exemption. Suggests that some cults may be taking advantage of religious status to further political and social goals and should be investigated. Notes.

554. New York. Assembly. Public Hearing on Treatment of Children by Cults. August 9-10, 1979; reprint ed., Lexington, Mass.: American Family Foundation, n.d.

Has 680 pages of sworn testimony from over twenty people, including scholars, deprogrammers, mental health professionals, and representatives from new religions. The intent of the hearing, which took place in the wake of Jonestown, was to assess the need for legislation to protect children in cults. Much of the testimony concerns the typical brainwashing and deception motifs; some strays into the realm of "children" over eighteen years of age.

555. Pierson, Kit. "Cults, Deprogrammers, and the Necessity Defense." <u>Michigan Law Review</u> 80(1981): 271-311.

Examines the necessity defense and its use by parents who have claimed that abducting their children from cults was necessary. Finds the necessity defense inadequate in deprogramming cases and suggests two variations. The "choice of evils" defense focuses on the necessity of deprogramming to prevent a greater harm but does not require that the harm be imminent, as in the necessity defense. The second variation, the "compulsion" defense, excuses the actors for acting as others might in the same situation. Notes.

556. Porter, Jack Nusan. "Kids in Cults: Some Legal and Political Problems." Paper read at the meeting of the Society for the Study of Social Problems, 1979, at Boston, Massachusetts. Photocopied.

An overview concentrating on issues such as brainwashing, kidnapping-rescue, tax-exempt status, and the reluctance of the U.S. Attorney General's office to bring charges against cults. Suggests local and individual action to stop the growth of cults.

557. Poythress, Norman G. "Behavior Modification, Brainwashing, Religion, and the Law." <u>Journal of Religion and Health</u> 17(1978): 238-243.

A brief but useful discussion of the free will philosophical perspective in our legal system, its religious origins, and the general opposition of the courts to behavior modification techniques that Poythress likens to religious indoctrination. References.

558. Reich, Walter. "Brainwashing, Psychiatry, and the Law." <u>Psychiatry</u> 39(1976): 400-403.

Reich argues persuasively that brainwashing defenses threaten the free will concept undergirding our judicial system. Claims that psychiatrists ought not to provide expert testimony in this area because not enough is known about socialization and group processes and theories conflict.

559. Richardson, Herbert W., comp. <u>Deprogramming: Documenting the Issue</u>. Toronto: Toronto School of Theology, 1977. Distributed by Edwin Mellen Press.

Collection of articles, interviews, and personal accounts dealing critically with deprogramming, prepared for the American Civil Liberties Union and the Toronto School of Theology Conferences on Religious Deprogramming held in 1977. Emphasizes the more brutal aspects of deprogramming, particularly in passages from a British

deprogramming manual subsequently alleged to be a
Scientology anti-deprogramming hoax.   A basic reference
for opponents of deprogramming.

560. Robbins, Thomas. "Cults and the Therapeutic State."
Social Policy, May/June 1979, pp. 42-46.

Discusses threats to civil liberties and right to
dissent that he sees in deprogramming and temporary
conservatorships. Legal control ought to be restricted
to violation of laws, according to Robbins.

561. Robbins, Thomas. "Even a Moonie Has Civil Rights."
The Nation, 26 February 1977,   pp. 238-242.

A vehement attack on legal deprogramming via temporary
conservatorships granted to parents in ex-parte
hearings from which the potential conservatee is
excluded and in which s/he is not represented.

562. Rosenzweig, Charles. "High Demand Sects: Disclosure
Legislation and the Free Exercise Clause." New England Law
Review 15(1979): 128-159.

Proposes state legislation requiring secular and
religious organizations which publicly recruit members
to disclose their identities to potential members.
Finds this form of regulation to be the least restric-
tive way to deal with cultic mind control.   Notes.

563. Shapiro, Robert N. "'Mind Control' or Intensity of
Faith: The Constitutional Protection of Religious Beliefs."
Harvard Civil Rights-Civil Liberties Law Review 13(1978):
751-797.

Shapiro argues that brainwashing is too diffuse a
term to serve as a basis for invalidating beliefs, and
an individual should be subjected to treatment only
when it is conclusively demonstrated that the person's
beliefs are both involuntary in origin and controlled
by others.   Notes.

564. Shepherd, William C. "The Prosecutor's Reach: Legal
Issues Stemming from the New Religious Movements." Journal
of the American Academy of Religion 50(1982): 187-214.

Surveys several cases involving First Amendment rights
and new religious movements and follows with a critique
of Richard Delgado's arguments justifying state intervention in religious beliefs.   Author cautions that
although some forms of indoctrination may involve
"mental and spiritual poison," they are not criminal.
References.

565. Siegel, Terri I. "Deprogramming Religious Cultists."
Loyola of Los Angeles Law Review 11(1978): 807-828.

Argues that compelling state interests have not been
shown to exist in cases where parents have sought
guardianships or conservatorships over their adult
children cult members and that therefore the state
should not intervene. Suggests that fraud in recruitment may be actionable under criminal statutes. Notes.

566. Slade, Margot. "New Religious Groups: Membership and
Legal Battles," Psychology Today, January 1979, p. 81.

Discusses the legal practices through which converts
are forcibly removed from cults and the legal attack
on these practices being made by the cults with the
backing of the American Civil Liberties Union.

567. Spendlove, Gretta. "Legal Issues in the Use of Guardianship Procedures to Remove Members of Cults." Arizona Law
Review 18(1976): 1095-1139.

568. State of New York. Charity Frauds Bureau. Final Report
on the Activities of the Children of God to the Hon. Louis
J. Lefkowitz, Attorney General of the State of New York.
Albany, N.Y.: 1974.

At the request of then Governor Rockefeller, the
Attorney General interviewed seventy-four persons in
some way connected with the Children of God and studied
some of its written materials. Highly critical of all
aspects of the COG, this report claims to expose the
group as only outwardly religious. One of the most
critical of all works about the Children of God.

569. "Sun Myung Moon and the Law." Church and State, January
1979, pp. 9-12.

Summarizes findings and recommendations of the investigation into the Unification Church by the Subcommittee
on International Organizations of the House International Relations Committee. (See item 571 for the
report.)

570. United States. Congress. House. Committee on Foreign
Affairs. The Assassination of Representative Leo J. Ryan
and the Jonestown, Guyana Tragedy. Washington: U.S. Government Printing Office, 1979.

An investigative fact-finding report. A short text is
followed by hundreds of pages of appendices, including
correspondence, opinions of scholars, and newspaper
and journal articles. Several sections are noted as
being "in classified version only."

571. United States. Congress. House. Committee on International Relations. Subcommittee on International Organizations. <u>Investigation of Korean-American Relations: Report of the Subcommittee on International Organizations of the Committee on International Relations, U.S. House of Representatives</u>. Washington: U.S. Government Printing Office, 1978.

> From 1976 through 1978 the Fraser subcommittee conducted an intensive investigation of Korean-American relations prompted by disclosures of major gifts to some members of Congress by Tongsun Park. Eighty-one pages in Part C of this report are devoted to "the Moon organization." The subcommittee found that Moon's enterprises constituted one international organization, with Moon having substantial control and the intent to establish a one-world government and religion.

572. United States. Congress. Senate. <u>Information Meeting on the Cult Phenomenon</u>. Special publications, U.S. Senate, S940-1. Washington, D.C.: Ace-Federal Reporters, 1979.

> Includes statements by Daphne Greene, Richard Delgado, Ted Patrick, and Neil Salonen.

573. United States. District Court. New Jersey. <u>TM in Court</u>. Berkeley, Calif.: Spiritual Counterfeits Project, 1978.

> Until this opinion, which found TM to be religious, TM had been taught in five New Jersey public schools. An example of how an anticult group, the Spiritual Counterfeits Project, achieved a court victory.

574. Weiss, Jonathan. "Privilege, Posture, and Protection: Religion in the Law." <u>Yale Law Journal</u> 73(1964): 593-623.

> Discusses the issue of fraud in religious representation, using as an example the case of United States v. Ballard, in which the leaders of the I AM movement were convicted of obtaining money through the mails by false pretenses. States that religious representations are protected by the First Amendment only in the realm of belief or manifestations affecting belief. Argues that courts should not define religion or make special religious exemptions for taxes or conscientious objectors; suggests other bases such as freedom to dissent in the case of conscientious objectors. Notes.

Personal Accounts

575. Allen, Steve. *Beloved Son: A Story of the Jesus Cults*.
Indianapolis: Bobbs-Merrill, 1982.

> In an attempt to understand his son's joining the Love
> Israel Family (also called Church of Armageddon), a
> famous entertainer discusses a number of communal cults.

576. Belfrage, Sally. *Flowers of Emptiness: Reflections on
an Ashram*. New York: Dial Press, 1981.

> A good-natured woman visits Rajneesh's controversial
> ashram in Poona, India, with two friends. Her some-
> times humorous and sometimes seriously questioning
> approach provokes thought.

577. Bharti, Ma Satya. *Death Comes Dancing: Celebrating
Life with Bhagwan Shree Rajneesh*. Boston: Routledge and
Kegan Paul, 1981.

> Autobiography by a disciple of Rajneesh, describing
> the transformation of a personality under the teacher's
> guidance. Valuable for anyone wanting to understand
> Rajneesh followers, many of whom now live in Oregon
> with Rajneesh, and what they do.

578. Brogan, Frankie Fonde. *The Snare of the Fowler*.
Lincoln, Va.: Chosen Books of the Zondervan Corporation,
1982.

> Brogan tells the story of her family's reactions to her
> son's brief involvement with the Children of God.
> One of the more thoughtful and compassionate works of
> this genre.

579. Brooke, Robert Taliaferro. Sai Baba, Lord of the Air.
New Delhi: Vikas Publishing House, 1979.

Brooke's search led him to India, where he joined
Sathya Sai Baba's inner circle of disciples. His posi-
tion there led to discoveries about the guru that
shocked him. In the wake of his crisis he embraced
Christianity.

580."Claudio Naranjo." San Francisco: New Dimensions Foundation, 1977. 2 audiocassettes.

A wide-ranging two-hour interview originally broadcast
on KQED-FM. Naranjo discusses his spiritual search and
involvement with Oscar Ichazo, Arica, SAT (Seekers
after Truth), Tarthang Tulku, and other new religious/
human potential groups.

581. Collier, Sophia. Soul Rush: The Odyssey of a Young
Woman of the 70s. New York: William Morrow, 1978.

A young woman's search for meaning through her involvement with the Divine Light Mission. Warm and insightful account of her spiritual journey from late high
school through her departure from the Divine Light
Mission at age twenty.

582. Davis, Deborah. "'Coming Out': The Testimony of
Deborah Davis." Berkeley, Calif.: Spiritual Counterfeits
Project, n.d. Audiocassette.

Her voice breaking with emotion, the daughter of Moses
David, leader of the Children of God, speaks before a
meeting of the Citizens Freedom Foundation about her
life in the movement from 1968 to 1978.

583. Edwards, Christopher. Crazy for God. Englewood
Cliffs, N.J.: Prentice-Hall, 1979.

Kidnapped and deprogrammed from his confusing and
unhappy affiliation with the Unification Church, Edwards
maintains he was brainwashed while in the UC and views
his life in the cult as a "nightmare."

584. Elkins, Chris. Heavenly Deception. Wheaton, Ill.:
Tyndale Publishers, 1980.

"Ex-Moonie's story"; Elkins points out the large
dropout rate in the Unification Church, warns against
deprogramming, and denies brainwashing.

585. Epstein, Perle. Pilgrimage: Adventures of a Wandering
Jew. Boston: Houghton Mifflin, 1979.

Raised in an Orthodox Jewish home, Epstein became
attracted to Hinduism and recounts her spiritual journey
through India and back to mystical Judaism.

586. Freed, Josh. <u>Moonwebs: Journey into the Mind of a Cult</u>. Toronto: Dorset Publishing, 1980.

A Canadian journalist writes the story of Benji Miller's (pseudonym) time in the Unification Church and his subsequent kidnapping and deprogramming. Bibliography.

587. Gerstel, David U. <u>Paradise, Incorporated: Synanon, a Personal Account</u>. Novato, Calif.: Presidio Press, 1982.

A former member's thoughtful account, based on his own experiences, interviews with other members, notes and transcripts, and records of legal proceedings. Includes an annotated list of sources.

588. Gibson, William. <u>A Season in Heaven</u>. New York: Atheneum, 1974.

Gibson, a writer noted for <u>The Miracle Worker</u>, chronicles his 1974 experiences at a Transcendental Meditation intensive in Spain. His mature observations of the Maharishi and devotees are sympathetic; the teachings receive criticism.

589. Hargrove, Robert A. <u>est: Making Life Work</u>. New York: Delacorte Press, 1976.

A former editor/publisher of <u>East West Journal</u>, pleased by his <u>est</u> training, writes of his experiences. Conveys well the language and activities of <u>est</u> seminars through reconstructed conversations. While writing the book he found the organization "very unwilling to communicate about itself."

590. Hultquist, Lee. <u>They Followed the Piper</u>. Plainfield, N.J.: Logos International, 1977.

About Children of God followers; one family's experiences and reactions to their daughter's involvement.

591. Hulme, Kathryn. <u>Undiscovered Country: In Search of Gurdjieff</u>. Boston: Little, Brown, 1972.

A personal memoir and tribute to the personality and teachings of Gurdjieff.

592. Kempton, Sally. "Hanging Out with the Guru." <u>New York Magazine</u>, 12 April 1976, p. 36.

A journalist tells of vague dissatisfaction with her life and how becoming a follower of Muktananda brought her renewed vitality and relief from "negative" emotions. Photographs of the guru with followers.

593. Kleps, Art. Millbrook: The True Story of the Early Years of the Psychedelic Revolution. Oakland, Calif.: Bench Press, 1975.

A vivid and uninhibited account of Kleps's counterculture years, including many inside stories of Timothy Leary's work as the guru of psychedelics.

594. Lerner, Eric. Journey of Insight Meditation: A Personal Experience of the Buddha's Way. New York: Schocken Books, 1977.

Working hard at not putting down roots anywhere, Lerner moves from drugs to India, back to the United States and marriage, back to India, and so on, recounting vividly the tortures of stilling the mind through vipassana meditation.

595. McManus, Una, and Cooper, John Charles. Not for a Million Dollars. Nashville: Impact Books, 1980.

McManus joined the Children of God when she was a drug-using fifteen-year-old and left five years later when she became shocked by the COG's unconventional sexual practices. Discusses her involvement and problems in getting her children out when she left.

596. Martin, Rachel. Escape. Denver, Colo.: Accent Books, 1979.

"The true story of a young woman caught in the clutches of a religious cult"; Rachel Martin tells the story of life with "Brother Evangelist" Jim Roberts.

597. Mills, Jeannie. Six Years with God. New York: A and W Publishers, 1979.

A former member of Peoples Temple offers a sensitive chronicle of her experience and that of her family.

598. Nazuna. Sai Dairy of a Traveling Zen Lady. San Diego: Birth Day Publishing Co., 1978.

Journal of a zen meditator and her encounter with Sathya Sai Baba, an Indian guru.

599. Olin, William F. Escape from Utopia: My Ten Years with Synanon. Santa Cruz, Calif.: Unity Press, 1980.

"I became swept up in this exhilarating movement, first with its unparalleled communication tools and later with its promise of an earthly paradise for me and my family." Then the paradise became "frightening fanaticism," and Olin left.

600. Owens, Claire Myers. Zen and the Lady. New York: Baraka Books, 1979.

   An intelligent and sensitive woman who began Zen meditation at the age of seventy-five describes her fulfilling personal experiences and also conveys Zen principles well.

601. Patrick, Ted. Let Our Children Go! New York: E.P. Dutton, 1976.

   Career autobiography of the earliest and most controversial deprogrammer. Fascinating reading. Includes photographs of some of Patrick's "successes."

602. Satya Bharti, Ma. Drunk on the Divine: An Account of Life in the Ashram of Bhagwan Shree Rajneesh. New York: Grove Press, 1980.

   The most explicit account to date of various encounter and meditation groups held at the Rajneesh ashram in Poona, India. Related through the experiences of several people.

603. Scott, R.D. Transcendental Misconceptions. San Diego: Beta Books, 1978.

   Scott tells of his six years as a teacher of Transcendental Meditation and how he left because he decided it was a "religious deception" and a "secret attack on the Constitution." Critique of TM teachings from an evangelical Christian perspective.

604. Underwood, Barbara. Hostage to Heaven. New York: Potter, 1979.

   A mother and daughter sort out the daughter's four years of membership in the Unification Church. An intimate if unfocused account with some attempt at social scientific analysis in the appendix.

605. Wood, Allen Tate. Moonstruck. New York: Morrow, 1979.

   A personal account of the months preceding membership in the Unification Church and a careful, often humorous treatment of life at the top. Superficial discussion of the decision and difficulties involved in leaving.

606. Yanoff, Morris. Where Is Joey: Lost Among the Hare Krishnas. Chicago: Swallow Press, 1981.

   A sixty-nine-year-old grandfather tells the story of retrieving his twelve-year-old grandson from the Hare Krishna movement.

607. Yee, Min S., and Layton, Thomas N. In My Father's House: The Story of the Layton Family and the Reverend Jim Jones. New York: Holt, Rinehart and Winston, 1981.

    A chronicle of the involvement of three Layton family members in the Peoples Temple. Both fascinating and embarrassing to read; the family members are frank about their intimate lives, but the reader will sense their lack of personal responsibility. Includes photographs.

608. Zweig, Paul. Three Journeys: An Automythology. New York: Basic Books, 1976.

    Zweig's third journey is the inner one, an intense, overwhelming series of experiences with Swami Muktananda which he claims added a new dimension to his life as a successful writer and happily married man.

Popular Studies

609. The Advisor. Lexington, Mass.: American Family Foundation, 1979- .

> A tabloid publication with a strong anticult stance.
> Very good source for news items from small newspapers
> throughout the country. Reports on scholarly studies
> also included. An insert, "The Collegiate Advisor,"
> reports on cult activities on college campuses.
> Published bimonthly.

610. Adler, Margot. Drawing Down the Moon: Witches, Druids,
Goddess-Worshippers, and Other Pagans in America Today.
New York: Viking Press, 1979.

> Fascinating look at Neo-Paganism in America today.
> The author visited a variety of groups and offers a
> thoughtful analysis of what's going on and the current
> literature. Easily understood by the general reader,
> Adler's work is particularly valuable because it is the
> only extended description of groups generally ignored.
> Appendices include rituals and resources, the latter
> (addresses of people, places, and newsletters)
> necessarily out of date by now. Notes provide sugges-
> tions for further reading. Index.

611. Anderson, Walt. Open Secrets: A Western Guide to Tibetan
Buddhism. New York: Viking Press, 1979.

> Good, popular introduction intended to render Buddhism
> intelligible to Westerners; uses parallels in Western
> thought. Basic ideas, illustrated exercises, and
> meditation practices are presented, mostly as taught
> at the Nyingma Institute in Berkeley, so much material
> concerns Tantric Buddhism. Discusses scriptures of
> several Buddhist lineages. Brief glossary of common
> terms, notes, and index.

612. Anderson, Walter Truett. The Upstart Spring: Esalen and the American Awakening. Reading, Mass.: Addison-Wesley, 1983.

 A chronicle of people and ideas associated with the
 birth of the human potential movement. Anderson
 writes from the viewpoint of both a sympathetic
 participant and a somewhat critical observer. Enjoyable, lightweight reading. Illustrations and index.

613. Anthony, Dick, and Robbins, Thomas. "A Demonology of Cults." Inquiry Magazine, 1 September 1980, pp. 9-11.

 Brief overview of several arguments the authors have
 developed fully elsewhere. They are against the
 generalizations about cults made by their critics,
 against the medical model used by mental health professionals, and in favor of a more self-reflective
 approach that focuses on what the growth of new
 religions says about our society.

614. Bancroft, Anne. Twentieth Century Mystics and Sages. London: Heinemann, 1976.

 Brief biographies and discussion of the teachings
 of several well-known spiritual teachers. Includes
 Alan Watts, Krishnamurti, Gurdjieff, Pak Subuh,
 Meher Baba, Chogyam Trungpa, Maharaj Ji, Maharishi
 Mahesh Yogi, and Rudolf Steiner. Photographs of
 most teachers and bibliographies of their writings.
 A useful general introduction. Index.

615. Banner, Bob. "In Search of Certitude." New Age Journal, May 1976, pp. 50-57.

 A very good journalistic account of the seductive
 appeal of certitude Banner experienced and rejected
 at a weekend workshop at the Unification Church's
 Ideal Community Ranch in Booneville, California.

616. Beauvais, Dave. "Jonestown: the Heart and the Jungle." Alternatives, January 1979, p. 26.

 Drawing on his personal experiences with New Age
 spiritual groups, Beauvais reflects on the dangers,
 sometimes unknown, of surrendering to spiritual
 leaders.

617. Boettcher, Robert. Gifts of Deceit: Sun Myung Moon, Tongsun Park, and the Korean Scandal. New York: Holt, Rinehart and Winston, 1980.

 Boettcher was staff director of a House Subcommittee on
 International Relations that investigated Korean-
 American relations. He contends that Sun Myung Moon
 was a main element in "Koreagate," although Moon's

role was obscured by the furor over congressional
bribery. Boettcher has been criticized for leveling
unsupported charges against Moon. Notes and index.

618. Butler, Katy. "Events Are the Teacher." CoEvolution
Quarterly, Winter 1983, pp. 112-123.

Butler tells how the San Francisco Zen Center dealt
with the unethical sexual behavior of its abbot.

619. Bromley, David G., and Shupe, Anson D., Jr.
Strange Gods: The Great American Cult Scare. Boston:
Beacon Press, 1981.

Two sociologists who have contributed significantly
to research on the Unification Church and the anticult movement present a work for the general public.
They dismiss the idea that there is a rapid growth
of cults that threatens American society; they view
cults as legitimating human identity. Origins, beliefs,
and lifestyles of several groups are described. Authors
discuss role of the media in formation of the "cult
scare," fund-raising controversies, and brainwashing.
Book has been strongly criticized by anticult reviewers.
Useful to read in conjunction with Melton and Moore's
The Cult Experience [item 672].

620. Bunt, Frederick. "Deprogramming and Religious Liberty."
The Humanist, September/October 1979, pp. 48-49.

Views deprogramming as a beneficial and benign process
of education that allows one to think freely again.
This is a response to Edd Doerr's article in the
January/February 1977 issue of same magazine. Rebuttal
by Doerr follows Bunt's article.

621. Campbell, Susan. "Alternative Communities: Are They
Working?" Yoga Journal, October 1981, p. 6.

Overview of life at several West Coast intentional
communities that Campbell visited as part of a
project to help communities network with each other.
Article serves as a reminder that there are many
small, spiritual communities that quietly continue to
thrive.

622. Cavell, Marcia. "Visions of a New Religion." Saturday
Review of Literature, 19 December 1970, p. 12.

In this thoughtful essay, Cavell criticizes the
counterculture for ignoring the lessons of history
and attempting to avoid guilt by accepting Eastern
religious views.

623. Chandler, Russell, and Marshall, Tyler. "Village
Uneasy: Guru Brings His Ashram to Oregon." Los Angeles Times,
30 August 1981, p. 1.

> Good, lengthy article on background, teachings, and
> followers of the controversial Bhagwan Shree Rajneesh,
> written soon after his arrival in central Oregon,
> where his organization had purchased a 64,000-acre
> ranch. Discusses the reactions of townspeople to
> their new neighbors. Photographs.

624. Chapman, Rick M. How to Choose a Guru. Berkeley:
White Horse Publishing, 1981.

> Written to help those seeking an authentic spiritual
> guide. Rather than evaluating individual teachers,
> Chapman gives general principles to use in discerning
> the genuine. Includes about eighty brief commentaries
> on topics ranging from "stereotypes" to "flattery,
> beware of." Very good aid for the seeker.

625. Chapman, Stephen. "Cult-Mongering." New Republic,
17 February 1979,   pp. 11-13.

> Critical of Senator Dole's hearing on cults and mind
> control [item 572]. Chapman contends that cults do
> perpetuate abuses but feels that mind-control arguments
> are the wrong approach to these problems.

626. Cinnamon, Kenneth, and Farson, Dave. Cults and Cons:
The Exploitation of the Emotional Growth Consumer. Chicago:
Nelson-Hall, 1979.

> Authors criticize human potential groups for encourag-
> ing dependency, exploiting the consumer market, and
> providing simplistic answers to life's complicated
> problems. Style is brash and humorous. Much
> reasonable advice is mixed in with simplistic descrip-
> tions of everything from Eastern philosophies to
> encounter groups. Index.

627. Citizens Freedom Foundation News. Hannacroix, New York:
Citizens Freedom Foundation, 1974- .

> The Citizens Freedom Foundation, primarily made up
> of concerned parents, was founded to "educate the public
> about the harmful effects of mind control as used
> by the destructive cults." Usually published monthly,
> the News used to reprint newspaper articles and was a
> good source for items not indexed anywhere. The format
> has changed and now includes brief summaries of
> news articles, CFF organizational news, and lists of
> recent anticult publications.

628. Clark, John G., Jr. "We Are All Cultists at Heart."
Newsday, 30 November 1978.

629. Clark, Tom. The Great Naropa Poetry Wars. Santa Barbara,
Calif.: Cadmus Editions, 1980.

> A history of Chogyam Trungpa Rinpoche and his Naropa
> Institute, an important Tibetan Buddhist institute.
> Emphasizes problems caused by Trungpa's use of "crazy
> wisdom," a form of authoritarian teaching that has
> included what many have perceived as arbitrary abuses
> of power. Of particular concern to Clark is the
> notorious party at which the Rinpoche had a noted poet
> and his companion stripped of their clothes. Peter
> Marin also comments on this incident in "Spiritual
> Obedience" (Harper's, February 1979). Primarily an
> expose; this short book is one of the few pieces
> critical of Naropa's spiritual director.

630. Collier, Peter. "Bringing Home the Moonies: The Brian
Snatch." New Times, 10 June 1977, pp. 25-29.

> Colorful, critical account of a case in which Judge
> Vavuris granted temporary conservatorships to the
> parents of five Unification Church members in order to
> have them deprogrammed.

631. Conway, Flo, and Siegelman, Jim. Snapping: America's
Epidemic of Sudden Personality Change. Phildelphia: J.B.
Lippincott, 1978.

> Provocative and sometimes sensationalistic account of
> sudden personality change that leads to "information
> disease." Conway, a communications specialist, and
> Siegelman, a journalist, point out that new religious
> groups and human potential groups share certain tech-
> niques; they consider these to be a threat to human
> development. Drawing on interviews with members of
> groups and contemporary communication theory, the
> authors maintain that "information disease" is a phy-
> sical alteration of the brain that destroys the
> individual's capacity to think critically. Mental
> health professionals are said to be incapable of
> coping with this new disease. Although authors
> do a good job of pointing out destructive aspects of
> cult life, they fail to distinguish between healthy
> and unhealthy religion. Intended for the general
> reader, who will most likely be unable to assess
> adequately the validity of the "information disease"
> theory. Bibliography and index.

632. Cooper, Paulette. The Scandal of Scientology. New York:
Tower, 1971.

> Highly critical expose of the beliefs and practices of

Scientology. Somewhat sensationalistic. Bibliography
lists many pre-1970 popular articles about Scientology,
but full citations are not given. Chapter notes at
end of volume are also incomplete.

633. Coser, Rose L., and Coser, Lewis. "Jonestown as Perverse
Utopia." Dissent 26(1979): 158-163.

Authors do a decent job of recounting methods Jim
Jones used to gain the loyalty of his followers, but
they fail to address the issue of why people stayed
in the Peoples Temple when they were abused.

634. Cox, Harvey. "Playing the Devil's Advocate, As It Were."
New York Times, 16 February 1977, p. A 25.

Cox values the new religions for the critical perspective they bring to our culture. He says oriental
religions particularly challenge America's capacity for
pluralism because they do not make clear distinctions
between religious behavior and other kinds of activity.

635. Decter, Midge. "The Politics of Jonestown." Commentary,
May 1979, pp. 29-34.

Decter maintains that Jim Jones was primarily a radical
left politician whose faults were overlooked because
the political climate of the country favored the success
of social causes. The rush of the press to blame the
deaths at Jonestown on cultic mind control is seen to
be the result of massive embarrassment over failed
radicalism.

636. Delgado, Richard A. "Investigating Cults." New York
Times, 27 January 1979, p. A 23.

Delgado argues that cult members are victims of deceit
and manipulation that has caused them to be unable to
think properly. Therefore he feels state intervention
is legitimate. See his later articles for the specific
forms cf intervention he recommends.

637. Doerr, Edd. "Deprogramming and Religious Liberty."
The Humanist, January/February 1977, pp. 44-45.

Criticizes forced deprogramming, particularly of
legal adults, as a serious encroachment on personal
liberty. Frederick Bunt responds to Doerr in the
September/October 1979 issue.

638. Dowling, Colette. "Confessions of an American Guru."
New York Times Magazine, 4 December 1977, p. 41.

Fascinating portrait of Ram Dass, formerly Richard
Alpert, who went on from 1960s experimentation with
drugs at Harvard to popularize Hinduism in America.

639. Drury, Nevill, and Tillet, Gregory. The Occult Source-book. London: Routledge and Kegan Paul, 1978.

Series of brief introductory articles on a wide variety of occult subjects such as spiritualism, Theosophy, witchcraft, Satanism, meditation, and ritual magic. "Who's Who of the Occult" section offers biographical sketches of important occultists. Authors are sympathetic to the possibilities for increasing human potential through the practices dscribed. Index of names. Each article has an annotated bibliography.

640. Edwards, Cliff. "Sun Myong [sic] Moon and the Scholars." Dialog: A Journal of Theology 21(1982): 56-59.

An enlightening description of activities and reactions of invited scholars at a Unification Church-sponsored conference on the island of Tenerife.

641. Endore, Guy. Synanon. Garden City, N.Y.: Doubleday, 1968.

Readable, anecdotal account of the people and life-style of Synanon in the late 1960s.

642. Ford, Arthur. "The Sun Myung Moon Sittings." In his Unknown but Known, pp. 113-138. New York: New American Library, 1969.

Transcriptions of two trance sittings, one with Moon present, during which the famous medium claims to have received messages concerning Moon's role as a prophet of the New Age.

643. Fracchia, Charles A. Living Together Alone: The New American Monasticism. San Francisco: Harper and Row, 1979.

Discusses new forms of monasticism and describes several communities including Gold Mountain Monastery, the Holy Order of MANS, Siddha Yoga Dham, and Vajradhatu. Fracchia allows members of the communities to speak for themselves. Short bibliographical essay at the end.

644. Gann, L.H. "The Fatal Assumption of Social Therapy." Worldview, April 1978, pp. 23-26.

A libertarian attack on "self-chosen elite(s)," including deprogrammers, who assume the task of subjecting others to therapy based on the belief that social deviants are acting involuntarily.

645. Garvy, Jack. "American-Born Guru, Bubba Free John Retires." East-West Journal, no. 7(1979), pp. 20-25.

Bubba Free John and his Free Communion Church have received little media and virtually no scholarly attention. Article introduces the reader to his complex and original teachings at a time when Free John was withdrawing from control over his organization to avoid formation of a personality cult.

646. Goleman, Daniel. "Good Grief! Gurdjieff." Psychology Today, September 1979, p. 16.

Two-page article points out a few salient features of Gurdjieff's life and the practices he developed that his contemporary followers use to realize his teachings.

647. Gordon, Suzanne. "Let Them Eat est." Mother Jones, December 1978, pp. 41-54.

Scathing investigative report that portrays est's Hunger Project as a recruitment and fund-raising arm of est.

648. Godwin, John. Occult America. Garden City, N.Y.: Doubleday, 1972.

Godwin, a journalist, has produced a lively picture of astrologers, witches, spiritual seekers, and other occultists in the Aquarian Age, based on his travels throughout the country and interviews with 300 people. Photographs and text are clearly indicative of the late 1960s. Author pays some attention to the history of occult practices and approaches his subject with sympathetic interest. Index.

649. Greeley, Andrew M. "There's a New-Time Religion on Campus." New York Times Magazine, 1 June 1969, p. 14.

650. Greenfield, Robert. The Spiritual Supermarket. New York: Saturday Review Press/E.P. Dutton, 1975.

Rambling and lively journalistic tour through the world of Eastern teachers and their followers. Features observations of people, events, and conversations from the point of view of a seeker and a writer.

651. Hedgepeth, William, and Stock, Dennis. The Alternative: Communal Life in New America. London: Collier-Macmillan, 1970.

Black-and-white photographs make up at least half of this book, providing glimpses into the counterculture communes of the 1960s. Texts and photographs emphasize

the excitement and perception of new possibility shared
by the communitarians.

652. Hefley, James C. The Youthnappers. Wheaton, Ill.: SP
Publications, 1977.

Brief descriptions of several popular cults, followed
by sketchy chapters about brainwashing and why cults
are attractive. Appears to be aimed at parents of
cult members. Hefley claims objectivity but actually
tends towards sensationalism and refers almost exclu-
sively to sources critical of cults.

653. Henderson, C. William. Awakening: Ways to Psycho-
Spiritual Growth. Englewood Cliffs, N.J.: Prentice-Hall,
1975.

Written as a guide for the seeker. Short, readable
descriptions, primarily of human potential movements
and Eastern religious groups. Henderson is sympathetic
to all the groups he discusses, issues few caveats,
and sees the groups as alternatives to suit different
needs. Ends with a list of names and addresses of
150 related groups.

654. Hentoff, Nat. "The New Body Snatchers." Playboy,
February 1978; reprinted in Playboy, March 1979, p. 61.

A civil libertarian argument against deprogramming,
reprinted as a counterpoint to Playboy's interview
with Ted Patrick in the March 1979 issue.

655. Hoffman, Eva. "est--the Magic of Brutality." Dissent
24(1977): 209-212.

Hoffman describes est as encouraging competitive
behavior through aggrandizement of the will and
insidiously offering relief from the dilemmas of
freedom by discouraging doubt, insight, and reflection.

656. Holzer, Hans. The New Pagans. Garden City, N.Y.:
Doubleday, 1972.

Holzer, known for his "ghost hunting" and psychic
meandering books, has produced a sympathetic account
of various forms of Neo-Paganism based on his meetings
with people involved. Conversational tone--the people
often speak for themselves--interspersed with descriptions of rituals. Holzer accepts the often-criticized
thesis that contemporary witchcraft can be traced
historically to pre-Christian Goddess worship.

657. Kilduff, Marshall, and Tracy, Phil. "Inside Peoples
Temple." New West, 1 August 1977, pp. 30-37.

An important piece of investigative journalism. Authors
briefly discuss Jim Jones's political power and social
programs in San Francisco in the mid-1970s. Ten former
Peoples Temple members also tell of the beatings,
humiliations, phony healings, and threats that were
more fully exposed after Jonestown.

658. Kirsch, Jonathan. "Beyond the Law: The Cults and the
Courts." New West, December 17, 1979, pp. 105-112.

Kirsch expresses dismay that a year after Jonestown,
the legal system still has not been able to make head-
way against "so-called religions."

659. Klineman, George; Butler, Sherman; and Conn, David.
The Cult that Died: The Tragedy of Jim Jones and the
Peoples Temple. New York: G.P. Putnam's Sons, 1980.

A journalistic account which the authors, convinced
that Peoples Temple would end in tragedy, had begun
to write in early 1978. Begins with Jones's childhood
and ends with the Jonestown tragedy. Much reconstructed
conversation lends an aura of realism. Lacks interpretation of the events.

660. Krause, Charles A. Guyana Massacre: The Eyewitness
Account. New York: Berkley Publishing, 1978.

Krause went to Jonestown as a reporter. Working with
other members of the Washington Post staff, he managed
to get this "instant" book published within weeks of
the tragedy. Krause's first-person account is inter-
spersed with third-person narrative. Includes photographs of the dead bodies at Jonestown.

661. Lane, Mark. The Strongest Poison. New York: Hawthorn
Books, 1980.

In this long account, a former Peoples Temple lawyer
minimizes the Jonestown tragedy by stressing media
and governmental conspiracy against Jones and himself.
Lane buttresses his arguments with documentation, but
the conspiracy theory does not ring true, although
it makes for engrossing reading. Lane is also too
concerned with vindicating himself. Index.

662. Lang, Anthony. Synanon Foundation: The People
Business. Cottonwood, Ariz.: Wayside Press, 1978.

First writer to produce an expose of Synanon. Portrays
founder Dederich as ruthless in his pursuit of power.

663. Lasch, Christopher. "The Narcissist Society." New York
Review of Books, 30 September 1976, pp. 5-12.

In this review article covering five books (including
Zweig's Three Journeys [item 608] and Schur's The
Awareness Trap [item 316]),Lasch contends that the
trend of the 1970s was therapeutic rather than religious because people hungered for health and psychic
security, not personal salvation. He discusses the
narcissistic personality, tendencies toward which he
sees throughout the human potential movement. He
claims these tendencies are brought on by feelings
of hopelessness about the future, a sense of the
dangerousness of the world, and disenchantment over
human relations. A strong and affecting, but perhaps
overstated, commentary.

664. Lieb. Raymond. "Cultists and Anti-Cultists, The
Difficult Search for the Easy Answer." TAT Journal, no. 2
(1979), pp. 73-76.

Lieb argues insightfully that fear of unusual religious
beliefs, which are perceived as a threat to society,
underlies the anticult movement. Since Jonestown, he
says, people have been tempted to use cults as scape-
goats.

665. Lifton, Robert Jay. "The Appeal of the Death Trip."
New York Times Magazine, 7 January 1979, pp. 14-16.

Lifton, an expert on thought reform, insightfully
maintains that Jim Jones was able to develop the
Peoples Temple's unique suicidal theology by using
thought reform methods and appealing to his followers'
desire for transcendence.

666. Malko, George. Scientology: The New Religion.
New York: Dell Publishing, 1970.

A journalist's readable and interesting account.
Although dated, the book is still valuable for its
thoughtful approach and description of techniques used
in Scientology courses. History and doctrines of the
church are also given.

667. Marin, Peter. "The New Narcissism." Harper's, October
1975, pp. 45-56.

Very good critique of the shallow and egocentric
aspects of human potential movements. Marin calls
for awareness of history and the larger world we live
in and moral action, not only individually but in
community.

668. Marin, Peter. "Spiritual Obedience." Harper's,
February 1979, pp. 43-58.

Chogyam Trungpa's Naropa Institute, where Marin spent
a summer teaching, is the subject of Marin's trenchant

criticism.   In addition to criticizing total obedience,
he attacks what he perceives as a retreat from conscience, politics, and history.

669. McKenzie, Bill; Ruberg, Ken; and Leach, Jim. "A Theo-
cracy from the Right: Reverend Sun Myung Moon and the
American Political Process." Ripon Forum, no. 1(1983),
pp. 8-16.

Authors point out political and financial connections
among the Unification Church, leaders of the New Right,
and other conservatives, warning that Moon will
exploit the other groups in order to set up a "quasi-
Christian theocratic regime."

670. Maslow, Abraham. "Synanon and Eupsychia." Journal of
Humanistic Psychology, no. 1(1967)., pp. 28-35.

Maslow visited Daytop Village, an offshoot of Synanon,
in 1965 and gave an impromptu talk that served as the
basis for this paper. His excitement about the
encounter group he saw appears naive now, as he himself
admits.

671. Mehta, Gita. Karma Cola: Marketing the Mystic East.
New York: Simon and Schuster, 1979.

Witty and cynical view of Westerners seeking enlightenment in India. Colorful vignettes of Indian daily life,
ashrams, and encounters with gurus.

672. Melton, J. Gordon, and Moore, Robert L. The Cult Experience: Responding to the New Religious Pluralism. New York:
The Pilgrim Press, 1982.

Authors have written a sensible book intended to ease
the concerns of relatives of cult members and aid professionals who offer counseling. They have combined
their personal experiences in working with anguished
families and their knowledge of scholarly research in
a refreshing perspective that respects both the religious needs of members of alternative religions and the
anxiety of their relatives. Conversion and deprogramming,
especially its more troubling aspects, are discussed,
and guidelines for seeking help are given. Brief,
nonjudgmental descriptions of several groups are
offered. Notes and bibliography.

673. Mitchell, Dave; Mitchell, Cathy; and Ofshe, Richard.
The Light on Synanon: How a Country Weekly Exposed a Cor-
porate Cult--and Won the Pulitzer Prize. New York: Seaview
Books, 1980.

The Mitchells, owner-editors of a weekly California
newspaper, The Point Reyes Light, and sociologist Ofshe

tell how they won the Pulitzer Prize for their investigative reporting of abuses and violence at Synanon.
Engrossing and disturbing reading. Includes photographs. Index.

674. Moorhouse, Geoffrey. "The Moonies Invade Gloucester."
Harpers, January 1981, pp. 46-52.

Describes how the Unification Church involved itself
in the fishing industry in Gloucester, Massachusetts.
Balanced and readable reporting of behavior of both
the residents and the Moonies.

675. Naipaul, Shiva. Journey to Nowhere: A New World
Tragedy. New York: Simon and Schuster, 1981.

Discussion of Guyana and its politics after the
Jonestown tragedy. Also describes the aftermath in
the United States through the eyes of those connected
with the Peoples Temple. Moves from Guyana to
California and commentary on the extremes of California
lifestyles. Bibliography and index.

676. Nolan, James. "Jesus Now: Hogwash and Holy Water."
Ramparts, August 1971, pp. 20-26.

Although Nolan is very critical of the fanaticism
of the Jesus Movement, he also notes the ways in which
the Jesus communes he observed helped aimless, drug-
using teenagers to lead productive lives.

677. Nugent, John P. White Night. New York: Rawson, Wade,
1979.

Nugent's account of Jim Jones's career and the Jonestown tragedy is fast paced and reads easily. The final
events in Guyana are the focal point of the story
and are well detailed. The work suffers from super-
ficiality in psychological interpretation of motives,
however. Nugent quickly passes over Jones's childhood
and simply brands him a crook and a racist, contributing
little to an understanding of why the mass suicides
and murders occurred. Bibliography and index.

678. Ornstein, Robert E. "Eastern Psychologies: The
Container vs. the Contents." Psychology Today, September 1976,
pp. 36-37.

Criticizes the commercialization of Eastern spiritual
practices in America, with particular attention to
Transcendental Meditation.

679. Ornstein, Robert E. The Mind Field: A Personal Essay.
New York: Grossman Publishers, 1976.

Drawing on his research on the two hemispheres of the brain, travel to Asia, Africa, and Europe, and acquaintance with spiritual systems, Ornstein comments on Sufism, Carlos Castaneda, parapsychology, consciousness, and what he sees as the good and bad aspects of new religious movements. Readable and well-informed. References.

680. "Playboy Interview: Ted Patrick." Playboy, March 1979, p. 53.

The notorious deprogrammer makes many outrageous statements about cults and mind control in this long, revealing interview.

681. Quebedeaux, Richard. "Korean Missionaries to America." New Conversations, Spring 1982, pp. 6-15.

Provides a general overview of Moon's life and The Divine Principle and offers reasonable rebuttals to some typical criticisms of the UC.

682. Reston, James, Jr., and Adams, Noah. "Father Cares: The Last of Jonestown." n.p.: National Public Radio, 1981.

Two 90-minute audiocassettes and a small teacher's booklet are intended for classroom use with adult students. The first cassette, a documentary of the events leading up to Jonestown, includes actual recordings made by Jones in Guyana. The second cassette is composed of excerpts from a call-in radio program with a panel of experts that followed the documentary's first broadcast. Jones's recordings are powerful and shocking.

683. Robbins, Thomas. "'Brainwashing' and Religious Freedom." The Nation, 30 April 1977, p. 518.

Taking his usual stand in support of civil liberties and freedom of religion, Robbins argues well against the temporary conservatorships that courts have granted to parents of cult members.

684. Rodarmor, William. "The Secret Life of Swami Muktananda." CoEvolution Quarterly, Winter 1983, pp. 104-111.

An important expose of the supposedly celibate Swami's sexual activities with women followers. Highlights the problem of followers rationalizing unethical behavior of their spiritual teachers.

685. Rosen, R.D. Psychobabble: Fast Talk and Quick Cure in the Era of Feeling. New York: Atheneum, 1978.

"Psychobabble" is Rosen's term for the style of language used by human potential groups such as est,

Primal Therapy, and Rebirthing. Rosen finds this language lacking in intellectual and emotional content, tedious, and unrelentingly confessional. Witty and reads easily. Bibliography.

686. Rowly, Peter. <u>New Gods in America</u>. New York: David McKay, 1971.

Brief chapters on a wide variety of new religious groups, focusing on conversations with members. Attributes the attractiveness of cults to perception of the world as materialistic, industrialized, and frightening. Written before the advent of the "brainwashing" argument. Bibliography, mostly of writings from teachers of these movements.

687. Rossman, Michael. <u>New Age Blues: On the Politics of Consciousness</u>. New York: E.P. Dutton, 1979.

In this series of provocative essays, Rossman, a 1960s political activist, comments on social implications of human potential and new religious movements. Discusses <u>est</u>, Ram Dass, psychics, Primal Therapy, and so on with a critical eye for phoniness and authoritarianism. Index.

688. Rudin, A. James, and Rudin, Marcia R. <u>Prison or Paradise? The New Religious Cults</u>. Phildelphia: Fortress Press,1980.

The Rudins begin with the assumption that the cults of today are substantially different from those of the past: never before, they say, have so many existed, never have cults been so geographically widespread, and never before have they used sophisticated mind-control techniques. Such sensational generalizations, teamed with their notion that there are between 1500 and 3000 cults in the United States, immediately discredit their work. This is unfortunate because they have a genuine concern for anxious parents (their primary audience) and distressed cult members. The nine best-known and most controversial cults are described in depth and chosen to represent all the others--a questionable tactic. Gives suggestions for countering cults. Index.

689. Rudin, Marcia R., and Rudin, A. James. "New Religious Movements: Cults or Continuum?" Paper read at the Conference on Conversion, Coercion, and Commitment in New Religious Movements, 11-14 June 1981, at Berkeley, California. Photocopied.

The Rudins' definition of a cult is summed up by two words--exploitation and deception. Basically a recitation of abuses, their discussion is confined to a few controversial organizations such as Hare Krishna, the Unification Church, and Children of God.

690. Sage, Wayne. "The War on Cults." Human Behavior,
October 1976, pp. 40-49.

A balanced look at the successes and failures of
deprogramming. Includes photographs.

691. Siegelman, Jim, and Conway, Flo. "Snapping: Welcome
to the Eighties." Playboy, March 1979, pp. 59, 217-219.

The authors describe the new mental illness they claim
cults cause, "information disease" (discussed more
fully in their book, Snapping [item 631]), and warn
that if the government does not crack down on cults,
"great masses of Americans" will be under mind control
in the 1980s.

692. Stoner, Carroll, and Parke, Jo Anne. All God's Children:
The Cult Experience--Salvation or Slavery? Radnor, Penn.:
Chilton Books, 1977.

Two reporters discuss the cult scene at length,
focusing on the most well-known groups. They discuss
why people join, deprogramming, and brainwashing.
Aimed primarily at parents, the book has a decided
slant against cults, but the authors are thoughtful
in their approach and demonstrate an appreciation for
all sides of the issues. One of the better of this
genre. Bibliography and index.

693. Streiker, Lowell D. The Cults Are Coming! Nashville:
Abingdon Press, 1978.

Streiker concentrates on the most popular cults and
common fears about them. Obviously aiming his rhetoric
at frightened parents, he offers meager advice on how
parents should communicate with their children. The
book may alarm more than help.

694. Streiker, Lowell D. The Jesus Trip: Advent of the Jesus
Freaks. Nashville: Abingdon Press, 1971.

Illustrated treatment covering Children of God,
Tony and Susan Alamo Christian Foundation, and other
Jesus Movement groups of the late 1960s. Coverage is
brief, focusing on experiences of those involved.

695. Tracy, Phil. "More on Peoples Temple: The Strange
Suicides." New West, 15 August 1977, pp. 18-19.

A short follow-up to Kilduff and Tracy's article
in the 1 August issue. Here Tracy mentions two strange
suicide cases and notes that Quentin Kopp, then
president of the San Francisco Board of Supervisors,
had asked then Mayor Moscone to investigate Peoples
Temple, which Moscone refused to do.

696. Vallee,Jacques. Messengers of Deception: UFO Contacts
and Cults. Berkeley: And/Or Press, 1979.

   Suggests that UFO cults are being manipulated and
   exploited by humans with certain political and
   social concerns. References to several UFO cults.
   Illustrations, bibliography, and index.

697. Wallis, Roy. "Fishing for Men." The Humanist, no. 1
(1978), pp. 14-16.

   Similar to author's "Recruiting Christian Manpower"
   [item 341].   In both articles, Wallis discusses the
   theological justifications given by Moses David
   and his Children of God for using sex, or "flirty
   fishing," to gain converts.   Here he considers how
   women can be persuaded to engage in such unconventional
   behavior and points out several reasons, including:
   1) the "sharing" behavior is acceptable to the COG;
   2) children born of the unions will be cared for by
   the COG; and 3) since the primary motive is love,
   the use of sex may be seen as a sacrifice.

698. Wooden, Kenneth. The Children of Jonestown. New York:
McGraw-Hill, 1981.

   Wooden brings together evidence from interviews,
   letters, memoranda, and other sources in this impassioned
   account of the nearly 300 children at Jonestown.
   Discusses how Jones obtained court guardianships over
   children and his abuse of them.   Wooden is very
   critical of the federal government and state of
   California for failing to rescue the children and
   calls for investigations into the treatment of
   children in other cults.   Includes photographs.
   Bibliography and index.

699. Yablonsky, Lewis. The Tunnel Back: Synanon. New York:
Macmillan, 1965.

   In this early description of Synanon and its therapeutic
   method, the author points to its success in rehabili-
   tating drug addicts. History, leadership styles, and
   types of members are discussed, using many reconstructed
   conversations. Synanon in prison is considered an
   important breakthrough.

New Religious Movements and the Spiritualization of Knowledge

Mysticism and Physics

700. Capra, Fritjof. The Tao of Physics: An Exploration of the Parallels Between Modern Physics and Eastern Mysticism. 2d ed. Boulder, Colo.: Shambhala, 1983.

Capra first discusses modern physics, then goes on to describe Hindu, Buddhist, Chinese, Taoist, and Zen mysticism, and finally discusses parallels between these two approaches to reality. Intended for the general reader, the book has enjoyed popular success. Some experts on both sides have found the work simplistic, albeit imaginatively constructed. The description of modern physics is accessible to the layperson. Good bibliography. Index.

701. Capra, Fritjof. The Turning Point: Science, Society, and the Rising Culture. New York: Simon and Schuster, 1982.

Claims that environmental, economic, and political problems are facets of a "crisis of perception" that derives from trying to apply outdated Cartesian concepts to a world that is interconnected in the way that modern physics describes for subatomic particles. Argues for a new holistic worldview that author sees beginning in medicine and healing, the integration of Eastern and Western psychologies, and economics and technology. This new paradigm is discussed at length. For the general reader. Notes, bibliography, and index.

702. Gardner, Martin. "Quantum Theory and Quack Theory." New York Review of Books, 17 May 1979, pp. 39-41.

Gardner discusses the questionable use of quantum

mechanics as a basis for explaining psychic phenomena.
Includes a letter from noted physicist John Wheeler,
whose writings have been quoted by paraphysicists such
as Jack Sarfatti but who thoroughly disdains attempts
to connect psi with physics.

703. LeShan Lawrence. The Medium, the Mystic, and the
Physicist: Toward a General Theory of the Paranormal.
New York: Viking Press, 1974.

LeShan presents an intriguing juxtaposition of ideas
gathered from the writings of mystics, physicists,
and mediums, along with his own personal experiences.
He brings the ideas together by proposing a unified
theory of the paranormal and a technique for psychic
healing. Notes but no index. A few of his articles
that were previously published elsewhere are included
in the appendices.

704. Mishlove, Jeffrey. The Roots of Consciousness:
Psychic Liberation through History, Science, and Experience.
New York and Berkeley: Random House/Bookworks, 1975.

Maintains that psychic experiences, occult and mystical
phenomena, and astral projection are real and may be
explained in the light of new theories in physics.
Large book divided into three sections: 1)"history
of the exploration of consciousness" from prehistory
through William James; 2) twentieth-century scientific
studies of psychic phenomena, UFOs,and physiology of
consciousness; and 3) physics and consciousness,
applications of psychic phenomena, and organizations
devoted to their study. Mishlove runs the gamut of
topics comprising the new study of consciousness. He
seems to believe in everything and is so impressed by
the connections he finds among events and ideas that
he is seldom critical. For the general reader. Attrac-
tively illustrated. References and index.

705. Toben, Bob. Space-Time and Beyond: Toward an Explanation of the Unexplainable. New York: E.P. Dutton, 1975.

A popular presentation of new concepts of universal
order and consciousness. Includes the structure of
space-time, paranormal phenomena, and the structure
of energy. Text is minimal, a few sentences on each
page illustrated by line drawings. All statements are
presented as fact, with no arguments or evidence to
account for them. A separate chapter by Jack Sarfatti
is devoted to scientific commentary. Useful annotated
bibliography at the end of the book.

706. Wilber, Ken. "Physics, Mysticism, and the New Holo-
graphic Paradigm: A Critical Appraisal." Re-Vision,
no. 2(1979), pp. 43-55.

In this complex article, Wilber, who has written on
consciousness and the mystical traditions, uses the
latter as a basis for criticising attempts to unite
physics and mysticism. Such attempts, he argues, are
imprecise, unclear, and simplistic; physics and mysticism, he says, operate on different levels of reality.
Hard reading for those unfamiliar with the concepts.
References do not include all items referred to in the
text.

707. Zukav, Gary. The Dancing Wu Li Masters: An Overview
of the New Physics. New York: William Morrow, 1979.

Although this book is primarily about quantum physics
and relativity, Zukav points out similarities he sees
between Eastern philosophies and physics. Written
for the general reader, the book conveys a great deal
of complex theoretical material in clear, readable
language. Illustrated with diagrams and photographs.
Bibliography and index.

Holistic Health Movement

708. Ardell, Donald B. High Level Wellness: An Alternative
to Doctors, Drugs, and Disease. Emmaus, Penn.: Rodale
Press, 1977.

An exploration of "wellness" as an approach to holistic
living that includes, but goes beyond, the medical
notion of "health." Provides concrete suggestions
for improving diet, managing stress, remaining physi-
cally fit, and having a low impact on the environment.
Includes a very useful annotated bibliography of
related books. For the general reader. Index.

709. Bry, Adelaide. Directing the Movies of Your Mind:
Visualization for Health and Insight. New York: Harper,
1978.

A popular and readable account of the creative use of
imagination in healing. Bry describes personal
experiences with visualization and gives directions
for achieving a relaxed state and working with
images in the mind to deal with a variety of problems.
Visualization is an important part of the holistic
trend in medicine. Very useful bibliography and
index.

710. Geis, Larry; Kelly, Alta Picchi; and Kelly, Aidan.
The New Healers: Healing the Whole Person. Berkeley:
And/Or Press, 1980.

Collection of sixteen essays provides a good introduction to a wide spectrum of holistic health concerns.

Noted healers represented include Moshe Feldenkrais, Linus Pauling, Irving Oyle, and Olga Worrall. Essays cover childbirth, dying, spiritual awareness, and methods such as biofeedback, vitamin therapy, massage, and movement therapy. They are easy reading and portray philosophies that the healers have developed primarily through experience.

711. Goldwag, Elliott M., ed. Inner Balance: The Power of Holistic Healing. Englewood Cliffs, N.J.: Prentice-Hall, 1979.

Most of the contributors to this collection of sixteen essays are medical doctors; some, such as Hans Selye and Malcolm Todd, have impressive credentials. In writing about stress and self-regulation through nutrition, meditation, and relaxation techniques they demonstrate the willingness of the established medical profession to incorporate alternative modalities. Marcus Bach, a noted author and teacher of comparative religion, and Julian Byrd, a hospital director of pastoral care, add perspectives on the spiritual dimension of health. Written in nontechnical language, this book is intended for the general reader. A bibliography for each paper appears at the end of the volume. Index.

712. Mattson, Phyllis H. "Holistic Health; an Overview." Phoenix, no. 2(1977), pp. 36-43.

Discusses the origins, growth, and ideology of the holistic health movement. Brief but useful and readable article. References.

713. Oyle, Irving. The New American Medicine Show: Discovering the Healing Connection. Santa Cruz, Calif.: Unity Press, 1979.

Oyle, a medical doctor, emphasizes the role the mind plays in disease. He discusses stress and a variety of psychosomatic ailments in a theoretical context, including recent research. Bibliography.

714. Samuels, Mike, and Bennett, Hal. The Well Body Book. rev. ed. New York and Berkeley: Random House/Bookworks, 1979.

Authors strike a balance between alternative and traditional healing methods in this large, practical handbook. Book includes chapters on diagnosis and treatment of many common ailments, giving yourself a physical exam, preventive medicine, using your doctor as a resource, and general information on drugs and rare diseases. Samuels is a medical doctor. Incorporates a number of physical and mental exercises for healing. Well illustrated with line drawings. Index.

715. "Self Healing." New Age, May 1979, pp. 28-51.

Several short articles by well-known writers, including
Jean Houston, Sam Keen, Gay Luce, and Irving Oyle.
Unity of mind and body is emphasized, especially the
role of positive thinking in healing disease. The
concept prevalent in metaphysical systems such as
Christian Science, that disease is the result of
negative thinking, is also prevalent here. The articles
contain many useful hints for leading a more relaxed
and healthy life.

716. Sobel, David, ed. Ways of Health: Holistic Approaches
to Ancient and Contemporary Medicine. New York and London:
Harcourt Brace Jovanovich, 1979.

A collection of twenty-two essays organized into
five sections: 1) "holistic approaches to health";
2) "ancient systems of medicine"; 3) "unorthodox
medicine"; 4) "techniques of self-regulation"; and
5) "an ecological view of health." Subjects include
Chinese medicine, Navaho medicine, biofeedback,
religious healing, homeopathy, yoga therapy, and
human ecology. The contributors are experts in their
subjects. Their essays are scholarly but generally
not too technical. A solid contribution. Useful
supplemental bibliography for each section.

Integration of Western Psychologies
and Eastern Religions

717. Brandon, David. Zen in the Art of Helping. London:
Routledge and Kegan Paul, 1976.

Director of a British project on homeless youth
writes poetically, thoughtfully, and practically about
incorporating Zen wisdom in the helping professions.
Notes.

718. Bregman, Lucy. "The Interpreter/Experience Split:
Three Models in the Psychology of Religion." Journal of
the American Academy of Religion. Supplement 46(1978): 115-
149.

One of the three models Bregman discusses is transpersonal psychology, which she finds rooted in human
potential movements and strongly influenced by the
influx of Eastern religions in the United States.
References.

719. Carpenter, J. Tyler. "Meditation, Esoteric Traditions--
Contributions to Psychotherapy." American Journal of Psychotherapy 31(1977): 394-404.

Gives brief descriptions of several Eastern forms of
meditation and therapy, which Carpenter believes may
enrich the practice of psychotherapy. References.

720. Coukoulis, Peter. Guru, Psychotherapist, and Self.
Marina del Rey, Calif.: DeVorss, 1976.

A comparative study of the guru/disciple relationship
and the Jungian analytic process. Coukoulis compares
Jungian concepts of the self and the guru-disciple
relationship with Eastern concepts as portrayed in
writings of Sri Aurobindo, Ramakrishna, and Milarepa.
He finds the meaning of the self to be essentially
the same in the two philosophies and also finds
many similarities in goals and in the guru-disciple,
analyst/analysand relationship. Not a very deep
study. Definitions of Sanskrit and Jungian terms
given at end. Bibliography.

721. Drury, Nevill. Inner Visions: Explorations in
Magical Consciousness. London: Routledge and Kegan Paul,
1979.

Intended to relate current interest in consciousness
research to various magical and esoteric systems.
Author views the contemporary search for mystery and
myth as a search for identity through creative
imagination. Discussion includes Western magical
systems, C.G. Jung, Tarot, and fantasy in contemporary
art and rock music. Bibliography for each chapter.
Index.

722. Deikman, Arthur J. The Observing Self: Mysticism
and Psychotherapy. Boston: Beacon Press, 1982.

Deikman attempts to provide a framework for understanding mystical science in Western psychological
terms so that mental health professionals may make use
of meditation and teaching stories as adjuncts to
psychotherapy. He maintains that the observing
self, or the self that is the center of experience,
has been ignored by Western psychology but is the key
element in the mystical traditions. In a very useful
appendix, Deikman warns the seeker about dangers in
spiritual groups that teach mystical techniques.
Notes.

723. Ferguson, Marilyn. The Aquarian Conspiracy: Personal
and Social Transformation in the 1980s. Los Angeles:
J.P. Tarcher, 1980.

Excited by the new possibilities she sees arising
from consciousness research, spiritual awareness,
holistic health, and new psychologies, Ferguson is
convinced that a benevolent "conspiracy" to transform

society is at work. Discusses areas in which she sees
change. Includes a wealth of names of people involved
in the "conspiracy" and lists organizations and publications to use as "resources for change." References
and index.

724. Fosshage, James L., and Olsen, Paul, eds. Healing:
Implications for Psychotherapy. New Directions in Psychotherapy, no. 2. New York: Human Sciences Press, 1978.

Collection of thirteen scholarly essays based in part
on a 1976 conference presented by the National
Institute for the Psychotherapies. Editors include
works of those researchers and clinicians they believe
to have made outstanding contributions to enlarging
the frontiers of healing. Influence of Eastern
philosophies is evident, particularly in the essays
concerned with using meditation in psychotherapy.
Split-brain and biofeedback research is also discussed.
All but one of the contributors are Westerners with
Ph.D.'s or M.D.'s; the notable exception is Chogyam
Trungpa, Rinpoche, a Tibetan Buddhist. Index.

725. Goleman, Daniel. Varieties of the Meditative Experience.
New York: E.P. Dutton, 1977.

Written by a psychologist, this book is a concise
intellectual integration that provides the reader with
an overview of several spiritual paths and the states
of consciousness they traverse. Over a dozen meditation forms from the major religious traditions,
including Christianity and Judaism, are described.
Author uses many special terms from each tradition.
but provides brief definitions in the text. Bibliography and index.

726. Goleman, Daniel. "Meditation and Consciousness: An
Asian Approach to Mental Health." American Journal of Psychotherapy 30(1976): 41-54.

Goleman recommends meditation as a complementary
adjunct to psychotherapy. He describes a classical
Asian model of consciousness, Abhidamma, which depends
upon meditation to regulate and train attention.
References.

727. Jacobs, Jane A. "Psychological Change Through the
Spiritual Teacher: Implications for Psychotherapy."
Ph.D. dissertation, California School of Professional
Psychology, Berkeley, 1974.

The work of a specific spiritual teacher in the
Eastern tradition was studied and compared with the
psychoanalytic tradition and client-centered therapy.
The spiritual teacher's approach is found to be limited

in several ways. Author feels that the spiritual
teacher should avail himself of the knowledge of
Western psychotherapy and that Western psychotherapists
should expand their present work by understanding
and selectively utilizing the unique strengths of the
spiritual teacher. Bibliography.

728. Naranjo, Claudio. The One Quest. New York: Viking
Press, 1972.

A unifying premise of what has come to be called
the human potential movement is that there is more
similarity than difference in the ways people grow.
In this classic statement of the interdependence of
psychological and religious approaches to growth,
Naranjo argues for a deeper understanding of the
underlying unity of all avenues to human fulfillment.
Notes and index.

729. Naranjo, Claudio, and Ornstein, Robert E. On the
Psychology of Meditation. New York: Viking Press, 1971.

Two long essays on techniques of meditation and
their implications for modern psychology. In the
first essay Naranjo discusses commonalities and
differences among forms of meditation from the major
world religions, giving attention to underlying
psychological processes. Ornstein, in the second
essay, attempts to translate the language of meditation
schools into that of modern psychology and discusses
possible medical and psychotherapeutic applications
of meditation. Notes and bibliography.

730. Needleman, Jacob, and Lewis, Dennis, eds. On the Way to
Self Knowledge. New York: Alfred A. Knopf, 1976.

Eight well-known psychiatrists, psychotherapists, and
spiritual leaders, including Viktor Frankl, James
Hillman, and Tarthang Tulku, explore and compare the
aims and methods of spiritual disciplines and psychotherapy. The essays grew out of a series of lectures
presented in 1975 at the University of California
Medical Center in San Francisco. Editors point out
the confusion some people feel concerning where to
seek help or whether to seek spiritual or therapeutic
help now that therapists are turning toward Eastern
religions. Readable and creative.

731. Netherton, Morris, and Shiffrin, Nancy. Past Lives
Therapy. New York: William Morrow, 1978.

Past lives therapy is based on the assumptions that
reincarnation exists and that people can trace mental
and physical problems to events in their earlier
lives. Netherton, a counseling psychologist, describes

his techniques and a few case histories. He believes
in reincarnation because his patients have reported
events, such as sea disasters and suicides, that
he claims that could not have known of in any other
way. The patients have an amazing ability to recount
scenes from supposed past lives after exchanging
only a few sentences with Netherton. Of course,
they may have very vivid imaginations. Past lives
therapy is one of the stranger examples of Eastern
influences on psychology.

732. Tart, Charles, ed. Transpersonal Psychologies.
New York: Harper and Row, 1975.

An important collection of articles relating Western
psychology to Christian, Sufi, Buddhist, Yogic,
Esoteric, and other spiritual traditions. By
"transpersonal" Tart means spiritual. He maintains
that Western psychology can apply the scientific
method to the transpersonal psychologies that are part
of certain spiritual traditions in order to create a
Western understanding of the spiritual. Tart provides
three general essays covering ways for science to
deal with spiritual psychologies, assumptions of
Western psychology, and the reality of the paranormal.
Eight essays on various spiritual disciplines as
psychologies follow, written by people versed both
scholastically and practically in the disciplines.
Bibliography and index.

733. van der Lans, Jan. "Meditation: A Comparative and
Theoretical Analysis." The Annual Review of the Social
Sciences of Religion 6(1982): 133-152.

Compares Eastern and Western forms of meditation,
finding strong similarities. Argues for a psychological model that recognizes the uniquely religious
transformations that meditation can bring. References.

734. Vaughan, Frances. "Transpersonal Dimensions of Psychotherapy." Re-Vision, no. 1(1979), pp. 26-29.

In this short article on the aims, values, and
attitudes of transpersonal therapy one can see
clearly its close relationship to human potential
groups and Eastern religions. It places high value
on an awareness of the unity of all life, the power
of self-healing, full responsibility for one's own
life, and the seeking of mystical experiences.
References.

735. Walsh, Roger N., and Vaughan, Frances. Beyond Ego:
Transpersonal Dimensions in Psychology. Los Angeles:
J.P. Tarcher, 1980.

Collection of twenty-five essays by major contributors
to transpersonal psychology. Essays are grouped in
six sections: 1) new paradigms, 2) nature of consciousness, 3) Eastern and Western concepts of well-being,
4) meditation, 5) transpersonal psychotherapy, and
6) implications for other disciplines. Intended as
a comprehensive introductory text. Most essays are
reprints, edited and condensed for a general audience.
Glossary, bibliography, and index.

736. Watts, Alan. Psychotherapy East and West. New York:
Random House, 1961.

Claims to be the first comprehensive study of parallels
between Western psychotherapy and Eastern philosophies,
including ways in which the two can benefit one another.
References.

737. Wilber, Ken. "Eye to Eye." Re-Vision, Winter/Spring,
1979, pp. 3-25.

A theoretical article in which Wilber discusses
transpersonal psychology as a synthesis of science,
philosophy/psychology, and religion/meditation.
Difficult reading for the neophyte. References.

738. Wilber, Ken. No Boundary: Eastern and Western
Approaches to Personal Growth. Whole Mind Series. Los
Angeles: Center Publications, 1979.

In this introductory synthesis of Eastern and Western
religious and psychological approaches to growth,
Wilber's theme is that awareness of oneness with all
creation is in the nature of humans. Suffering
results from failing to see this. He explores levels
of consciousness leading up to "unity consciousness"
and ways that different approaches can aid in
transformation. Wilber is an important theoretician
of transpersonal psychology. Written for the general
reader. Index.

Appendix: Selected New Religious Movements Publishers

Ananda Cooperative Village

Ananda Publications
14618 Tyler Foote Road
P.O. Box 900
Nevada City, California 95959

American-born disciple of Paramahansa Yogananda, Donald Walters, now called Swami Kriyananda, is spiritual director of Ananda Cooperative Village. The Village's press publishes his writings, talks, and musical compositions in printed and audio formats.

Association for Research and Enlightenment

P.O. Box 595
Virginia Beach, Virginia 23451

This organization, devoted to the teachings of Edgar Cayce, makes available his psychic readings. Lecture tapes by members of the organization are available, also.

Church of Scientology

Bridge Publications
1414 North Catalina Street
Los Angeles, California 90027

Bridge publishes the writings and lectures given by L. Ron Hubbard, founder of the Church of Scientology.

Dharma Realm Buddhist Association

    Buddhist Text Translation Society
    City of 10,000 Buddhas
    P.O. Box 217
    Talmage, California 95481

The City of 10,000 Buddhas is the headquarters and main
center of the Dharma Realm Buddhist Association, a Chinese
Buddhist organization. The Buddhist Text Translation
Society has been translating into Spanish, English, and
Zhung Wen, and publishing the Chinese Buddhist Canon. All
of the translated works are accompanied by interlinear
commentaries by Tripitaka Master Hsuan Hua, founder of the
Association. Other publications include books on all forms
of meditation, virtuous conduct, poetry and biographies
of Buddhist Masters. A monthly journal of orthodox
Buddhism, Vajra Bodhi Sea, is also available.

Himalayan International Institute of Yoga Science and
    Philosophy

    RD 1, Box 88-A
    Honesdale, Pennsylvania 13431-9706

Swami Rama directs the Himalayan International Institute of
Yoga Science and Philosophy. The Institute's publishing
house makes available his writings in book form and
lectures on audio tapes. Like many other new religious
movements' publishers, Himalayan emphasizes holistic
living and includes scholarly and practical titles by a
variety of writers concerned with diet, nutrition, meditation, psychology, yoga, and homeopathic remedies. All
items are well-described in the catalogue.

International Society for Krishna Consciousness

    Bhaktivedanta Book Trust
    3764 Watseka Ave.
    Los Angeles, California 90034

Bhaktivedanta Book Trust publishes the writings of Swami
Prabhupada, deceased spiritual director of the International
Society for Krishna Consciousness. Other publications
include translations, commentaries and summaries of Indian
classics such as the Bhagavad-Gita, the Puranas, and the
Upanisads.

Eckankar

    IWP Publishing Company
    P.O. Box 2449, Department B-1
    Menlo Park, California 94025

IWP presents the teachings of Eckankar through the writings

of Paul Twitchell and Darwin Gross. Several titles are
available as talking books on audiocassettes.

Johannine Daist Communion

> Laughing Man Institute
> Dawn Horse Press
> Clearlake, California 95422

American-born Franklin Jones, known as Da Free John, is
the spiritual director of the Johannine Daist Communion.
His teachings are based on the wisdom tradition as it has
appeared throughout history and do not represent a particular religious tradition. A prolific writer, Free John
has produced about twenty books since 1973. In addition
to those writings Dawn Horse Press publishes The Laughing
Man, a quarterly periodical, in cooperation with The
Laughing Man Institute.

Meher Baba Lovers

> Sheriar Press
> 1414 Madison Street
> North Myrtle Beach, South Carolina 29582

Sells books and pamphlets by and about Meher Baba.
Pamphlets, stationery, posters and audio recordings are
also available, along with a few children's books.

Naropa Institute

> Naropa Institute Bookstore and Vajradhatu Recordings
> 2011 10th Street
> Boulder, Colorado 80302

Chogyam Trungpa is the spiritual director of Vajradhatu, an
association of Tibetan Buddhist centers in the United
States. His writings and talks, on audiocassettes, are
sold through the bookstore and its catalog. Talks given
by Thomas F. Rich, known as Osel Tendzin and chosen by
Trungpa to be his successor, are available on audiocassette.
In addition, the Bookstore carries a wide variety of
scholarly titles on all aspects of Buddhism. Naropa
Institute has held conferences on Christian and Buddhist
meditation annually since 1981; conference proceedings
are published on audiocassettes.

Neo-Pagan and Witchcraft Network

> Circle
> Box 9013
> Madison, Wisconsin 53715

Circle is an organization that gathers resources pertaining
to Witchcraft, Goddess worship, Neo-Paganism, and Shamanism.

Their periodical, <u>Circle Network News,</u> provides news,
notices, rituals, and other information related to those
subjects. <u>Pagan Circles</u>, a newsletter, lists Wisconsin
area Pagan events. An annual publication, <u>Circle Guide to
Wicca and Pagan Resources</u> is the only reference book of its
kind.

Nyingma Institute

Dharma Publishing
2425 Hillside Avenue
Berkeley, California 94704

Dharma Publishing presents Tibetan Buddhist teachings and is
part of the Nyingma Institute, directed by Tarthang Tulku.
The Tibetan Translation Series has offered representative
works from early Buddhist literature. A major undertaking
has been a reprint edition of the Tibetan Buddhist Canon.
Tarthang Tulku has written several books adapting Tibetan
teachings for Western practitioners. Other publications
include the journal <u>Crystal Mirror</u>, <u>Gesar Magazine</u>, books
on Tibetan Buddhism by various authors, and art reproduc-
tions.

Rajneesh Foundation International

Zarathustra Road
P.O. Box 9
Rajneeshpuram, Oregon 97741

This publisher makes available the teachings of Bhagwan
Shree Rajneesh. Many of Rajneesh's discourses given before
he entered silence have been printed in book form, over
1500 audiotapes are available, and a growing number of
videotapes. Music and meditation tapes are published.
The discourses have also been translated into several
languages.

Satchidananda Ashram - Yogaville

Integral Yoga Publications
Distribution Division
P.O. Box 108
Pomfret Center, Connecticut 06259

Publishes books, audio tapes, and records by Sri Swami
Satchidananda, founder and director of the Satchidananda
Ashram - Yogaville. Also distributes books by Swami
Sivananda, Paramahansa Yogananda, Swami Vivekananda, and
other Hindu teachers. Photographs, T-shirts, posters,
films, videotapes, and devotional items may be purchased.
Issues of <u>Integral Yoga Magazine</u> are also available.

Shasta Abbey

Shasta Abbey Books and Gifts
P.O. Box 199
Mt. Shasta, California 96067

Shasta Abbey is the headquarters of the Order of Buddhist
Contemplatives of the Soto Zen Church. Roshi Jiyu-Kennett
founded and directs the activities of the Abbey. She has
written books and delivered lectures that are published by
the Abbey. Other books concerning Buddhism are available,
along with the bi-monthly Journal of Shasta Abbey. A wide
variety of devotional items, jewelry, notecards and posters
are for sale, also.

Siddha Yoga Dham Foundation

SYDA Foundation
Box 600
South Fallsburg, New York 12779

Swami Muktananda, former spiritual director of Siddha Yoga
Dham Foundation died in 1982. His two successors are Swami
Chidvilasananda and Swami Nityananda. The SYDA Foundation
catalog includes books, periodicals, audio and video tapes,
and devotional items. Several books and pamphlets are
available in Spanish, Hindi, French, German, and Italian
from the organizations' publishing houses in Europe,
Mexico, and India.

Sikh Dharma

Sikh Dharma Book Suppliers
1050 North Cherry Avenue
Tucson, Arizona 85719

Offers a small selection of books concerning Sikh poetry,
literature, and history from India.

Sri Aurobindo

Auromere
1291 Weber Street
Pomona, California 91768

Auromere distributes Indian publications in the United
States and publishes a wide variety of spiritual writings
concerned with health, meditation, Hindu thought, metaphysics, and philosophy. The Indian publications include
writings of Sri Aurobindo, The Mother, and their disciples,
along with spiritual and cultural texts. Children's books,
diaries, calendars, greeting cards, incense and Ayurvedic
health care products are also available.

Sufi Order

Omega Press
1570 Pacheco St.
Santa Fe, New Mexico 87501

Publishes books by Hazrat Inayat Khan and books and audio
cassettes by Pir Vilayat Inayat Khan, the current Murshid
of the Sufi Order in America. Items in the catalog are
described thoroughly.

Theosophy

Theosophical University Press
Post Office Bin C
Pasadena, California 91109

This publisher reprints the writings of H.P. Blavatsky
and William Q. Judge, co-founders of the Theosophical
Society. Other Theosophists' writings are also represented.
Sunrise, a bimonthly periodical, presents articles,
interviews, and book reviews.

3HO Foundation

1620 Pruess Road
Los Angeles, California 90035

The Sikh teachings of Yogi Bhagan and the activities of
his Healthy, Happy, Holy Organization are reported in the
quarterly periodical Beads of Truth available from the
above address.

Unification Church of America

Rose of Sharon Press
G.P.O. Box 2432
New York, New York 10116

Rose of Sharon Press distributes publications of the
Unification Church and its affiliated organizations.
Many of the books are collections of papers read by
scholars at meetings sponsored by the New Era Research
Association. Divine Principle, containing teachings of
Reverend Moon and doctrines of the Church is also
available.

Yasodhara Ashram

Timeless Books
Box 60
Portill, Idaho 83853

Timeless Books publishes the teachings of yoga as interpreted by Swami Sivananda Radha, founder and spiritual
director of Yasodhara Ashram in British Columbia, Canada.
Books and audiocassettes are available.

Author and Title Index

Chandler, Russell, 623

Chapman, Rick M., 624

Chapman, Stephen, 625

"Charisma and Conversion,"
  483

"Charisma, Pseudo-Certainty
  and Grace," 378

"Charismatic Cults," 124

"Charistmatic Leader and the
  Violent Surrogate Family,
  The," 396

"Charismatic Religious Sects
  and Psychiatry," 358

Chidester, David, 456

Child Development Abstracts
  and Bibliography, 020

"Child Law and Religious
  Extremists," 532

Children of Doom, 270

Children of Jonestown, The,
  698

Chorover, Stephen L., 351

Christ and the New Consciousness, 512

Christ, Carol, 457

"Christian Church and the
  New Religious Movements,
  The," 517

Christianity and est, 520

"Christian Response to the
  New Religions, The," 518

Christian Zen, 506

"Church of Satan in the
  United States, The," 452

"Church, State, and Cult,"
  159

Cinnamon, Kenneth, 626

Circle Guide to Wicca and
  Pagan Resources, 010

Citizens Freedom Foundation
  News, 627

Civil Liberties, "Brainwashing" and "Cults," 042

Clarie, Thomas C., 031

"Clarifying the Cult," 201

Clark, John G., Jr., 352-
  353, 400-401, 628

Clark, Tom, 629

"Claudio Naranjo," 580

"Client and Audience Cults
  in America," 115

"Clinical Profiles of Hare
  Krishna Devotees," 445

"Clinical Study of Four
  Unification Church Members,
  A," 425

Coercive Persuasion, 385

"Coercive Persuasion (Brainwashing), Religious Cults,
  and Deprogramming," 389

Coleman, James, 137

Coleman, John, 499

Coleman, Lee, 535

Collective Search for
  Identity, 146

Collier, Peter, 630

Collier, Sophia, 581

Coming Out, 582

Subject Index

Underlined numbers refer to pages. Other numbers are citations in the bibliography.

Yoga, <u>10</u>, 034, 036, 048, 117
  Kundalini, 481

Yoga Association of Self-
  Analysis, 290

Zazen, 335

Zen Buddhism. <u>See</u> Buddhism
  Zen

Zen Center of San Francisco,
  098, 347, 618

About the Compiler

DIANE CHOQUETTE is Head of Public Services and Special Collections at the Graduate Theological Union Library in Berkeley, California.